Race and the Suburbs in American Film

THE SUNY SERIES

HORIZONS OF CINEMA

MURRAY POMERANCE | EDITOR

Race and the Suburbs in American Film

∽

Edited by

Merrill Schleier

Cover: Tony Espinoza and Noah Jupe in *Suburbicon* (Black Bear Pictures, Dark Castle Entertainment, Huahua Media, Silver Pictures, Smokehouse Pictures, 2017), directed by George Clooney. Courtesy of Photofest.

Published by State University of New York Press, Albany

For information, contact State University of New York Press, Albany, NY
www.sunypress.edu

Library of Congress Cataloging-in-Publication Data

Name: Schleier, Merrill, editor.
Title: Race and the suburbs in American film / Merrill Schleier.
Description: Albany : State University of New York Press [2021] | SUNY series, Horizons of Cinema | Includes bibliographical references and index.
Identifiers: ISBN 9781438484471 (hardcover : alk. paper) | ISBN 9781438484488 (ebook)
Further information is available at the Library of Congress.

Library of Congress Control Number: 2021938473

10 9 8 7 6 5 4 3 2 1

Contents

Illustrations

Acknowledgments

This collection has been several years in the making. It is an outgrowth of my abiding interest in cinema and the built environment, especially urban spaces, and their relationship to representations of gender, class, and race. In 2016, I was invited by Stefano Baschiera and Miriam De Rosa to contribute to their anthology *Film and Domestic Space* (2020), in which I explored Japanese American masculinity in post–World War II cinematic interiors in general and the suburbs in particular. I want to extend my thanks to the authors for providing the initial impetus for this project. My chapter in their book led, in turn, to my panel on "Race, Ethnicity, and the Cinematic Suburbs" in 2018 at the Society for Cinema and Media Studies conference, of which the present collection is an outgrowth. Subsequently, I was invited to contribute to Angel Daniel Matos, Paula J. Massood, and Pam Robertson Wocjik's collection, *Crossroads: Intersections of Space and Identity in Screen Cultures* (2021) in which I continued my interest in race and the suburbs, by exploring the intersection of whiteness and queerness in *Crime of Passion* (Oswald, 1956). I presented this research in 2019 at an SCMS panel, presided over by Elizbeth A. Patton, entitled "Screening Intersectional Spaces." I would like to acknowledge the aforementioned editors for sharpening my thinking about race, domestic space, and the suburbs. Appreciation is also extended to the numerous audience members who had wonderful suggestions and recommended additional suburb films to view.

I extend further recognition to Elizabeth A. Patton and Amy Lynn Corbin for our numerous discussions during the genesis of this project at several Society of Cinema and Media Study annual conferences. Appreciation is also due to SCMS's Urbanism/Geography/Architecture Scholarly Interest Group for the intellectual stimulation provided by its members, several of whom are represented herein.

In addition, I want to express my gratitude to several others who read various portions of my work pertaining to cinema and suburban space during the duration my research, namely Elizabeth A. Patton, Paula J. Massood, Alison McKee, and Steven Cohan. All of them helped improve the book in innumerable and significant ways.

This collection would never have been possible without the efforts of Murray Pomerance, the Horizons of Cinema editor at the State University of New York Press, who believed in this project from the outset. His sage advice on all matters pertaining to it and the generous allocation of his time were valuable gifts. Gratitude is extended to James Pelz, codirector of the State University of New York Press, for the expeditious and professional manner in which he handled the publication of this book. I was also fortunate to have excellent referees whose suggestions improved the quality of the manuscript. I would also like to acknowledge the invited scholars represented in this volume for the high quality of their essays.

Finally, special appreciation is also due to my husband, Dr. Glenn Lapp, who was kind enough to provide feedback on all aspects of this project from its inception to its completion. He watched numerous suburb films with me, offered perspicacious insights and advice, and was always willing to read numerous drafts.

Introduction

Race and the Suburbs in American Film

MERRILL SCHLEIER

*L*OST *BOUNDARIES* (WERKER, 1949) was released two years after the
completion of the first Levittown suburb in Long Island, New
York, which was a harbinger of the massive postwar expansion of
such dwellings. Based on a true story that occurred in the 1920s, the film
largely takes place in a small, white New England town and concerns Dr.
Scott Carter (Mel Ferrer), an African American physician and his family
who pass for white, but whose identities are unearthed when he tries
to enlist as an officer during World War II and is rejected. The subsequent discovery by the townspeople and Dr. Carter's own children of his
long-held secret prompts everyone's soul searching, before the venerable
physician is embraced anew by his all-white patients, culminating in a
sanctifying church service. The Colonial town with its lily-white homes
and public buildings may serve as a synecdoche for the emerging suburb's
little white houses, environs, and inhabitants.

Yet the community's embrace of Dr. Carter is not consonant with
the reactions of whites to African Americans' efforts to integrate the
country's newly built postwar suburbs. Hence the film's producer, Louis
De Rochemont, believed that *Lost Boundaries* could have an ameliorative
effect on current race relations and their concomitant spatial divisions,
that it "might help white Americans turn away from outmoded 'separate

1

but equal' legislation" and change the country's racial dynamics, a hope that proved elusive. But the fact that De Rochement envisioned the film for white audiences served only to reinforce prevailing racial hierarchies.[1] Karen Bowdre argues further that the producer's use of white actors to play African American characters underscored the film's valorization of whiteness and the replication of the country's racial caste system.[2] By focusing the narrative on a singular and exceptional African American family at a time when race riots over housing were roiling the nation, *Lost Boundaries* served as only a liberal plea for limited integration. Its story of token inclusion through a conformist philosophy of racial assimilation, ostensibly told from the point of view of an African American family, foreshadows the manner in which most subsequent suburb films reproduced whiteness.

This anthology's chronological parameters begin during the postwar era when housing shortages altered the physical landscape of the United States, which resulted in a "suburban explosion," according to historian David M. P. Freund, and when a massive government-sponsored resegregation of the nation was underway.[3] Between 1950 and 1970, the population of the suburbs doubled to nearly seventy-four million, and by 2018 it rose to 175 million people. Even though suburbs developed in America in the early nineteenth century as a way for whites to retire to more salubrious, semirural locations, in part to avoid what they deemed riffraff in the increasingly more crowded and diverse urban centers, the far-reaching post–World War II exodus from cities to suburbs irrevocably changed the nation's geography and racial demography. The emergence of what has variously been referred to as suburb or suburban films, which continue up to the present, began soon after the war when these material changes coincided with political events—the suburban postwar housing boom with its concomitant racial restrictions and the civil rights movement's targeted focus on the integration of housing and social space. The book ends in the present when suburbs have increased exponentially with more diverse architectural and spatial typologies and inhabitants, but when segregation, discriminatory practices, and racialized income inequality still haunt their parameters.

Race and the Suburbs in American Film focuses on narrative films since they differ from television and other media in their initial representations of the suburbs. Postwar television shows were poised to satisfy sponsors and advertisers, often presenting, until not far in the past, a utopian, affirmative image of white nuclear families in such locales (e.g., *Leave It to Beaver, Father Knows Best, Ozzie and Harriet*); while suburb films were concerned more frequently with subject matter rife with conflict or with neighborhoods under siege, fabricated to garner wider audience members. This book commences with the premise that Hollywood cinematic iterations have not encompassed the suburbs' complexities—neither its varied typologies nor its heterogeneous inhabitants—nor do they address America's diverse audiences at the level of inclusion, production, or reception.[4] Up until recently many of those considered white, middle class, and heterosexual enjoyed the privilege of imagining themselves in such cinematic tales of suburban nostalgia, but despite the ability of Blacks, Latinx, Asian Americans, and other minorities to project themselves into these fictional settings, they possessed neither the luxury of inhabiting such locations nor of entering or leaving them at will.

Several studies concerning the suburb in film, television, and fiction in the last two decades precede this anthology, but the majority do not concentrate on race in American cinema exclusively. Perhaps the first to explore racialized representations of the suburbs in American literature was Catherine Jurca, focusing predominantly on the construction of whiteness. She claims that fictional portrayals of the suburbs frequently portray its privileged, dysfunctional middle-class white denizens as placeless victims at a time when African Americans were suffering real discrimination in matters of housing.[5] Amy Marie Kenyon's book *Dreaming Suburbia: Detroit and the Production of Postwar Space and Culture* (2004) followed; it explores spatial themes in suburban film and fiction, including the tensions produced by the racialized suburbs and their counterpart, the cities.[6] Both Robert Beuka's *Suburbia Nation: Reading Suburban Landscape in Twentieth-Century American Fiction and Film* (2004) and David R. Coon's *Look Closer: Suburban Narratives and American Values in Film and Television* (2014) address utopian and dystopian suburban variants in cinema, and the "idea" of the suburbs, with single chapters on race.[7] Timotheus Vermeulen's *Scenes from the Suburbs* (2014) acknowledges rightly the need for an analysis of race and ethnicity in more theoretical and aesthetic terms, and includes a short treatment of the television show *Desperate Housewives*.[8] Recently Amy Lynn Corbin's *Cinematic Geographies and Spectatorship in America* (2015) asserts, in an excellent chapter devoted solely to suburb films, that the display of otherness in the suburbs is often accomplished through displacement; for example, themes of teen rebellion or alien invasion may serve as metaphors for racial and cultural difference.[9] In the last five years, several other books that treat film and the suburbs in an international context have appeared but have not concerned themselves with race as their primary focus.[10]

Suburb Films—From Cycle to Genre

American suburb films emerged in Hollywood in the late 1940s and lasted for about ten years during a time of intense debate concerning the viability of white middle-class suburban living and a vexed period of racial apartheid when overt and covert racial violence was employed to protect white suburban domestic space from Blacks, Asian Americans, Latinx, and those deemed other. These include such post–World War II examples as *Pitfall* (De Toth, 1948), *Desperate Hours* (Wyler, 1955), *The Man in the Gray Flannel Suit* (Johnson, 1956), *Rebel Without a Cause* (Ray, 1956), and *Crime of Passion* (Oswald, 1956). Suburb films rely on the suburban environs (place), which may include the negotiation of its domestic interiors (space), as a motivating force in the cinematic plot in significant ways, whether thematically, through character development, or spatial logic. Defying cinema's traditional categories and periodizations, suburb films include but are not limited to melodramas, film noirs, social problem films, comedies, science fiction, and horror films. These diverse examples of suburb films are part of a cinematic cycle, according to Amanda Klein's definition, sharing similar "images, characters, settings, plots, or themes."[11] According to Klein, cycles are short-lived and topical and may emerge from a single film, continuing beyond their original source only if they are critically successful and garner a large audience, ever attendant to the latter's desires, while pointing to films' commercial or use value. Preceding genres, film cycles are concerned especially with the way cultural discourses by filmmakers, audiences, reviewers, and current events interact with cinematic texts.

Since cycles are linked to current events or material conditions, it is necessary to historicize them in their cultural, political, economic, and material milieus.[12] Suburb films from the late 1940s until the late 1950s accord with Klein's assertion that cycles emerge in response to contemporary discussions taking place in the mass media, in this case the widely debated nature of suburban life after World War II. Contemporary boosters, politicians, and real estate interests promoted the suburbs as utopian, wholesome, and exclusive, while social critics such as David Riesman, William H. Whyte, and Betty Friedan decried variously their putative soul crushing conformism and commodity fetishism for middle-class white people, while remaining conspicuously silent on the suburb's effects upon racialized others.[13] Most suburb cycle films begin by establishing the insufficiencies of white middle-class suburban life; but even at their most disparaging and destabilizing, these seemingly dystopian tales opt for suburban restoration or rehabilitation. For example, *No Down Payment* (Ritt, 1957) explores a Japanese American family's effort to move into the all-white Sunrise Hills in Southern California's Orange County, far from Los Angeles's dense urban population and diverse inhabitants. Despite the cinematic suburb's upbeat moniker, wholesome architectural façades, and seemingly friendly nuclear families, dysfunctional men and their accommodating wives—an alcoholic philanderer, a sadistic former sergeant turned rapist, and an ineffectual organization man—occupy the cloistered enclave. At the film's denouement, the rapist is killed, the husbands regain their professional standing, and the churchgoing Japanese American family is allowed to move in by ellipsis, thus restoring the promise of the suburb.[14]

Suburb films have surprisingly continued after the cycle's initial decade and up to the present with similar syntactical and semantic elements, thus rendering them more akin to Rick Altman's theorization of genres. But Altman cautions us not to assume that all genres operate in the same manner or in universal terms; some begin slowly, assuming familiar patterns, while others go through various paradigms, but always in dialogue with the flow of time.[15] Generic suburb films include but are not limited to *Bachelor in Paradise* (Arnold, 1961), *The Stepford Wives* (Forbes, 1975), *Ordinary People* (Redford, 1980), *Pleasantville* (Ross, 1998), *American Beauty* (Mendes, 1999), continuing into the twenty-first century with *Donnie Darko* (Kelly, 2001), *Revolutionary Road* (Mendes, 2008), and *Suburbicon* (Clooney, 2016). Many of their syntactical and semantic features, which commenced in previous cycle films, have been identified in several of the aforementioned cinematic suburb studies. Key themes include the appearance of a white, dysfunctional middle-class family unit, often consisting variously of emasculated male homeowners, bored housewives, and rebellious teenagers who seek independence from their surroundings, often in the city, all of whom are subject to the overwhelming character of suburban conformity and the quest for consumer goods occasioned by a belief in the American Dream. Even the few midcentury suburb films about the provisional, and problematic, inclusion of minorities, such as *No Down Payment* (Ritt, 1957) and *Take a Giant Step* (Leacock, 1959), or minority assimilation, transgression, and rebellion in the later *Better Luck Tomorrow* (Lin, 2002) and *Amreeka* (Dabis, 2009), explore newcomers' negotiations of predominantly white spaces and their challenging attempts at assimilation. These thematic features are accompanied by such semantic elements as placelessness and entrapment, which are prompted, in part, by the homogeneity and seeming pervasiveness of the built environment. Placelessness is often represented by downward tilt shots or bird's-eye views of nondescript prefabricated houses as far as the eye can see, engendering a sense of social and existential alienation among its largely white denizens. While I do not seek to interrogate all of the syntactical and semantic elements and narrative conventions of typical suburb films, it is necessary to problematize them in order to excavate their racialized underpinnings. That said, films situated in African American, Asian American, Latinx, and immigrant suburbs have been understudied, excluded from the canon, prompting a reevaluation, if not an expansion, of the suburb film's cyclical and generic parameters, and a reconsideration of what we mean by a suburb film.

There is no consensus concerning what constitutes a real suburb since they have changed so dramatically over time, including edge cities, ethnoburbs, and planned sprawl. Nevertheless, Hollywood has appropriated and focused repeatedly on a particular variant—privately owned, generic looking homes in planned, decentralized communities where white heteronormative families reside. Yet since the 1970s the suburb's shifting demographic, geographic, and diverse architectural character calls for a critical analysis of Hollywood's stubborn adherence to outdated suburban stereotypes, constituting a veritable cultural lag. The film industry's selective depictions of demographic and architectural sameness prevail even though working-class and racially, ethnically, and architecturally diverse suburbs have existed in Los Angeles, Baltimore, and Washington, DC for decades.[16] Becky M. Nicolaides and Andrew Wiese in their magisterial *Suburb Reader* point to the suburbs' multiplicity and the particularized experiences of its varied residents—African Americans, Latinx, Asian American, and working-class suburbanites.[17] Just as the suburbs were engaged in the politics of racial exclusion, in a parallel process Hollywood has habitually occluded others' points of view from its suburban-inspired boundaries, often reducing them to ancillary characters that occupy the margins of the narratives. Nicolaides and Wiese claim that these representations remain "one legacy of a long history of imagineering in the mass media in which whites were the only suburbanites who mattered."[18] In addition to interrogating whiteness, this book adapts Nicolaides and Wiese's important query to suburb films, "How did the 'other suburbanites' ascribe meaning to their own living spaces?"[19]

The Racialized Spatial Turn:
Suburban Typologies, Suburban Neighborhoods

Race and the Suburbs in American Film's contributors open up suburb films to spatial theorization whether through an analysis of location shooting, production design, or characters' habitation and negotiation of such places and spatial arrangements. Even though films are not passive reflections of material or social reality, they engage in a dialogue with their actual counterparts and inform cinematic adaptations. In this way, this book expands upon my own *Skyscraper Cinema* (2009) and Pamela Robertson Wojcik's excellent books *The Apartment Plot* (2010) and *The Apartment Complex* (2018), with a focus on the constructed cinematic environment's spatiality as a crucial component of investigation rather than relying on traditional genre or auteurist analyses.[20] As urban geographer David Delaney argues, space is an "enabling technology" through which race is produced—for example, it may be the result of such diverse ideologies as colorblindness, race consciousness, integrationist, assimilationist, separatist, and nativist, among others. Delaney encourages us to interrogate the spatial conditions under which one absorbs an assigned racial category and how one learns to negotiate its spaces. When we take such racialized spaces seriously, he continues, we must also consider such "race-making events" as "displacement, dislocation, and relocation."[21] It is well known that post–World War II suburbs were built on the principle of the exclusion of those deemed nonwhite, enshrined in racial covenants, redlining, and Federal Housing Administration rules and further enforced by physical barriers such as walls, cul-de-sacs, dead ends, and greenbelts; even freeways were constructed to separate the city from suburban neighborhoods to safeguard whiteness. Yet most of cinema's suburban cinematic narratives focus instead on the spatial travails of their white inhabitants, rather than the white suburb's more urgent sufferers, while ignoring the heterogeneous suburbs and their diverse inhabitants.[22]

For example, the semantics of placelessness seen in many suburb films is not simply an illustration of feelings of spatial alienation experienced by monolithic suburb dwellers, as several scholars claim, but it affects diverse populations and cinematic characters differently.[23] One way to understand the racial underpinnings of placelessness is to problematize the suburb's uniformly styled houses peopled by similar, conforming inhabitants who mirror their generic dwellings as well as their cinematic representations. We must bear in mind that real estate developers like William Levitt adopted architectural sameness in part as a purposeful tactic to valorize whiteness and the assimilation of racial and ethnic differences—a ploy copied by Hollywood filmmakers and production designers to signify the suburbs. Architectural historian Dianne Harris explores how such unacknowledged whiteness and its connection to property ownership permeated all aspects of the ideological and physical construction of the midcentury suburbs—its standardized classical revival and ranch style architecture, house plans, and interior design principles—which were then repeatedly reinforced in the media as a form of publicity and pro-paganda, instructing suburban residents how to perform and assimilate to whiteness in their suburban abodes and surrounding environs.[24] Writing in 1955, housing expert Charles Abrams demonstrates that architectural consistency was supposed to extend to a house's inhabitants—suburban middle-class denizen were "told to be homogeneous, not to mix with the rich or poor, and to use 'restrictions' to keep the 'wrong people' out" because "inharmonious racial, national or income groups" led to a decrease in property values.[25] Thus Harris insists that no exploration of the suburbs or its various representations in popular culture, and I argue in Hollywood cinema, are valid without a discussion of race even when it seems invisible.[26]

Filmmaker Jordan Peele explores placelessness in an exclusive, white suburban space from the perspective of African American city dwellers in *Get Out* (2017), employing the horror genre to underscore his point. An anonymous Black man in the film's initial nocturnal scene feels trepida-tion while traversing a generic suburban neighborhood in Connecticut, indicating that de facto segregation and Jim Crow are still prevalent in the putatively liberal Northeast. Sensing that he is out of his element, the man describes the neighborhood's look-a-like dwellings and the con-founding spatiality of its cul-de-sacs as a "confusing-ass suburb," where Edgewood Way and Edgewood Lane are indecipherable. As architectural historian Barbara Miller Lane explains, the layout of these suburbs—the large picture-windowed houses facing one another in circular cul-de-sacs, featuring ample front lawns without boundary fencing, which extended to the street—were purposely planned as confounding spaces, in part to keep such unwanted visitors out.[27] Soon the man's anxiety assumes tan-gible form as a color-coded white vehicle begins to track his movement down the street before a masked Ninja emerges and removes him forcibly, recalling the body snatching occasioned by slavery, police violence, and the white suburban resistance that accompanied integration.

Augmenting the work of David Delaney, George Lipsitz challenges us further to assess the relationship between the spatial dynamics of racial segregation and racial representation. He argues that "racism takes place" and that social relations "take on their full force and meaning when they are enacted physically in actual places" such as the suburbs, which shape and reproduce the significance of race.[28] He further posits the idea of white and Black racialized spatial imaginaries, in material spaces and in fictional, artistic, and, by implication, cinematic representations. For instance, the white spatial imaginary, of which the suburb serves as an archetype, structures feelings as well as social institutions. "It idealizes 'pure' and homogeneous spaces, controlled environments and predictive patterns of design and behavior."[29] According to Lipsitz, suburbs promote the values of individual escape and private acquisition (e.g., home ownership and commodities), which he refers to as a "possessive investment in whiteness" rather than collective action seen in the Black spatial imaginary that benefits all, serving as the locus for exchange value and the exclusion of nonnormative others.[30] While his paradigm is useful for the analysis of such spaces in cinema, we must also recognize that racialized spatial imaginaries are neither transhistorical nor perpetual and must be interrogated to identify how they operate temporally and in discreet locations.

Most Hollywood-produced suburb films are predicated on such white spatial imaginaries, and have until recently been composed of generic neighborhoods that house heteronormative families, which either exclude or jettison people of color and those considered other from their boundaries, both narratively and spatially. *Crime of Passion* (1956), for example, tells the story of queer, white San Franciscan Kathy Ferguson (Barbara Stanwyck) who begins the film as an accomplished journalist, supporting a community of distinct women through her newspaper column, but marries her way to a lowbrow, all-white Los Angeles suburb in the San Fernando Valley where social conformity and architectural monotony prevail.[31] The now stymied housewife soon covets a majestic Westwood suburban home like the one owned by chief inspector Tony Pope (Raymond Burr), her husband's boss, a way of "trading up" to attain success, wholly absorbing the values of the American Dream and its spatial analogue, a better white suburb. A failed extramarital affair with Pope to achieve her quest for upward mobility leads to a criminal act, hence her ineluctable downfall, transferring her from the perceived carceral spaces of the suburbs to the penitentiary, thereby jettisoning her from the former's environs. *Crime of Passion*'s spatialized white imaginaries of two suburbs, its syntactical elements (e.g., emasculated husband, dissatisfied wife, dysfunctional family unit) and semantic features (e.g., placelessness, entrapment, surveillance) remain the bulwark of most Hollywood suburb films.

In addition to suburban typologies, we may apply Lipsitz's notion of racialized imaginaries to specific geographies, neighborhoods, and places that have discreet histories. Several contributors to this anthology demonstrate that suburb films include such wide-ranging settings as the decentralized neighborhood of Los Angeles's Sugar Hill, the older suburbs of upstate New York, or in the urban fringes of Chicago. As I have previously argued, it is vital to excavate the built environment's embedded character to discover its hidden layers, following Walter Benjamin's example in his discussion of the Paris Arcades.[32] Architecture and its surrounding environs often serve as a palimpsest, preserving both a diachronic and synchronic relationship to present structures and their accompanying ideologies in culture.[33] Yet one must expand on Benjamin's project by excavating the impact of race on cinema's built environment, in this case the suburbs' domestic abodes and neighborhood milieus. Architect and architectural historian Craig E. Barton notes that architecture and its contiguous spaces have the capacity to serve as repositories of our individual as well as our collective racial pasts, encouraging scholars to recover these lost histories and inner meanings.[34] Thus middle-class Connecticut suburbs composed of white Neocolonial homes redolent of both the nation's founding and its slave-owning legacy in the films *Take a Giant Step* (1959) and *Get Out* (2017), the once utopian but now decayed suburb of Liberty City outside Miami in *Moonlight* (Jenkins, 2016), and the location-shot and production designed working-class ethnoburb of Quincy, Massachusetts in the independent film *Children of Invention* (Chun, 2009) and the challenges it presents for its newly arrived Chinese immigrants, present vastly dissimilar architectural and spatial histories that have implications for their inhabitants' identities.

One must bear in mind that African Americans, Asian Americans, and Latinx home seekers were formerly steered to older, well-established open access neighborhoods that whites had vacated rather than the newly built Levittown-like suburbs. These established localities were filled with variously styled houses (e.g., Victorian, Craftsman, Mission Revival) that were sometimes situated over the redline, not the little white, classically inspired dwellings and manicured lawns found in the new subdivisions that were pitched to white Americans. Historical suburbs possess their own repositories of memories and associations, which may include afterimages of slavery and recollections of racialized oppression. Thus, films about Black suburbs and their inhabitants, for example, may emit haunted presences that serve as specters of suffering or even death as illustrated in *Ganja and Hess* (Gunn, 1973), *To Sleep with Anger* (Burnett, 1990), and *Get Out*, constituting a subgenre. Coextensive with such geographical locations and styles are the interior spaces of such suburban houses—their circumscribed plans and layouts, rooms, walls, doorways, and other architectural features—which are occupied and mediated by their inhabitants, and may either reinforce or challenge Hollywood's racial stereotypes.

History of the Racialized Suburbs: American Dreams/American Nightmares

Race and the cinematic suburbs must be considered extra-cinematically, especially in view of the racialized ideologies that inform material places and their inhabitants, which were often adopted by Hollywood. Robert Beuka and others point out that suburbs became stereotypical images of the American Dream after World War II, with the popular media proffering "glowing images of American life to an emerging sense of the suburbs as the promised land of the American middle class."[35] Such superficially promising views, despite their drawbacks, are intrinsic to cinematic suburban discourses, and are often conflated with notions of the American Dream—the valorization of individual achievement realized by the ownership of a private, detached home, or a more upscale variant, a stable heteronormative family, and the acquisition of consumer appliances and an automobile. Such is the premise of *Mr. Blandings Builds His Dream House* (H. C. Potter, 1948), *Crime of Passion* (1956), and *Love, Simon* (Berlanti, 2018). Even immigrants and minorities who move to the suburbs are in pursuit of the American Dream in *Towelhead* (Ball, 2008), *Amreeka*, and *Better Luck Tomorrow*, albeit with different obstacles placed in their paths. But as Vermeulen argues, this façade often hides a dark and sinister underbelly, but how and for whom?[36] If the American Dream is but a provisional mirage that requires a rehabilitative intervention as staged in suburb films, why have they largely considered its impact on white denizens or through strategies of assimilation?

Procuring a suburban house was also regarded as the quintessential symbol of American citizenship, a fulfillment of a patriotic adherence to capitalist principles amid the fear of Communist or alien infiltration, especially during the Cold War. Many postwar suburban cycle films present such aspects of the American Dream under threat or siege by swarthy criminals (*Desperate Hours*), urban marauders (*Pitfall*, *The Reckless Moment*), or even mental instability (*Bigger Than Life*) which required extirpation in order to restore suburban equanimity, hence the Dream. Viewing these films through a racial lens during the prevailing attempt by civil rights organizations to integrate the suburbs may suggest the metaphorical incursion of "others" into the suburbs and a concomitant desire to maintain its racial purity.

While American Dream propaganda reached fruition after World War II, its racialized foundations were already apparent in the earlier pronouncements of President Herbert Hoover. In a 1930 speech delivered at the Conference on Building and Home Ownership, he waxed poetic about suburban home acquisition as the realization of racialized citizenship, albeit articulated in coded terms: "Those immortal ballads . . . such as 'Home Sweet Home' . . . were not written about tenements or apartments. They are expressions of racial longing, which find outlet in the living poetry and songs of our people. . . . That our people should live in their own homes is a sentiment deep in the heart of our race and of American life."[37] Realtors, bankers, and elected officials knew full well that Hoover's allusions to race meant that such houses were meant for middle-class white citizens only, far removed from the problems of the urban sphere. Architectural historian John Archer points out that one of the animating forces of the American Dream was escape from the "pressure, congestion, and corruption of urban life" to locales that resembled more readily the salubrious open spaces of the country.[38] Whites employed segregation as a strategy to effect this purifying regime, according to Archer, constructing homogeneity by race and class, thereby more readily preserving their rights as individuals.[39] By juxtaposing suburban homes with tenements and apartments, Hoover relied on an established trope of distinguishing and separating them in the spatial imaginary from diverse cities where people of color and lower-class ethnics resided.

Postwar suburbs were deliberately planned and built as segregated spaces for returning white veterans and their families by private developers with the aid of federal subsidies, demonstrating the manner in which race, the built environment, and real estate are mutually constitutive.[40] Yet legal scholar Cheryl I. Harris argues that the inextricable link between whiteness, private property, and value was foundational to the United States, predating the advent of suburbs; Blacks were treated as property while white ownership of property (e.g., land, dwellings, possessions) was validated, while accruing such additional privileges as human rights, liberties, and immunities, and the right to exclude others not deemed white.[41] Indeed, even a neighborhood's worth was thought of as intrinsic to those that inhabited it; locations with white occupants were appraised higher than those with predominantly African Americans, Latinx, and Asian Americans. Charles Abrams asserted that real estate law even regarded upscale Blacks who wished to provide their children with a college education and "thought they were entitled to live among whites" as poised to "instigate a form of blight," reinforcing the idea that real estate value was superimposed on racialized bodies.[42]

Thus the postwar Levittowns and Lakewoods of America and their suburban offspring followed established racialized traditions enshrined in legal doctrine (e.g., racial covenants, racial zoning, redlining); updated during the Depression with the formation of the Home Owner's Loan Corporation and continued by the Federal Housing Administration, and the Veterans Administration after World War II, which denied FHA and VA loans to Blacks; administered and solidified by physical barriers; and reinforced and codified by de facto practices (e.g., steering and blockbusting by realtors), which were all constructed to bar African Americans, Latinx, Asian Americans, and other minorities while sanctioning European ethnics to become white through assimilation. Suburban white homeowners often augmented such state authorized and private business practices by embracing NIMBY (not in my neighborhood) policies, which were invented ostensibly to protect their investments, in turn creating a generation of mostly white suburban dwellers who were hostile to the civil rights movement and to those they deemed nonwhite. Many suburbs were consequently produced and maintained as racialized spaces in which private property rights were valorized over nondiscriminatory human rights, serving as the material manifestations of the "set of practices, cultural norms, and institutional arrangements that both reflect and help create and maintain race-based outcomes in society."[43] However, many suburb films persist in addressing the adverse effects of the American Dream upon whites rather than upon African Americans, Asian Americans, Latinx, immigrants, and ethnic minorities, the real victims of its de facto and de jure practices.

But the premise that the American Dream, of which the suburban house was a bulwark, was available to anyone if they simply exerted the requisite effort needs to be problematized in both material reality and cinematic representations. Only recently have suburb films begun to address the suburban genre's dystopian syntax and semantics for people of color in such films as *Amreeka*, *99 Homes*, and *Get Out*. But as early as 1964 Malcolm X took issue with the mythos of the American Dream, arguing that African Americans were neither the beneficiaries of American democracy nor its institutional privileges, but rather of its hypocrisies. "We didn't see any American Dream," he charged. "We experienced only the American nightmare."[44] For African Americans, this was especially applicable to the purchase of a suburban home. While it is accurate that token Black families were admitted to some white suburbs, beginning in the postwar period, realtors steered most African Americans to open access or to all Black suburbs, preserving the country's racial apartheid, a practice that is still prevalent today. The segregation of most suburban neighborhoods, and the lower wages and the banning of subsidized loans for African Americans and other minorities, precluded their entrance to white suburban neighborhoods, which enjoyed higher tax revenues, better schools, available jobs, and enhanced services. While middle-class African American and Latinx suburbs were established, they often had private economies that were less prosperous than their white counterparts.

Thus middle-class prosperity and respectability did not necessarily benefit the minority house seeker or owner; rather, their achievement was often exploited by predatory lenders to plunder their resources further in the secondary loans markets after World War II and beyond, as Ta-Nehisi Coates and others have observed. African Americans in particular paid more than whites for comparable houses and were compelled to buy contract loans at higher interest rates, with no ability to accrue equity, hence wealth accumulation, like their white counterparts.[45] Before the 2008 housing crisis and subsequent economic meltdown, for example, lenders such as Wells Fargo and Countrywide Financial (now Bank of America) targeted African Americans and other minorities for predatory loans, even forging relationships with church and community groups to achieve their goals. For example, Blacks with "sterling credit ratings" were charged higher fees and rates on mortgages and steered into subprime and adjustable loans when they could afford cheaper ones compared to white borrowers with similar credit profiles.[46]

Developing Malcolm X's notion of the American Nightmare, Kee-anga-Yamahtta Taylor begins by exposing the Dream's underbelly—that when people fail at attaining the promise of American exceptionalism and opportunity, their personal failures, rather than a racist and class based system, serve as the explanation. In response to then governor Ronald Reagan's valorization of the plentitude occasioned by the American Dream in 1974, Taylor argues that it was "wholly contingent on the erasure or rewriting of three themes in American history—genocide, slavery, and the massive exploitation of waves of immigrant workers."[47] In her book *Race for Profit* (2019), she investigates further the continued exploitation of African Americans in the acquisition of privately owned homes after the passage of the Fair Housing Act of 1968. That is, despite the federal government's purported desire to provide more Blacks the opportunity to purchase houses, they were often located in economically depressed urban locations, in an effort to preserve the lily whiteness of most suburbs. But the government abrogated the program's supervision to private industry, to the very lenders that had hitherto preyed upon African Americans, in effect allowing the wolf to guard the henhouse. Mortgage lenders used the program as an opportunity to further extract monies from already economically disadvantaged Black communities. Additionally, federal inspection standards were loosened, paving the way for so-called "zombie homes" that would never accrue equity, and sold with HUD assistance to the unsuspecting poor, often Black welfare mothers who could ill afford them and their inevitable repairs.[48] Houses were thus repossessed and sold again, with the government guaranteeing the mortgage broker's initial investment while disadvantaging the homeowner, who lost everything. Taylor refers to these practices as a form of the "predatory inclusion" of African Americans in the so-called American Dream. Similar rapacious practices commenced in the 1990s and continued until the economic meltdown of 2008.[49] Lenders targeted poor minorities with subprime or what was referred to in internal memos as "ghetto loans," fully aware that when the interest rates rose, their victims would default.[50]

The American Nightmare also extended to various types of antagonism perpetrated against people of color especially in the suburbs, from microaggressions to overt acts of hostility against those who dared traverse its white designated spaces. As Andrew Wiese has noted, "When it came to race, arson was as suburban as the backyard barbeque grill during much of the postwar period.[51] Yet these acts of explicit aggression were purposely suppressed in the mass media, according to historian Arnold R. Hirsch, leading him to refer to the mid-twentieth century as an era of "hidden violence" against African Americans in particular, but also perpetrated against Asian Americans and other minorities who tried to gain entrance to the white suburbs.[52] While microaggressions in the white suburbs are seen in many postwar suburb cycle films, including *Take A Giant Step*, *Rebel Without a Cause*, and *No Down Payment*, blatant acts of racial violence perpetrated by whites against Blacks are likewise omitted.

Racialized Production and Distribution of Suburb Films

Just as the real suburbs were engaged in the politics of racial exclusion, Hollywood has habitually occluded others' points of view from its suburban-inspired boundaries, often reducing them to secondary characters. (e.g., *Mr. Blandings*, *Reckless Moment*, *Rebel Without a Cause*). Hollywood preferred white suburbanites while creating and reinforcing an audience of white, middle-class consumers, believing them to be the most lucrative revenue stream. If cinema's houses entail a vicarious form of property ownership, habitation, and emplacement, as John David Rhodes claims in his book *The Spectacle of Property* (2016), then Hollywood's cinematic suburbs have omitted people of color from its parameters in a similar manner.[53]

This volume aims to remedy these exclusions by problematizing the very notion of the suburb or suburban film by reinserting those that have been neglected, rendered marginal, or invisible whether through lack of analysis, funding, distribution, or promotion. Benjamin Wiggins identifies the manner in which the racialization of cinematic suburban space occurs at the level of distribution and promotion in such films as *Boyz n the Hood* (Singleton, 1991) and *Menace II Society* (Hughes and Hughes, 1993) while urging us to think beyond traditional genre categories. For example, despite *Boyz*'s location in the suburbs of Inglewood, California, it was nevertheless marketed as an inner city and urban film, which reflects a "conservative, imaginative geography put forth by Hollywood's marketing department, which render the systematic problems of race as confined to the urban sphere."[54] In order to fully understand the plight of its Black cinematic suburban protagonists and their often economically depressed environs, one must begin to situate such films in the context of governmental policies of redlining, the purposeful defunding and disinvestment of neighborhoods, and the introduction of low income public housing, which altered their racial and class makeup.

Beginning in the 1970s and continuing to the mid-1980s and beyond, a group of independent Black filmmakers, such as Charles Burnett, Bill Gunn, and Kathleen Collins, to name a few, began to explore African American suburban spaces and family life, which were created in part as a reaction to Hollywood's Blaxploitation films and renditions of the Black rural experience. Recent research on the L.A. Rebellion and East Coast Black independent filmmakers offers an antidote to the representation of stereotypical white suburban subdivisions.[55] We discover in works by African American filmmakers another suburb that did not require whiteness, but might reveal what Ellen C. Scott refers to as "colonial entanglements, back migration, or tangled domestic and familial concerns" explored through domestic abodes.[56] Often apprehended through their own life experiences in domestic spaces, Black filmmakers reveal the L.A. group's socially conscious commitment to "the real world material, psychological and spiritual challenges that Black people face in a racist society." As Allyson Field, Jean Christopher Horak, and Jacqueline Najuma Stewart have recently contended, they created and circulated films free from the restrictions that made "commercial 'official cinema' corrupt and conservative in style and politics, such as manipulative narrative conventions, high budgets, censorship, and prohibitive distribution and exhibition systems."[57] Most Black filmmakers were not able to obtain Hollywood backing from producers who routinely rejected their scripts and from distributors who refused to carry their independently made and financed films.[58] Scholarship on the Los Angeles independent school of filmmakers offers a paradigm for other marginalized independent cinemas to recover productions that have been left out of cinema studies discourses, leading to a reevaluation of traditional cycle and genre categories, to which this anthology gestures.

Race and Bodies in Space

In accord with Henri Lefebvre, this book also differentiates between place and space: place refers to a material location, and social space is produced by human activity.[59] Critical race theorists build upon the work of Lefebvre by acknowledging how race is also constructed and performed in the world. Sociologists Michael Omi and Howard Winant claim that race is an artificial process of "making people up," while reminding us that these ideological constructions are subject to change in lived experience.[60] Likewise, Karen E. Fields and Barbara J. Fields caution us to be leery of even the concept of race, which has its genesis in bio-determinism, and is often conflated with racism, although they belong to "different families of social construction." Inventing the term "racecraft," they claim that it is a mental process akin to witchcraft and subject to all forms of irrationality. This accords with Omi and Winant's claim that race exists in both the imagination and in human action, hence in space.[61]

Race and the Suburbs in Postwar American Film considers how the suburb's cinematic inhabitants affect such locations through their own agency, sometimes as a form of resistance to white hegemony and its

assimilationist project. Adapting Lefebvre's theorizations of human conduct
to the spaces of cinema, the book's contributors pay particular attention
to how racialized bodies negotiate their ways in and through cinematic
spaces, which can alter and disrupt physical environments. Real and
imagined suburban locations are occupied by bodies, which may appear
phenotypically and culturally different from one another and perform and
negotiate their identities through interaction with others. Thus, this book
considers how people of color, minorities, and nonconforming whites
negotiate spatial politics in various suburban settings, including physical
and psychological exclusion, isolation, containment, and entrapment,
variations of the ideological and spatial barriers operative after World
War II and beyond. Yet there is a mediation of and a resistance to such
obstacles, demonstrating a sense of agency and cultural power. Geographers
Wilbur Zelinsky and Barrett Lee employ the term "heterolocalism," or
the ability of immigrants to maintain their distinctive cultural or ethnic
identities in the suburbs despite the pressure to conform to white hegemonic standards.[62] Likewise, African Americans, Asian Americans, and Arab
Americans and others forge new versions of the suburbs, infusing them
with their own spatial practices and cultural or ethnic histories through
the introduction of art, food, and music, thereby creating new suburbs
by altering their formerly white parameters.

In the last twenty-five years, suburbs have become new immigrant
gateway communities, further problematizing issues of race and ethnicity
in their environs. Urban geographer Susan W. Hardwick has even gone so
far as to refer to this period as a time when the United States became a
"suburban immigrant nation."[63] Additionally, the emergence of ethnoburbs
from the effects of globalization, the struggles between nations, and shifts
in immigration policy has led to a new Asian American global citizenry,
which has changed the assimilation imperative in some suburbs.[64] At the
same time, suburbs vary considerably in their treatment of those perceived
as nonwhite, including immigrants, migrants, and asylum seekers, to either
occupy the public square or seek shelter. Laws and ordinances may be
passed to either preserve or alter its majority, white demographic. Films
about the suburbs have not caught up sufficiently with such ever-changing
places, particularly in light of the resurgence of nativism, accompanied
by xenophobic and racist rhetoric and new legal restrictions in many
suburbs, which escalated in the age of former President Donald Trump.
Before the 2020 election, Trump sought to appeal to white suburban
voters with anti-Black and anti-immigrant racist speech, attempting
to frighten them into believing that a vote for Biden would mean the

incursion of Black Lives Matter protestors—who he labeled violent—into their neighborhoods. But according to the Brookings Institution, Biden's presidential win was due largely to his capturing the votes of those in diverse suburbs and smaller metropolitan areas in several swing states, demonstrating that Trump's strategy had not only failed, but that his view of a nation of mostly white suburbs was an anachronism.[65]

Contributions

My research has long focused on urban architecture and environs in cinema, especially how such spaces and bodies are mediated by gender, class, and race. In my book *Skyscraper Cinema*, for example, I explored the manner in which the postwar suburbs were seen as counterparts to lofty office buildings, employed as spaces of containment for white organization men. In addition, I showed that in such silent films as *Safety Last* (Newmeyer and Taylor, 1923), the Boy's (Harold Lloyd) white, middle-class ascension to the skyscraper's crest, a test of his masculine mettle, is buttressed narratively and spatially by the film's African American and Jewish characters. As previously stated, my interest in race and the suburban environs in cinema was stimulated by an invitation to contribute to Stefano Baschiera and Miriam de Rosa's anthology, *Film and Domestic Space* (2020), in which I examined Japanese Americans' efforts to inhabit white domestic and suburban spaces.[66] But my concern for race's embeddedness in such environs goes deeper, prompted by my personal memories of the white, middle-class suburban housing project where I grew up in the 1950s and early '60s, a segregated environment that was created by the New York City Housing Authority, a government agency.

The current book collection continues my abiding interest and represents the first sustained effort to interrogate race in the suburbs in American film, although it is not meant to be all-inclusive or comprehensive, but rather to open the subject up to further examination. Each of the chapters employs a different combination of strategies and methodological approaches to interrogate the manner in which the suburb and race are imbricated. Several of the themes that wind their way throughout, but are not limited to, include the new racial and ethnic complexity of suburban environments in contemporary films; the interaction of seemingly homogeneous suburban neighborhoods and diverse metropolitan locales in forging identities; the effects of slavery, Jim Crow, and racial trauma on the Black suburban experience; intersectional notions of race, ethnicity, and identity formation among suburban inhabitants; suburban inclusion and visibility versus exclusion and invisibility; the links between race and neoliberalism in suburban space; and the vexed experiences of new immigrant populations in the suburbs, among others. Several authors explore how racial and ethnic characteristics coalesce with class, sexual identity, and gender to disclose the manner in which identities are overdetermined especially as they interact with the built environment. It is my aim that this volume will inspire further scholarship in the aforementioned areas of inquiry, while serving as an impetus to interrogate other issues relating to racialized bodies and racialized places and spaces in the cinematic suburbs.

John David Rhodes explores the Black female domestic servant as a cipher of the house's racialized spatiality, at a time when their emplacement in Hollywood films echoed Black actors' underpaid bit parts and anonymous roles as extras. Rhodes theorizes that the Black maid's body graphs the terrain of the suburban house, including its spatial parameters in *Mr. Blandings Builds His Dream House* (1948) and as an autonomous, and spatially defined agent in *The Reckless Moment* (1949), consonant with director Max Ophuls's mobile camerawork.

Merrill Schleier focuses on the travails of the Scotts, the first Black family to move into an all-white northeastern suburb in *Take a Giant Step* (1959). Experiencing what Omi and Winant refer to as various scales of racism, Schleier argues that the Scotts are subjected to the racialized ruptures between institutional, social, and private domestic space for middle-class African Americans in the white suburbs. These unequal spatial divisions ensure their racial containment, prompting their feelings of isolation, placelessness, and even entrapment, which are determined by both race and class. Schleier analyzes production design, architectural style, and prop placement as indicators of white material and ideological spaces in which the family is ensconced.

Through Bill Gunn's independent horror film *Ganja and Hess* (1973), Ellen C. Scott examines the understudied Black cinematic suburbs as a place of lush landscapes and gothic-styled homes that are replete with the traumas of colonialism and migration, far removed from Hollywood's standardized white depictions. In a suburban home of multiple rooms replete with art objects that bear the stain of European oppression and African memories alike, whites haunt the interior as spectral presences of death. As Scott demonstrates, Gunn locates the class divisions that trouble its Black suburban inhabitants in *Ganja and Hess*, rendering them at once predators and prey. She suggests that the despite the Black suburb's haunting, it contains the possibilities of healing and self-discovery.

In accord with Scott, Josh Glick considers the magic realism of *To Sleep with Anger* (1990) by the independent filmmaker Charles Burnett who broke from Hollywood's hackneyed, largely urban, and criminalized portrayals of Black family life. Glick looks at the Sugar Hill suburb of Los Angeles, which became a dwelling place for successful Black residents amid the contentious battles to integrate the California suburbs. Yet the Butler family must also reconcile their contemporary suburban experience with their traumatic rural southern past, which is visited upon them by the trickster Harry (Danny Glover), a past friend and coworker. Glick also explores the distribution and reception of the film to demonstrate the manner in which such suburb films were formerly sidelined and misrepresented.

Timotheus Vermeulen discusses the appearance of an interracial couple, a surprisingly uncommon trope in suburb films, in the comedic *Guess Who* (Sullivan, 2005), based on the earlier social melodrama *Guess Who's Coming to Dinner* (Kramer, 1967). In accord with Rhodes and Scott, Vermeulen maps the movement of racialized bodies through the porous boundaries of the suburban house via cinematography by relying on Edward Soja and Henri Lefebvre's theories of space. Vermeulen claims that Blacks and whites are treated in oppositional, essentialized terms in *Guess Who*, leaving the viewer with a depoliticized, retrogressive depiction of racialized difference in the suburbs.

Both Helen Heran Jun and Amy Lynn Corbin examine the immigrant experience in the suburbs. Focusing on two Asian American tales, the films *Better Luck Tomorrow* (2002) and *Children of Invention* (2009), Jun uncovers the contradictions in discourses on assimilation and socioeconomic mobility implied by suburbanization. As Jun demonstrates, despite their divergent settings, both films show Asian American suburban aspiration as rife with dysfunction and loss. Jun argues that the neoliberal ideology of success characterized by entrepreneurship and instrumentalized logic is marketed to Asian Americans and other immigrant communities as a way to neutralize their ethnic identities. Amy Corbin examines the Arab American immigrant experience in *Towelhead* (2007) and *Amreeka* (2009) from the perspective of several suburban cinematic tropes, including conformity, isolation, and teenage alienation. Borrowing from Jane Gaines's theory that Black silent films may "inhabit" rather than imitate traditional white genre categories, Corbin shows that both films are mediated through Arab Americans' cultural and political experiences at a time of increasing hostility toward Middle Eastern immigrants and Muslims in the post

9/11 era. In accord with Jun, Corbin asserts that the cinematic suburbs remain largely alienating white domains for immigrants.

Paul J. Massood analyzes the Academy Award–winning *Moonlight* (2016) through the lens of its suburban setting, Liberty City outside Miami, as a way to help "reimagine both the definitions and the representations of suburbia, of ghettoes, and of real and imagined spaces." In accord with the main character, Chiron, Liberty City is replete with contradictions, at once both beautiful and miserable. According to Massood, director Barry Jenkins explores the intersection and performance of Black masculinity and sexuality, attendant to the way class, criminality, and urban geography are implicated in the construction of identity. Massood concludes that *Moonlight* may not be a suburb film after all; rather, that genre construction is not based solely on location but on how difference is conveyed within representation.

Elizabeth A. Patton employs the concept of the palimpsest to illustrate that the white suburbs are laden with the memories and stains of slavery, racial terror, and racial essentialism in Jordan Peele's horror film *Get Out* (2016). Patton explores how director and screenwriter Peele challenges neoliberal racism and colorblindness that obscure the lingering impact of structural racism. Identifying the film's white suburb as a veritable Sundown town, Patton explores the way Black bodies are disappeared and neutralized through abduction, terror, and incarceration, harkening back to past anti-Black racist practices. In accord with Scott and Glick, Patton shows that Black bodies are still haunted by past traumatic histories and contemporary realities as they try to negotiate their way through suburban spaces.

In his analysis of *Suburbicon* (2016) and *99 Homes* (2014), Nathan Holmes makes sense of suburbs as social rather than predominantly racialized spaces, eschewing the idea that suburban whiteness is a transhistorical essence. Holmes adopts Marshall Berman's idea of avidity as a template to find new social formations in the suburbs. As Holmes argues, *Suburbicon* explores the 1957 riots that accompanied the integration of Levittown by psychologizing whiteness. In contrast, *99 Homes* examines the psychic and economic dynamics of the 2008 housing crisis, which, Holmes argues, regards homeowners as atomized entrepreneurs who are victimized by the vicissitudes of neoliberalism.

Angel Daniel Matos likewise interrogates whiteness, by considering the ways suburban spatiality and modernity affect its connection with queerness in *Love, Simon* (2018). Even though the film ostensibly reflects a universal appeal in its staging of teenage Simon's seemingly normal life in a typical suburban house, signified, in part, by a station wagon that is gifted to him, Matos regards it as a film in crisis. He argues that the nostalgia and traditional values associated with suburbs are pressured by the mobility and the privacy offered through the suburban car, which provides its main character a liberatory space to reveal his gay identity, inexorably altering his suburban whiteness.

Notes

1. Louis De Rochemont quoted in J. Dennis Robinson, "History Matters: The 'Story' behind 'Lost Boundaries'," March 5, 2018, https://www.seacoastonline.com/news/20180305/history-matters-story-behind-lost-boundaries.

2. Karen Bowdre, "Passing Films and the Language of Racial Equality," *Black Camera* 5 (Spring 2014): 22.

3. David M. P. Freund, *Colored Property: State Policy and White Racial Politics and Suburban America* (Chicago: University of Chicago Press, 2010), 4.

4. See Samuel G. Freedman's prescient article, "Suburbia Outgrows Its Image in the Arts," *New York Times*, February 28, 1999, https://www.nytimes.com/1999/02/28/arts/suburbia-outgrows-its-image-in-the-arts.html.

5. Catherine Jurca, *White Diaspora: The Suburb and the Twentieth-Century Novel* (Princeton, NJ: Princeton University Press, 2001).

6. Amy Marie Kenyon, *Dreaming Suburbia: Detroit and the Production of Postwar Space and Culture* (Detroit: Wayne State University Press, 2004).

7. Robert Beuka, *SuburbiaNation: Reading Suburban Landscape in Twentieth-Century American Fiction and Film* (New York: Palgrave Macmillan, 2004); David R. Coon, *Look Closer: Suburban Narratives and American Values in Film and Television* (New Brunswick, NJ: Rutgers University Press, 2014).

8. Timotheus Vermeulen, *Scenes from the Suburbs: Suburban Space in US Film and Television* (Edinburgh: Edinburgh University Press, 2014).

9. Amy Lynn Corbin, *Cinematic Geographies and Multicultural Spectatorship in America* (New York: Palgrave Macmillan, 2015), 170.

10. Other books include Stephen Rowley, *Movie Towns and Sitcom Suburbs* (New York: Palgrave Macmillan, 2015); David Forrest, Graeme Harper, and Jonathan Rayner, eds., *Filmurbia: Screening the Suburbs* (New York: Palgrave Macmillan, 2017); and Philippe Met and Derek Schilling, *Screening the Paris Suburb: From the Silent Era to the 1990s* (Manchester: Manchester University Press, 2018).

11. Amanda Klein, *American Film Cycles: Reframing Genres, Screening Social Problems, and Defining Subcultures* (Austin: University of Texas Press, 2011), 4.

12. Klein, *American Film Cycles*, 4–12.

13. David Riesman, et al., *The Lonely Crowd: A Study of the Changing American Character* (New Haven: Yale University Press, 1950); William H. Whyte,

The Organization Man (New York: Simon and Schuster, 1956); Betty Friedan, *The Feminine Mystique* (New York: W. W. Norton and Co., 1963).

14. See my chapter "Whiteness, Japanese American Masculinity and Architectural Space in the Mid-century Cinematic Suburbs," in *Film and Domestic Space: Architectures, Representations, Dispositif*, ed. Stefano Baschiera and Miriam De Rosa (Edinburgh: University of Edinburgh Press, 2020).

15. Rick Altman, "A Semantic/Syntactic Approach to Film Genre," *Film Journal* 23 (Spring 1984): 8.

16. Jonathan Fricker and Donna Fricker, "Louisiana Architecture: 1945–1965 Post-War Subdivisions and the Ranch House," 2010, Louisiana Division of Historic Preservation, http://www.crt.state.la.us/hp/nationalregister/historic_contexts/ranchhousefinalrevised.pdf.

17. Becky M. Nicolaides and Andrew Wiese, eds., *The Suburb Reader*, 2nd ed. (New York: Routledge, 2016). See also Becky M. Nicolaides, *My Blue Heaven: Life and Politics in the Working Class Suburbs of Chicago, 1920–65* (Chicago: University of Chicago Press, 2002).

18. Nicolaides and Wiese, *Suburb Reader*, 7.

19. Nicolaides and Wiese, *Suburb Reader*, 194.

20. Merrill Schleier, *Skyscraper Cinema: Architecture and Gender in American Film* (Minneapolis: University of Minnesota Press, 2009); Pamela Robertson Wojcik, *The Apartment Plot: Urban Living in American Film and Popular Culture, 1945 to 1975* (Durham, NC: Duke University Press, 2010); Pamela Robertson Wojcik, ed., *The Apartment Complex: Urban Living and Global Screen Cultures* (Durham, NC: Duke University Press, 2018). See my bibliography for a consideration of the voluminous scholarship on cinema and the built environment.

21. David Delaney, "The Space That Race Makes," *Professional Geographer* 54, no. 1 (2002): 7.

22. In *White Diaspora*, 9, Catherine Jurca points out that in suburb novels, in a feature appropriated by Hollywood films, white flight is perceived as the result of persecution, rendering the occupants' multiple possessions as evidence of their spiritual emptiness and oppression, thereby treating privileged homeowners as the victims of their obvious success.

23. Beuka, *SuburbiaNation*, 2; Corbin, *Cinematic Geographies*, 172.

24. Dianne Harris, *Little White Houses: How the Postwar Home Constructed Race in America* (Minneapolis: University of Minnesota Press, 2013).

25. Charles Abrams, *Forbidden Neighbors: A Study of Prejudice in Housing* (New York: Harper and Brothers, 1955), 163.

26. Harris, *Little White Houses*, 15. See Richard Dyer, "White," *Screen* 29 (Autumn 1988): 46.

27. Barbara Miller Lane, *Houses for a New World: Builders and Buyers in the American Suburbs* (Princeton, NJ: Princeton University Press, 2012), 9–15, 24–27.

28. George Lipsitz, *How Racism Takes Place* (Philadelphia: Temple University Press, 2011), 5.

29. Lipsitz, *How Racism Takes Place*, 29

30. George Lipsitz, *The Possessive Investment in Whiteness: How White People Profit from Identity Politics* (Philadelphia: Temple University Press, 1998).

31. See my chapter "Queerness, Race, and Class in the Mid-Century Suburb Film *Crime of Passion* (1956)," in *Crossroads: Intersections of Space and Identity in Screen Cultures*, ed. Angel Daniel Matos, Paula Massood, and Pam Robertson Wojcik (Durham, NC: Duke University Press, 2021).

32. Walter Benjamin, *The Arcades Project*, trans. Howard Eiland and Kevin McLaughlin (Cambridge, MA: Belknap Press of Harvard University Press, 1999).

33. Schleier, *Skyscraper Cinema*, xii.

34. Craig E. Barton, ed., *Sites of Memory: Perspectives on Architecture and Race* (New York: Princeton Architectural Press, 2001). See also *Race and Modern Architecture: A Critical History from the Enlightenment to the Present*, ed. Irene Cheng, Charles L. Davis II, and Mabel O. Wilson (Pittsburgh: University of Pittsburgh Press, 2020).

35. Beuka, *SuburbiaNation*, 5–6.

36. Vermeulen, *Scenes from the Suburbs*, 2.

37. Abrams, *Forbidden Neighbors*, 147.

38. John Archer, *Architecture and Suburbia: From English Villa to American Dream House, 1690–2000* (Minneapolis: University of Minnesota Press, 2005), 253.

39. Archer, *Architecture and Suburbia*, 300.

40. Gwendolyn Wright, *Building the Dream: A Social History of American Housing* (Oxford: Oxford University Press, 1981); Kenneth Jackson, *Crabgrass Frontier: The Suburbanization of the United States* (New York: Oxford University Press, 1985); Clifford Clark, *The American Family Home, 1800–1960* (Chapel Hill, NC: University of North Carolina Press, 1986); Dolores Hayden, *Building Suburbia: Green Fields and Urban Growth, 1820–2000* (New York: Vintage Books, 2003); Stephen Grant Meyer, *As Long as They Don't Move Next Door: Segregation and Racial Conflict in American Neighborhoods* (Lanham, MD: Rowman and Littlefield, 2000); Lynn Spigel, *Welcome to the Dream House: Popular Media and Postwar Suburbs (Console-ing Passions)* (Durham, NC: Duke University Press, 2001); Archer, *Architecture and Suburbia*; Andrew Wiese, *Places of Their Own: African American Suburbanization in the United States*, new ed. (Chicago: University of Chicago Press, 2005); Charlotte Brooks, *Alien Neighbors, Foreign Friends: Asian Americans, Housing, and the Transformation of Urban California* (Chicago: University of Chicago Press, 2009).

41. Cheryl I. Harris, "Whiteness and Property," in *Critical Race Theory: The Key Writings That Formed the Movement*, ed. Kimberlé Crenshaw, Neil Gotanda, Gary Peller, and Kendall Thomas (New York: New Press, 1995), 278, 283.

42. Nathan William MacChesney, *The Principles of Real Estate Law* (New York: Macmillan Company, 1927), 586, quoted in Abrams, *Forbidden Neighbors*, 157.

43. John A. Powell, *Racing to Justice: Transforming Our Conceptions of Self and Other to Build an Inclusive Society* (Bloomington: Indiana University Press, 2012), 4.

44. Malcolm X, "The American Nightmare," 1964. https://sites.psu.edu/jld5710/2012/10/02/1964-the-american-nightmare/.

45. Ta-Nehisi Coates, "The Case for Reparations," *Atlantic* (June 2014), 196. See also Beryl Satter, *Family Properties: How the Struggle over Race and Real Estate Transformed Chicago and Urban America* (New York: Picador, 2010).

46. Ylan Q. Mui, "Ex-Loan Officer Claims Wells Fargo Targeted Black Communities for Shoddy Loans," *Washington Post*, June 12, 2012, https://www.washingtonpost.com/business/economy/former-wells-fargo-loan-officer-testifies-in-baltimore-mortgage-lawsuit/2012/06/12/gJQA6EGtXV_story.html; Rick Rothacker and David Ingram, "Wells Fargo to Pay $175 Million in Race Discrimination Probe," Reuters, July 12, 2012, https://www.reuters.com/article/us-wells-lending-settlement/wells-fargo-to-pay-175-million-in-race-discrimination-probe-idUSBRE86B0V220120712.

47. Keeanga-Yamahtta Taylor, *From #Black Lives Matter to Black Revolution* (Chicago: Haymarket Books, 2016), 29.

48. Keeanga-Yamahtta Taylor, *Race for Profit: How Banks and the Real Estate Industry Undermined Black Home Ownership* (Chapel Hill: University of North Carolina Press, 2019), 19.

49. Taylor, *Race for Profit*, 17–18.

50. Richard Rothstein, *The Color of Law: A Forgotten History of How Our Government Segregated America* (New York: Liveright, 2017), 109–113.

51. Wiese, *Places of Their Own*, 100.

52. Arnold R. Hirsch, *Making of Second Ghetto: Race and Housing in Chicago* (Chicago: University of Chicago Press, 1998), 53.

53. John David Rhodes, *Spectacle of Property: The House in American Film* (Minneapolis: University of Minnesota Press, 2017).

54. Benjamin Wiggins, "Race and Place at the City Limits: Imaginative Geographies of South Central Los Angeles," *Ethnic and Racial Studies* 39 (2016): 2585–2586. See also Josh Sides, "Straight into Compton: American Dreams, Urban Nightmares, and the Metamorphosis of a Black Suburb," *American Quarterly* 56 (September 2004): 583–605.

55. Allyson Field, Jan-Christopher Horak, and Jacqueline Najuma Stewart, eds., *L.A. Rebellion: Creating a New Black Cinema* (Berkeley: University of California Press, 2015).

56. Ellen C. Scott, chapter 3 in this volume.

57. Field, Horak, and Stewart, *L.A. Rebellion*, 3, 17.

58. Recently, more films and videos by these independent Black filmmakers have been located and made available, which will lead to a broader definition of the suburban cycle film.

59. Henri Lefebvre, *The Production of Space* (1974), trans. Donald Nicholson-Smith (Oxford: Blackwell, 1999).

60. Michael Omi and Howard Winant, *Racial Formations in the United States*, 3rd ed. (New York: Routledge, 2014), 105.

61. Karen E. Fields and Barbara J. Fields, *Racecraft: The Soul of Inequality in American Life* (New York: Verso, 2012), 101, 18.

62. Wilbur Zelinsky and Barrett Lee, "Heterolocalism," *International Journal of Popular Geography* 4 (1998): 1–18.

63. Susan W. Hardwick, "Toward a Suburban Immigrant Nation," in *Twentieth-First Century Gateways: Immigration Incorporation in Suburban America*, ed. Audrey Singer, Susan W. Hardwick, and Caroline B. Bretell (Washington, DC: Brookings Institution Press, 2008), 31–50.

64. Wei Li, *Ethnoburb: The New Ethnic Community in Urban America* (Honolulu: University of Hawai'i Press, 2012).

65. William H. Frey, "Biden's Victory Came from the Suburbs," November 13, 2020, https://www.brookings.edu/research/bidens-victory-came-from-the-suburbs/.

66. Baschiera and De Rosa, *Film and Domestic Space*.

References

Abrams, Charles. *Forbidden Neighbors: A Study of Prejudice in Housing*. New York: Harper and Brothers, 1955.

Aitkin, Stuart C., and Leo Zonn. *Place, Power, Situation and Spectacle: A Geography of Film*. Lanham, MD: Rowman and Littlefield, 1994.

Altman, Rick. "A Semantic/Syntactic Approach to Film Genre." *Film Journal* 23 (Spring 1984): 6–18.

Archer, John. *Architecture and Suburbia: From English Villa to American Dream House, 1690–2000*. Minneapolis: University of Minnesota Press, 2005.

Barton, Craig E., ed. *Sites of Memory: Perspectives on Architecture and Race*. New York: Princeton Architectural Press, 2001.

Benjamin, Walter. *The Arcades Project*. Translated by Howard Eiland and Kevin McLaughlin. Cambridge, MA: Belknap Press of Harvard University Press, 1999.

Beuka, Robert. *Suburbia Nation: Reading Suburban Landscape in Twentieth-Century American Fiction and Film*. New York: Palgrave Macmillan, 2004.

Bowdre, Karen. "Passing Films and the Language of Racial Equality." *Black Camera* 5 (Spring 2014): 21–43.

Brooks, Charlotte. *Alien Neighbors, Foreign Friends: Asian Americans, Housing, and the Transformation of Urban California*. Chicago: University of Chicago Press, 2009.

Carpio, Genevieve, Clara Iraza Bal, and Laura Pulido. "Right to the Suburb: Rethinking Lefebvre and Immigrant Activism." *Journal of Urban Affairs* 33 (May 2011): 185–208.

Coon, David R. *Look Closer: Suburban Narratives and American Values in Film and Television*. New Brunswick, NJ: Rutgers University Press, 2014.

Corbin, Amy Lynn. *Cinematic Geographies and Multicultural Spectatorship in America*. New York: Palgrave Macmillan, 2015.

Delaney, David. "The Space That Race Makes." *Professional Geographer* 54, no. 1 (2002): 6–14.

Dyer, Richard. "White." *Screen* 29 (Autumn 1988): 44–65.

Field, Allyson, Jan-Christopher Horak, and Jacqueline Najuma Stewart, eds. *L.A. Rebellion: Creating a New Black Cinema*. Berkeley: University of California Press, 2015.

Fields, Karen E., and Barbara J. Fields. *Racecraft: The Soul of Inequality in American Life*. New York: Verso, 2012.

Forrest, David, Graeme Harper, and Jonathan Rayner, eds. *Filmurbia: Screening the Suburbs*. New York: Palgrave Macmillan, 2017.

Freedman, Samuel G. "Suburbia Outgrows Its Image in the Arts." *New York Times*, February 28, 1999, https://www.nytimes.com/1999/02/28/arts/suburbia-outgrows-its-image-in-the-arts.html.

Freund, David M. P. *Colored Property: State Policy and White Racial Politics in Suburban America*. Chicago: University of Chicago Press, 2010.

Fricker, Jonathan, and Donna Fricker. "Louisiana Architecture: 1945–1965 Post-War Subdivisions and the Ranch House." 2010. Louisiana Division of Historic Preservation, http://www.crt.state.la.us/hp/nationalregister/historic_contexts/ranchhousefinalrevised.pf.

Harris, Cheryl I. "Whiteness and Property." In *Critical Race Theory: The Key Writings That Formed the Movement*, edited by Kimberlé Crenshaw, Neil Gotanda, Gary Peller, and Kendall Thomas, 276–291. New York: New Press, 1995.

Harris, Dianne. *Little White Houses: How the Postwar Home Constructed Race in America*. Minneapolis: University of Minnesota Press, 2013.

———, ed. *Second Suburb: Levittown Pennsylvania*. Pittsburgh: University of Pittsburgh Press, 2010.

Hayden, Dolores. *Building Suburbia: Green Fields and Urban Growth, 1820–2000*. New York: Vintage Books, 2003.

Hirsch, Arnold R. *Making of Second Ghetto: Race and Housing in Chicago*. Chicago: University of Chicago Press, 1998.

Jackson, Kenneth. *Crabgrass Frontier: The Suburbanization of the United States*. New York: Oxford University Press, 1985.

Jurca, Catherine. *White Diaspora: The Suburb and the Twentieth-Century Novel*. Princeton, NJ: Princeton University Press, 2001.

Kenyon, Amy Marie. *Dreaming Suburbia: Detroit and the Production of Postwar Space and Culture*. Detroit: Wayne State University Press, 2004.

King, Martin Luther, Jr. *Where Do We Go from Here? Chaos or Community*. New York: Beacon Press, 1967.

Klein, Amanda. *American Film Cycles: Reframing Genres, Screening Social Problems, and Defining Subcultures*. Austin: University of Texas Press, 2011.

Kruse, Kevin M., and Thomas Sugrue. *The New Suburban History*. Chicago: University of Chicago Press, 2006.

Lane, Barbara Miller. *Houses for a New World: Builders and Buyers in the American Suburbs*. Princeton, NJ: Princeton University Press, 2012.

Lefebvre, Henri. *The Production of Space*. Translated by Donald Nicholson-Smith. Oxford: Blackwell, (1974) 1999.

Lipsitz, George. *How Racism Takes Place*. Philadelphia: Temple University Press, 2011.

———. *The Possessive Investment in Whiteness: How White People Profit from Identity Politics*. Philadelphia: Temple University Press, 2016.

Li, Wei. *Ethnoburb: The New Ethnic Community in Urban America*. Honolulu: University of Hawai'i Press, 2012.

Met, Philippe, and Derek Schilling. *Screening the Paris Suburb: From the Silent Era to the 1990s*. Manchester: Manchester University Press, 2018.

Meyer, Stephen Grant. *As Long as They Don't Move Next Door: Segregation and Racial Conflict in American Neighborhoods*. Lanham, MD: Rowman and Littlefield, 2000.

Nicolaides, Becky. *My Blue Heaven: Life and Politics in the Working-Class Suburbs of Los Angeles, 1920–1965*. Chicago: University of Chicago Press, 2002.

Nicolaides, Becky M., and Andrew Wiese, eds. *The Suburb Reader*. 2nd ed. New York: Routledge, 2016.

Omi, Michael, and Howard Winant. *Racial Transformations in the United States*. 3rd ed. New York: Routledge, 2014.

Powell, John A. *Racing to Justice: Transforming Our Conceptions of Self and Other to Build an Inclusive Society*. Bloomington: Indiana University Press, 2012.

Rhodes, John David. *Spectacle of Property: The House in American Film*. Minneapolis: University of Minnesota Press, 2017.

Robinson, J. Dennis. "History Matters: The 'Story' behind 'Lost Boundaries'." March 5, 2018. https://www.seacoastonline.com/news/20180305/history-matters-story-behind-lost-boundaries.

Rothstein, Richard. *The Color of Law: A Forgotten History of How Our Government Segregated America*. New York: Liveright, 2017.

Rowley, Stephen. *Movie Towns and Sitcom Suburbs*. New York: Palgrave Macmillan, 2015.

Satter, Beryl. *Family Properties: How the Struggle over Race and Real Estate Transformed Chicago and Urban America*. New York: Picador, 2010.

Schleier, Merrill. "Queerness, Race, and Class in the Mid-Century Suburb Film *Crime of Passion* (1956)." In *Crossroads: Intersections of Space and Identity in Screen Cultures*, edited by Angel Daniel Matos, Paula Massood, and Pam Robertson Wojcik. Durham, NC: Duke University Press, 2021.

———. *Skyscraper Cinema: Architecture and Gender in American Film*. Minneapolis: University of Minnesota Press, 2009.

———. "Whiteness, Japanese American Masculinity and Architectural Space in the Mid-century Cinematic Suburbs." In *Film and Domestic Space: Architectures, Representations, Dispositif*, edited by Stefan Baschiera and Miriam de Rosa. Edinburgh: University of Edinburgh Press, 2020.

Sides, Josh. "Straight into Compton: American Dreams, Urban Nightmares, and the Metamorphosis of a Black Suburb." *American Quarterly* 56 (September 2004): 583–605.

Singer, Audrey, Susan W. Hardwick, Caroline B. Bretell, eds. *Twentieth-First Century Gateways: Immigration Incorporation in Suburban America*. Washington, DC: Brookings Institution Press, 2008.

Spigel, Lynn. *Welcome to the Dream House: Popular Media and Postwar Suburbs (Console-ing Passions)*. Durham, NC: Duke University Press, 2001.

Taylor, Keeanga-Yamahtta. *From #Black Lives Matter to Black Revolution*. Chicago: Haymarket Books, 2016.

———. *Race for Profit: How Banks and the Real Estate Industry Undermined Black Home Ownership*. Chapel Hill: University of North Carolina Press, 2019.

Vermeulen, Timotheus. *Scenes from the Suburbs: Suburban Space in US Film and Television*. Edinburgh: Edinburgh University Press, 2014.

Wiese, Andrew. *Places of Their Own: African American Suburbanization in the United States*. New ed. Chicago: University of Chicago Press, 2005.

Wiggins, Benjamin, "Race and Place at the City Limits: Imaginative Geographies of South Central Los Angeles." *Ethnic and Racial Studies* 39 (2016): 2585–2586.

Wojcik, Pamela Robertson, ed. *The Apartment Complex: Urban Living and Global Screen Cultures*. Durham, NC: Duke University Press, 2018.

———. *The Apartment Plot: Urban Living in American Film and Popular Culture, 1945 to 1975*. Durham, NC: Duke University Press, 2010.

Wright, Gwendolyn. *Building the Dream: A Social History of American Housing*. Oxford: Oxford University Press, 1981.

X, Malcolm. "The American Nightmare." 1964. https://sites.psu.edu/jld5710/2012/10/02/1964-the-american-nightmare/.

Zelinsky, Wilbur, and Barrett Lee. "Heterolocalism." *International Journal of Popular Geography* 4 (1998): 1–18.

1

Passing Through

The Black Maid in the Cinematic Suburbs, 1948–1949

JOHN DAVID RHODES

IN DOUGLAS SIRK'S 1959 *IMITATION OF LIFE* (a remake of John Stahl's eponymous 1934 film, both adapted from the novel by Fannie Hurst), the material success of its protagonist Lara Meredith (Lana Turner), a hardworking actress on the New York stage, is measured by her move to a large house in the suburbs. Lara brings to the house her daughter Susie (Sandra Dee), her faithful African American maid Annie (Juanita Moore), and Annie's mixed-race daughter Sarah Jane (Susan Kohner). In her new, spaciously luxurious surroundings Lara has also employed a tuxedoed African American butler (Napoleon Whiting) who only fleetingly appears in the film, smoothly passing through the image in the nearly wordless execution of his tasks. In one throwaway moment that leads up to a dramatic confrontation between Lara and Sarah Jane (an argument having to do with Sarah Jane's racial identity), we catch a brief glimpse of the butler going about his well-oiled business. We are in the house's large, open-plan living room. A low-angle shot, tilt-panning down, left to right, on a smooth diagonal shows us first Lara, walking briskly, left to right, along the upstairs balcony, then, as the camera tilt-pans down, we immediately see the butler, moving in the same direction across the floor of the living room. The camera follows his movement, keeping his figure in extreme close-up as he carries and deposits some undisclosed object on a coffee table (just out of frame), turns on a table lamp, and then exits screen right, just as the encounter between Lara and Sarah Jane begins. This almost apparitional vision of the African American servant, despite or perhaps because of this film's extended meditation on race and racism through the lives of Annie—another servant—and Sarah Jane, might be read as a metacommentary on the marginality of such representations in Hollywood cinema. African Americans were, almost without exception, allotted marginal roles in Hollywood filmmaking. These roles, in turn, most frequently portrayed fictional maids and servants—characters that mirrored, often in cartoonish and caricatured portrayals, the lived marginality of African American citizens. This double marginality is the subject of this chapter's investigation of the representation of African American servants in two films produced in the 1940s, a decade before the well-meaning, civil rights era liberalism of Sirk's *Imitation of Life*.

In a short reflection on his own practice as a filmmaker, the African American documentary filmmaker St. Clair Bourne writes that "because the purpose of the Africans brought here by Europeans as slaves was to provide service and nothing more, the art and media images of these slaves were also created and used to rationalize and reinforce their place in society."[1] Bourne makes an implicit ontological link between the practice of enslavement—particularly the enslavement of Black bodies and the market in Black human chattel—that brought Africans to the American continent and the representation of blackness in American media, especially in Hollywood cinema. This is to say, more bluntly, that African Americans were brought to America to perform labor—agricultural, menial, domestic—for their white owners, and that this history lived on in the practice of putting Black bodies on the film screen in Hollywood cinema in order so that these bodies could represent servants for white employers. The image of a Black maid is an afterimage of a Black slave. Frank B. Wilderson III has written that "the Black" is "a subject who is always already positioned as a slave."[2] This provocative ontological formulation provokes us to keep the slave in sight when all we are presented with might be the spectacle of an amiable, reliable, and loving domestic servant. And, as I myself argue elsewhere, "any image of property" is "an image, or least an afterimage, of slavery."[3] Thus the figure of the Black servant working in a suburban house in a Hollywood film presents us with a highly condensed and charged set of relations. Suburban space

was constructed around various flights from ethnically and racially heterogeneous urban contexts into homogeneous white enclaves that, once
established, were carefully monitored so as to prevent minorities, and
especially African Americans, from entering (much less living in) in them.
Thus, the appearance onscreen of the Black servant in white suburban
space (architectural and domestic), while it is normalized through its
recurrence in classical Hollywood filmmaking, remains a quietly and often
spectacularly racist trope that demands close analysis and consideration.

The questions that I want to pursue in what follows are predicated
on the ontological conditions and connections I have outlined above,
but that see the Black domestic servant as a spatial agent, one who
makes visible certain regimes of spatial inhabitation, and who is subject
to the laws and norms of who can occupy various forms of private
(and to a lesser degree, in the films I analyze, public) space. The Black
servant may also usurp or disrupt the hegemonic functioning of (racist)
spatial practice, but my interest here is not in tracing possibilities for
disruption inside representations or tracing connections between the
cinematic representation of disruption and the actual destabilization
of oppressive norms in social reality. This is not because I believe it is
impossible to pursue such readings or to posit causal relations between
the representational and the real. Rather, and quite simply, I want to
describe the movement (or immobilization) of the Black servant so that
we can see this figure vividly.

The figure of the maid in Hollywood cinema summons into view
questions of the marginalized labor of the Black actor that runs in parallel to the marginalized labor of African American domestic servants.
On the subject of the employment as extras in Hollywood cinema of
the 1930s and '40s, Charlene Regester has written that "those [African
Americans] hired to assume domestic roles were relegated to 'bit' roles,
while those employed in individual or what was referred to as 'mammy'
roles were characterized as landing 'parts.' Parts were distinguished from
other roles because they allowed actors to be photographed in close-ups
and remain prominently visible in the film."[4] Regester's straightforward
account hints at something remarkably complex: that the Black body's
presence on camera exerted a pressure on cinema, a pressure both formal and social, and that cinema, in turn, responded to this pressure by
strictly delimiting the appearance of the Black body both in terms of the
roles such bodies were allowed to inhabit and how much of the camera's
attention they could claim, how much of onscreen space they could be
allowed to occupy. Complaints about the poverty of roles available to

high-profile Black actors were often voiced in mainstream African American publications. An article entitled "Movie Maids" and published in *Ebony* in August 1948 notes with dismay that "for all its self-professed reforms of recent years, Hollywood is still sticking to the same old stereotypes of moon-faced maids and grovelling menials . . . in casting Negroes."[5] The article quotes Hattie McDaniel as saying that she would continue to play in such roles as long as African Americans work "in real life as menials."[6] Whatever resignation of the spirit McDaniel's position might seem to index, it also points to the way in which Hollywood filmmaking itself has been understood as a secure, if nonetheless abstractly artificial, index of social reality, including the intractability of American racism.

Even inside this depressing set of coordinates, the figure of the Black domestic servant opens up interesting possibilities both for assessing the aesthetics of Hollywood narrative cinema as a racializing medium or mode of production and for testing the figure of the servant—most often, in classical Hollywood cinema of the 1930s, '40s, and '50s, a Black servant—as a medium for the registration of class and wealth as these things are indexed by and in domestic, suburban architectural space. The Black maid's body is the body that graphs the terrain and the expanse of the terrain of the house itself. The occupation of space is not a neutral activity for African Americans in the way it is for whites. African Americans have always been subjected to a terrible regime of displacement and emplacement, one that began with the horrors of the transatlantic slave trade. Enslaved people were forced to live where they were owned, unless accompanying their owners on a trip away from the plantation. The imaginary of the escape from slavery was, therefore, more spatial than temporal: it was about being outside or beyond the reach of the enslaver—somewhere else, in the North, in Canada. And in the long and uneven history of injustice that has succeeded the emancipation of Blacks from formal, legal slavehood, and still, very much up to this day, occupying the wrong space or being in the wrong place at the wrong time could mean death for African Americans.

The history of suburban growth in the postwar period is a history of racial (and racist) spatialization—of the racist demarcation of who could live where. In her study of the construction of the suburban home as a racialized space of whiteness, architectural historian Dianne Harris has argued that the "invisibility" of "nonwhites in mass-media images of newly constructed postwar houses" is "one of the key signals that indicates the operation of racialization in the popular consciousness."[7] The nonappearance of nonwhites in Hollywood cinema, apart from their mostly minor roles as servants, was congruent with their nonappearance in white suburban areas and the houses therein. But the spatial segregation of race in postwar America, which saw the rapid growth of all-white suburbs surrounding city centers that became increasingly abandoned to a nonwhite urban poor, was not a contingent feature of this period in American history. Rather, this racial apartheid was the result of postwar government policy that hid itself behind a fig leaf of free market capitalism. The historian David M. P. Freund writes that there is among historians a "consensus that the early postwar era saw the emergence of a new kind of racial conservatism, a precursor to the better-known backlash politics of the 1960s and the rise of the New Right, fuelled by white's preoccupation with protecting their neighborhoods, status, and privileges from minorities."[8] Freund argues that "whites' racial thinking itself changed during the years that the United States became a predominantly suburban and home-owning nation."[9] He traces a shift from a spatial separation of white and Black residential areas on the basis of an assumed and biologically determined white racial superiority to a continued separation that, in the postwar period, was articulated in terms of property values and the "rights" of (white) property owners to safeguard such values.[10] Freund writes that "by 1949 . . . the state's most influential housing programs focused on subsidizing the construction and sale of single-family homes, in the suburbs, for white people while refusing to offer loans for Blacks in white neighborhoods."[11]

The irony of the appearance of the maid in Hollywood cinema of the postwar period consists in the fact that while these years saw an enormous increase in home ownership among whites (and modest increases in home ownership among African Americans), the same period saw a decline in households that were able to afford live-in or full-time domestic servants, domestic laborers who most often were from racialized classes. The image of the new middle-class home in 1940s and 1950s America was the product of a concentrated set of ideological representational practices articulated across a vast range of media that included women's magazines, shelter publications, design manuals, and government policies, as well as cinema and television. According to Harris, the illusion of spaciousness, one of the most desirable conquests of white middle-class housing, distanced itself from "crowded living conditions" or urban life that "signalled ethnic origins."[12] Harris writes that "images of stylistically modern homes . . . were . . . about containing and eliminating the signs of ethnic difference and attaining class status."[13] Advertisements in magazines from this period "did not depict or include people of color."

However, there did proliferate at the same time "material culture artifacts of . . . slaves, servants, and minstrels, but configured as cups, planters, salt and pepper shakers, maple syrup containers, and so on—Black 'figures' made to serve in some capacity and to substitute for the absence of actual slaves and servants of color."[14]

Harris's point about material culture is interesting when set alongside the persistence of the trope of the Black servant in postwar Hollywood cinema. Do these representations, regardless of the period in which a film is set, but perhaps especially in those films set in the historical present of the period of their production, also speak a language of compensatory substitution, in which a white spectator, who in this period is highly likely now to be a suburban property owner, can indulge in a phantasmatic enlargement of any real race, racialized, and racist privilege? Cinema allows the extension and reinvention of the prerogatives of white racist privilege in the face of the diminishment of the purely economic claims to such privilege.

In what follows, I intend to provide brief accounts of the work and movement of the Black servant in two postwar Hollywood films set in suburban milieus, all made during the period in which, as Freund writes, "the United States became a predominantly suburban and home-owning nation," and in which the movement from tenancy to ownership was a privilege bestowed on white citizens and barred from most Black citizens.[15] The house and home ownership could be said to be among the most powerful media through which anti-Black racism in the postwar period organized and articulated itself. The Black servant—most often a woman—that we so often see in Hollywood cinema is herself, to borrow Markus Krajewski's terms, a medium. The server, a privileged modality of which is the domestic servant, is a type of medium, a mediatic figure, a figure that mediates. Krajewski writes that "the servant is a figure of the in-between, an intermediary moving between different spheres and a medium that systematically slips through the mesh of fixed categories."[16] Krajewski's is a cunning reframing of a mode of labor and the agents of that labor, a proposition that is predicated on the servant/server as a figure that is animated by language, the language of commands. I want to take the ontological claims of contemporary critical race theory and Krajewski's media-archaeological understanding of the servant in order to see how the mediatized image of the Black servant helps us to understand postwar racism—both on- and off-screen—as a mediator of a spatial regime of racism embodied and enforced by suburbia and the suburban house.

Mr. Blandings Builds His Dream House

A satire on the subject of postwar suburban aspiration, *Mr. Blandings Builds His Dream House* (H. C. Potter, 1948) is an adaptation of Eric Hodgins's 1946 novel of the same name. The film features Cary Grant as Jim Blandings, a moderately successful ad man in New York City where he lives in a cramped apartment in a high-rise building with his wife, Muriel (Myrna Loy), and their two daughters. The film's opening set piece introduces the viewer to these characters and their constricted living conditions. Moving among them in these circumscribed quarters is Gussie, their live-in African American maid, played by Louise Beavers, a prolific actress whose most famous role is that of Delilah in John Stahl's *Imitation of Life*, based on the (again, eponymous) novel by Fannie Hurst, first published in 1933.

The film poses the desire to move to suburban Connecticut as primarily a question of space, not merely of social aspiration. The film uses a long tracking shot to make its point about the compression of the Blandingses' living space. The shot follows Mr. Blandings as he opens the door of his and Muriel's bedroom (itself already shown to be crammed with furniture, objects, and clothing that have to be navigated like an obstacle course) and walks down the long narrow hallway, moves through the living room and dining room, before pausing at the kitchen doorway at which appears, on cue, Gussie, who greets him with good morning and a glass of orange juice, which he drinks in one gulp, before handing him a cup of coffee, which he carries with him first to the front door, which he opens so as to retrieve the morning paper, and then back toward the bedroom (where, following a cut to the inside of the bedroom, he offers it to Muriel). The shot graphs the entirety of all of the apartment's spaces so as to make the point that will compel the narrative: the Blandingses need more room.[17] Gussie is defined, in part, by the limits of the space afforded to her. The one room that the camera never really ventures into, whose threshold it does not cross, is the kitchen (and Gussie's bedroom, if she has one, which is something the film does not directly imply or deny). Her appearance at the very margins of the frame emphasizes Gussie's size, almost as if she does not quite fit inside the apartment, even less than the Blandingses themselves and their furniture. When she moves around the dining room, she is shown having to squeeze herself in between the chairs and the sideboard in order to deliver the plates to the table. Moving to the suburbs, perhaps, would be as spatially liberating for her as it would be for the rest of the family.

The film mostly preoccupies itself with the comical misfortunes of the Blandings family as they first purchase a Colonial-era house that, due its structural instability, has to be demolished and then replaced with a Colonial Revival house whose construction runs into a seemingly infinite and costly set of obstacles. When the family does finally make the move to Connecticut, we are shown the family in their large convertible trailing behind two large moving trucks. The convertible pulls behind it a rickety wooden open flatbed trailer, at the back of which, facing backward, sit Gussie and Cole (Melvyn Douglas), the Blandingses' loyal friend and the film's pseudonarrator, both clutching a precarious-looking rope that is there is to prevent them from being thrown out onto the road. Cole—who at this moment provides again the voice-over narration—is carried to Connecticut by the same pejorative means of conveyance as Gussie, but given his quasi-authoritative control of the film's narration, his position is merely ironic, while she functions purely as a visual gag.

Gussie's appearances across the film are few in number, functioning almost as more of an extra (along the lines described by Regester) than a supporting player. She appears twice during the part of the film set in New York—first, as the film opens, as I have described above and then serving breakfast a bit later, and another time serving dinner—and only four times in Connecticut: her arrival in the trailer, in the kitchen as the family unpacks their belongings, in the final scene (the only scene in Connecticut in which she is given dialogue), and in an epilogue sequence. The lines of dialogue she is given are similarly few in number, marginal to the plot's development, but central to its conclusion. One of the film's running gags is that Mr. Blandings's creativity has failed him in coming up with a clever campaign for his newest account—a tinned ham product called "Wham." At the dinner table sequence in the New York flat, he complains to Gussie about her having served it to them again. She protests and offers that the girls and Mrs. Blandings like it. When he sarcastically reels off its virtues, she responds, in a tone that mixes irony with gullibility, "You don't have to sell me—I like it!" In the final scene, when Mr. Blandings returns home, following an all-nighter in the office wracking his brains for a new slogan for Wham, he assumes his failure to do so may cost him his job. Gussie announces that breakfast is ready and when asked by Joan what they are having, she replies, "Orange juice, scrambled eggs, and you know what?!" "Ham?," one of the girls asks. Gussie, in close-up, responds in mock indignation, "Not ham! Wham! If you ain't eating Wham, you ain't eating ham!" Mr. Blandings, overhearing this, realizes that Gussie has just given him the ad campaign that has so far eluded him. "Muriel, Darling, give Gussie a ten dollar raise," he exclaims as he lifts his wife in an embrace, and the shot dissolves into a shot of an open magazine revealing a full-page ad with a photograph of Gussie in a giant chef's hat serving up a platter of Wham and the slogan she (not Mr. Blandings) has created splashed beneath her (figure 1.1). The final shot shows Mr. Blandings, who is holding the magazine in his lap, closing it and picking up a copy of Hodgins's novel, as the camera pulls back to reveal Muriel and Bob at his side, the girls playing in the middle background, and Gussie, who can be glimpsed in the far background, busy doing some work on the patio next to the house (figure 1.2).

Mr. Blandings's scene of appropriation is a scene of double appropriation: it represents the appropriation of Gussie's creative and linguistic labor, but in doing so it appropriates Hurst's novel's and Stahl's film's narrative of appropriation. Weirdly, by casting Beavers as Gussie, it also relies on the same actor (as in *Imitation of Life*) to enact the role of alienated Black

Figure 1.1 Gussie (Louise Beavers) foregrounded as a literally two-dimensional figure, her labor extracted twice over in *Mr. Blandings Builds His Dream House* (H. C. Potter, RKO Pictures, 1948). Digital frame enlargement.

Figure 1.2. Gussie (Louise Beavers) is remanded to the background in the final shot of *Mr. Blandings Builds His Dream House* (H. C. Potter, RKO Pictures, 1948). Digital frame enlargement.

domestic worker. In *Imitation of Life* Bea (Claudette Colbert), the white entrepreneur and Delilah's employer, builds a small commercial empire on the appropriation of both Delilah's pancake recipe and her visual image. This appropriation is at least acknowledged overtly and worked through, to some extent, by the film's diegesis, whereas in *Mr. Blandings* the appropriation of Gussie's one-liner is sudden, played purely for comedy, and provides the film with a means of resolving its crisis with a kind of ferocious brevity. It is significant to acknowledge that the novel from which *Mr. Blandings* is adapted did not feature the character of Gussie; she is an invention of the film and its screenplay. The film's teleological focus on suburban Connecticut—as narrative destination and site of ideological fulfilment, however gently satirized—could be read as exercising an ambiguous mode of incorporating Gussie into its story, only for the story of her appropriated labor suddenly to swing into view as a deus ex machina that solves the family's financial woes and summons the film's denouement.

In a brilliant essay on the film that understands it as an attempt by Hollywood to demonstrate its loyalty to the American ideals of family and private property, Catherine Jurca has trenchantly observed that "Black woman in this film are devoted consumers of hams so that white families may be devoted consumers of homes."[18] While the ordeal of building the house provides the film's primary plot line, Mr. Blandings's difficulty in selling Wham is the secondary narrative, and we are given to understand that his failure would mean the family's financial ruin and possible eviction from their ramshackle suburban idyll. Gussie's infrequent appearances across the film can be characterized thus: first as hardly anything more than an extra—the "maid," a stock character or human prop—then as the solution to the narrative's crisis, next as a two-dimensional image in a racist ad campaign—basically an actual prop—and finally, again, as an extra hovering, as extras do, in the background. This trajectory suggests that her place in the suburbs, if she has a place, is to blossom into highly exploitable creative and cognitive labor from which enormous value is extracted by her white employer, only to be folded back into menial, hourly paid two-dimensionality (figure 1.2). While Gussie embodies, however fleetingly, what Krajewski calls the servant as "superior epistemic agent," she is also subject to the containing force of the white household, which threatens to convert her vibrant three-dimensional personhood into a two-dimensional abstraction (the photograph in the magazine). Her image and her words, pressed together on the page of a magazine, are obviously much more valuable than the paper abstraction—her ten dollar raise—she is offered in return. Her appearance as a household prop also resonates with Harris's analysis of the postwar period's racist household objects that "substitute for the absence of actual slaves and servants of color." It is unlikely that a family like the Blandings, stretched to their financial limits by their move to the suburbs, could actually afford a live-in maid like Gussie. But the film offers a fantasy scenario whereby the economic implausibility of Gussie's presence in the Blandingses' dream house provides the grounds for generating a plausible solution to how they might go on affording to pay for her labor—which is by appropriating the better part of it as unpaid. Her linguistic fecundity drops from her mouth like fruit from a tree; Mr. Blandings need only scoop it up and put it to use. The film's magical narrative resolution, performed unwittingly by the underpaid Black servant, who also mirrors the conditions of the film's production, whereby Beavers (and actors like her) would be paid considerably less than their white peers, despite the fact that their presence in the film was deemed crucial to a film's commercial success.[19]

The Reckless Moment

Max Ophuls's 1949 film *The Reckless Moment* is an adaptation of Elizabeth Sanxay Holding's story "The Blank Wall," which was published first as a story in *Ladies Home Journal* in 1947 and later that year as a novel. Like *Mr. Blandings*—both the novel and the film—*The Blank Wall* and *The Reckless Moment* are preoccupied with the precarity of suburban middle-class existence. Unlike Hodgins's novel, however, Holding's book presents at its center a Black servant, the character Sybil, the trusted employee of Lucia Holley, whose husband Tom is away at the war front, and who is raising two children on her own, with the help of her father. The novel and subsequent film's plot centers on Lucia's attempts to maintain her family's security and good name following her daughter's involvement with the unsavory Ted Darby. When Darby pays an unwanted visit to the Harper household, Lucia's father throws Darby into the lake behind the Holley house. Her father does not realize that he has inadvertently killed Darby, and so Lucia tries to dispose of the body and protect her family's innocence, which is not made easy by visits from Mr. Donnelly, a blackmailer who starts by attempting to extort money from Lucia in return for keeping secret the cause of Darby's death. Lucia and Mr. Donnelly, however, end up in a kind of sympathetic friendship, and Donnelly ends up falling on his sword to protect Lucia and her family.

Sybil (Frances E. Williams) is crucial to the film's development, despite the fact that in many ways she is restricted in terms of the amount of dialogue she is given and the fleshing out of her interiority. Her position in the film might be described as marginally central, or centrally marginal: she is always near the center of the action in the Harper home, but she is never a primary agent in the film's action, apart from the last scene in which she accompanies Lucia (Joan Bennett) in pursuit of Donnelly (James Mason), who dies in a car crash and takes with him the secret of her daughter Bea's (Geraldine Brooks) guilt. Sybil's marginal centrality, however, did not result in a credited title for the actor who portrays her, Frances E. Williams, whose performance subtly evokes a psychological intensity—indeed, something like a personality—that is belied by the few lines given to her to deliver. It's almost as if in order to pay for the right to be exempt from the spectacle of mammy-fication that Beavers is subject to in *Mr. Blandings*, Williams must allow her labor to be invisibilized, at least in the film's credits.

In a perceptive and sensitive reading of *The Reckless Moment* as a film that is preoccupied by the accumulation and removal of waste, most notable Darby's corpse, Karl Schoonover writes that "the film's interest in debris and its abatement means, though, that *The Reckless Moment* cannot spatially marginalize Sybil and her labor with quite the same rigor as other Hollywood films. Sybil is often found at the center of shots."[20] Schoonover comments that, despite her attractive force, her ability to be at the center, at least spatially, of the film's narrative, Sybil "remains a compromised and flat character."[21] I would argue—and not to award any special credit to the film or to Ophuls—that Sybil is no more or less "flat" than David or Mr. Harper. What seems more significant about Sybil, and as Schoonover's more interesting point about the impossibility of marginalizing her suggests, is her consistent appearance in the film at all or most of its key narrative junctures. Moreover, she tends to function as a medium through which information is passed, as well as a mediating force that delays and diverts threats to the Harper family. In these respects, she demonstrates many of the capacities attributed by Krajewski to the servant who is useful and adept at "anticipating, controlling, events, allowing for significant interventions into the course of destiny and history." Sybil's signal role in mediating and regulating some of the film's narrative developments presents an interesting example of a representation of a Black servant at work in a suburban home that does not merely conform to racist stereotyping. Rather, thanks both to the way she has been written into the script, the way Ophuls's cinematography frames her, and the way in which she is brought to life by Williams, Sybil's character presents a hermeneutic challenge. Her blackness and her role as domestic servant in the Harper household pushes her into inevitable proximity to the mammy/servant figure, but her sympathetic engagement with Lucia's dilemma and her clockwork-like appearance across the film make her into something else. She has a total of fifteen significant appearances across the film's short duration of only seventy-nine minutes.

The film—like most texts, it is true—pivots on a system of binaries. It begins with Lucia leaving what the voice-over narrator tells us is "a charming community called Balboa, fifty miles from Los Angeles" and driving her car into the city. The film, in pleonastic style typical of the Hollywood mode of production, gives us, in succession, a shot of the car crossing a wooden bridge, leaving Balboa, a close-up, shot inside the car (using rear projection to depict the passing scenery outside), of

Lucia driving, and another shot of the car on the highway. The shot pans with the direction of the car, left to right, and then stops on a highway sign that confirms that Lucia is driving toward Los Angeles. Next there is another traveling shot taken from a moving vehicle traveling behind Lucia's car; we see the Los Angeles skyline with Los Angeles City Hall clearly prominent in the distance. The film italicizes the movement from the (distant) suburbs to the city while, already in these very first few seconds of the film, pitting these two locations against one another melodramatically.[22] City-country, public-private, corrupt-pure, male-female, age-youth, single-married: these are only a handful of the binary tensions that organize the film's narration. The film, of course, also works to blur the coherence of these binaries. Following Darby's death and Lucia's (unsuccessful) disposal of his corpse, she is drawn into a world of criminality that rubs off on her. Likewise, the more Donnelly comes to know Lucia and her family, the more he distances himself from the corruption of his associates and ultimately sacrifices himself for the security of the Harper family. At least part of the film's mission, it seems, is to set up rigid binaries so as to undo them. Ophuls's own style, which emphasizes fluidity and movement, often through the use of his signature tracking, dollying, and crane shots, is responsible, at the level of form, for helping to create a sense of temporal and spatial transit and transition in which we see binary oppositions put into play, but also see their instability. Suspended in and traversing some of these binary tensions is Sybil. Her blackness is clearly melodramatically opposed to—or different from—the whiteness of the Harper family. However, Ophuls's tracking and dollying movements—the fluid cinematography that acts as his signature—has the effect of granting Sybil almost the same degree of spatial autonomy, of movement in and through space, that is allowed to the other characters.

The flux of Ophuls's camera was apposite the nature of the material and also meshed with the sensibilities of the screenwriters, Henry Garson and Robert Soderberg, who had worked together on family comedy serial programs for radio. Garson recounts: "We had the same thoughts in the way you'd like to do a picture: movement, not just standing still." And Soderberg's recollection of their collaboration with Ophuls strikes the same notes: "On radio, we had been doing a family living in an apartment. So we were conscious of the flow within in a house, very conscious of a lack of privacy . . . in the American home."[23] These reminiscences of the film's production also reveal how an interest in suburban domesticity, which is more shown than told, was felt to be an implicitly important subtext of the film's action. Sybil operates inside the system of Ophuls's cinematography and narration in a strange way. Sybil is a figure past which the camera frequently sweeps, as it does when we see her vacuuming the stairs of the Harper house just as Lucia returns from her visit to Los Angeles, where she has unsuccessfully tried to warn Darby off from seeing Bea and thus unintentionally mired her family more firmly in his squalid demimonde of lowlifes and crooks (figure 1.3). In a sequence that serves to introduce us to the interior spaces of the house and the lives of the characters therein, Lucia enters the house bearing a load of parcels while the camera, which is already inside, follows her movements, left to right, as she moves through the kitchen, across a doorway (at which point the film discreetly cuts on action), and through the entry hall and up the stairs, the camera all the while dollying and tilting to keep track of her movements. The camera's skill in effortlessly tracing her movements through wild artifice, which is

Figure 1.3. Sybil (Frances E. Williams) vacuuming as Ophuls's mobile camera sweeps past her in *The Reckless Moment* (Max Ophuls, 1949, Columbia Pictures). Digital frame enlargement.

meant to efface itself, reverberates with Lucia's own attempts casually to bat away her father's questioning of her trip to the city. As she ascends the stairs, midway up she passes Sybil who is wrestling with a noisy vacuum cleaner. "Sybil, can you turn that vacuum cleaner off? I can't hear the race results," Mr. Harper complains. Sybil responds while also greeting the returning Lucia: "I don't know why you want to hear 'em Mr. Harper—hello Mrs. Harper!—you never win anyhow!" Everything could not be more *in medias res,* least of all Sybil, who is between floors and whose activities stand between Mr. Harper and the media he wants to consume. She is also in a position to undermine gently his desire for media, for the racing news. Sybil closely fits Krajewski's description of the servant as the "in-between, an intermediary." Lucia asks her just seconds later where Bea is, and Sybil responds with affectionate, efficient knowing: "She's in your room, Mrs. Harper, using your shower again." Sybil sees Lucia leaving the house early on the morning that she discovers Darby's corpse—"You're up awful early this morning." When Lucia returns from her ordeal, heroically attempting to appear as if nothing is the matter, like she has not just been getting rid of a corpse, Sibyl asks her where the shopping list is, so that she can add something to it. Lucia struggles to find it in her pocket, "I have it right here. . . . Well, I had it." Sybil interjects, "I know, you put it in your pocket so you wouldn't forget it like the last time." She calls Lucia in to receive phone calls, she brings her dinner up to her bedroom. When Lucia returns home from her last meeting with Donnelly in Los Angeles, Sibyl meets her outside the house to tell her that she has (wisely and intuitively) diverted Donnelly's boss, the blackmailer Mr. Nagel, to wait in the boathouse for Lucia.

In several scenes in which deep-focus cinematography allows the viewer to observe action in several planes of the image, Sybil is often given to occupy the background, where she is busy cooking or dusting. But she is just as likely to reemerge as a figure, an agent in the narration of a film in which everything is always already in flux (figure 1.4). Sybil's anticipatory, intercepting, delaying, intuiting strategies—in short, her deft management of the Harper household—aids and abets the film's "happy" ending. (The ending is happy, that is, insofar as the family survives intact, despite the fact that Lucia will likely never recover from the intimacy she has shared with Donnelly or from the sadness of his death.) She both activates and delays various narrative outcomes; she mediates the meetings between characters, and thus mediates the narrative's temporality, as well as the resolution of its plot. In short, she is both caught up in the

Figure 1.4. Sybil (Frances E. Williams) occupies the background while dusting in *The Reckless Moment* (Max Ophuls, 1949, Columbia Pictures). Digital frame enlargement.

movement of Ophuls's stylized narration in movement and also acts as a sort of counterforce to its boundless forward motion.

Williams's comments about Ophuls's directorial style add some anecdotal flesh to these observations: "He got to know us well enough to *know* us . . . knowing what they had to give and how they would blossom into what he wanted. . . . The flow and tempo were very important. He was aware of the whole, always, of what fit into what and what flowed into what."[24] (Her description, in fact, actually makes Ophuls sound something like a Sybil, or a Jeeves—the consummate servant who knows what is needed before the employer does.) Williams's performance, often when she is pictured in the background, is characterized by an open-ended range of expressive facial gestures, whereby and according to the content of the scene, she conveys sympathetic surprise or sadness, as well as gentle consternation. These responses are not the typical stock-in-trade expressions associated with a mammy-type role. Instead, they suggest a skeptical, but emotionally engaged human subject. Williams said of the feeling on the set: "It was a good family, a good film family."[25]

Sibyl functions as an agent of delay who produces small eddies of temporal stasis. She helps to maintain the sense of otium that is promised by suburban space; she defends a kind of decelerated temporality against the encroachments of those avatars of the city (Darby, Donnelly, and Nagel) who would otherwise succeed in hastening life in the Harper household to a conclusion better suited to the tempo of an urban noir.[26] But the postwar suburb was itself a site of accelerated temporality. Dolores Hayden has written that what she calls the "sitcom suburbs" of the 1950s, the period that immediately follows the moment of *The Reckless Moment*'s production and release, "were constructed at great speed."[27] Moreover, such suburbs—the most iconic and exemplary instance of which is surely Levittown, New York—were built to facilitate the speedy, autonomous traversal of the automobile, like the one we see screeching out of Balboa when Lucia breaks the artificial harmony of the suburbs on her unenviable and reckless errand to the city. In safeguarding the Harper family, and preventing them from going to ruin, one could say that Sybil safeguards them as a useful unit of consumption. Lucia will survive to compile more shopping lists; the suburban home's aura of repose will endure. But with her facility in serving the needs of the family and its sustainability, Sybil participates in the ongoing normalization of conditions that will keep people like herself from owning for herself a house like the Harpers' in a town like Balboa.[28]

Sybil takes an active part in the film's suspenseful conclusion. Donnelly has arrived at the Harpers' boathouse just in time to defend Lucia from Nagel, who he kills, while also seriously injuring himself. Lucia runs to the house to get something to dress his wound, but comes out to discover Donnelly racing away, intent on expunging any trace of his and Nagel's world from the life of the Harpers' Balboa. Lucia calls out for Sybil to bring her the car keys, and we see them both in pursuit of Donnelly. When he runs off the road and fatally injures himself, he explains to Lucia, who tearfully attempts to help him, that the accident will allow him to take the blame for both Nagel's and Darby's deaths. He convinces her to leave the scene of the accident so that his plan will work. When she returns to the car, Sybil helps her inside and surprisingly says, "Come on, Mrs. Harper. I'll drive." And so she does. She drives them home, in time for the film's final scene. This reckless moment of film directing propels Sybil into a novel narrative configuration, a slight transgression of spatial coordinates, and a reassignation of roles. Of course, this quick script reshuffle is also merely a mode of minor compensation for remanding Williams to her role as "movie maid." As a gesture, it did not create better roles for actors like Williams, much less could it help to dislodge a government-backed system of property purchase and ownership, one that insured that Sybil's counterparts would never be allowed to live in a suburb like Balboa in 1949.

This drive home with Sybil at the wheel registers like a more dignified and more progressive role than that granted to Gussie in the final shots of *Mr. Blandings Builds His Dream House*. Both Gussie and Sybil are granted forms of limited agency that are imagined in specifically spatial registers. Gussie saves the Blandings family from financial ruin, but can only be shown to do so by making her representation conform to a racist and marginalizing stereotyping. Sybil's much more dignified portrayal across *The Reckless Moment* is perhaps less offensive, but its poignancy (if we want to call it that) derives from the fact that its small and important differences impress us because of the strength of the racist representations from which her character subtly differs. In both films the static framings and minor movements of the African American maid tell us much about the intransigence of racism and white privilege in the United States, and their manifestation and maintenance in regimes of spaces both real and represented.

Notes

1. St. Clair Bourne, "The African American Image in American Cinema," *Black Scholar* 21, no. 2 (March–April–May 1990): 12.

2. Frank B. Wilderson III, *Red, White, and Black: Cinema and the Structure of U.S. Antagonisms* (Durham, NC: Duke University Press, 2010), 14.

3. John David Rhodes, *Spectacle of Property: The House in American Film* (Minneapolis: University of Minnesota Press, 2017), 5.

4. Charlene Regester, "African American Extras in Hollywood during the 1920s and 1930s," *Film History* 9 (1997): 96.

5. "Movie Maids: Eight New Hollywood Films Backtrack to Hack Racial Stereotypes in Casting Negro Actors as Maids and Menials," *Ebony* 3, August 1948, 56.

6. "Movie Maids," 57.

7. Dianne Harris, *Little White Houses: How the Postwar Home Constructed Race in America* (Minneapolis: University of Minnesota Press, 2013), 13.

8. David M. P. Freund, *Colored Property: State Policy and White Racial Politics in Suburban America* (Chicago: University of Chicago Press, 2007), 6.

9. Freund, *Colored Property*, 8.

10. Freund, *Colored Property*, 8–9.

11. Freund, *Colored Property*, 177.

12. Harris, *Little White Houses*, 103.

13. Harris, *Little White Houses*, 92.

14. Harris, *Little White Houses*, 92–93.

15. The scope of the essay does not permit me to mount a thorough survey of such representations in this period, but the analyses that follow demonstrate some of the variety in films made in these years. We might count Louise Beavers's portrayal of Delilah Johnson in Stahl's *Imitation of Life* (1934) as a high-water mark for its sensitivity relative to other films from 1930s, such as the Mae West vehicle *She Done Him Wrong* (Lowell Sherman, 1933) in which Beavers plays Pearl, a racist mammi-fied caricature. Hattie McDaniel's performance as Hester in *George Washington Slept Here* (William Keighley, 1942) shows that the mammy stock character survived into wartime filmmaking, and, as we will see, Beavers's performance as Gussie in *Mr. Blandings Builds His Dream House* is merely a variation on this racist trope. Douglas Sirk's *Imitation of Life* probably marks the point at which such performances became less comfortable for Hollywood. For a comprehensive study of the stereotyped roles given to Blacks in Hollywood cinema, see Donald Bogle's pathbreaking and canonical *Toms, Coons, Mulattoes, Mammies, Bucks: An Interpretive History of Blacks in American Films*, 5th ed. (New York: Bloomsbury, 2016), esp. 29–88. (This book was first published in 1973.)

16. Markus Krajewski, *The Server: A Media History from the Present to the Baroque* (New Haven: Yale University Press, 2018), 30.

17. This point is made by Catherine Jurca in her brilliant essay on the film, "Hollywood, the Dream House Factory," *Cinema Journal* 37, no. 4 (Summer 1998): 23.

18. Jurca, "Hollywood, the Dream House Factory," 28.

19. For a fascinating consideration of Beavers's performances that departs in some significant ways from the line of argumentation that I am following, see Karen Beavers, "Everybody Has a Mammy: The Productive Discomfort of Louise Beavers' Movie Maids," *Genders* (July 2, 2010), https://www.colorado.edu/genders archive1998-2013/2010/07/02/everybody-has-mammy-productive-discomfort-louise-beavers-movie-maids.

20. Karl Schoonover, "The Cinema of Disposal: Max Ophuls and Accumulation in America," *differences: A Journal of Feminist Cultural Studies* 29, no. 1 (2018): 44.

21. Schoonover, "The Cinema of Disposal," 44.

22. In some ways Balboa is ambiguously suburban. It was developed in the late nineteenth and early twentieth century as a resort/recreation and residential neighborhood of Newport Beach. Thus, the actual town did not originate as a suburb per se. But in the film, the ease and frequency with which Lucia moves between it and Los Angeles sutures it to the imaginary of suburbia.

23. Lutz Bacher, *Max Ophuls in the Hollywood Studios* (New Brunswick, NJ: Rutgers University Press, 1996), 272. Bacher's chapter on the making of *The Reckless Moment* is a kind of production microhistory.

24. Bacher, *Max Ophuls* 292.

25. Bacher, *Max Ophuls*, 298.

26. Whether *The Reckless Moment* is a woman's film, or a melodrama, or a noir is an open question, and in this ambivalence it resembles a film like *Mildred Pierce* (Michael Curtiz, 1945), which similarly pits mother against daughter in the confines of the cramped suburban home in which Mildred's (Joan Crawford) story begins.

27. Dolores Hayden, *Building Suburbia: Green Fields and Urban Growth, 1820–2000* (New York: Vintage, 2003), 128.

28. At the same time, built into Sybil's representation in the film, however, is an implausibility that recalls that of Gussie's employment in the Blandingses' household. How does Lucia pay for Sybil's wages? A family of such modest means would be unlikely to be able to maintain a live-in servant. This is a question the film does not really answer.

References

Bacher, Lutz. *Max Ophuls in the Hollywood Studios*. New Brunswick, NJ: Rutgers University Press, 1996.

Beavers, Karen. "Everybody Has a Mammy: The Productive Discomfort of Louise Beavers' Movie Maids." *Genders* (July 2, 2010), https://www. colorado.edu/gendersarchive1998-2013/2010/07/02/everybody-has-mammy-productive-discomfort-louise-beavers-movie-maids.

Bourne, St. Clair. "The African American Image in American Cinema." *Black Scholar* 21, no. 2 (March–April–May 1990): 12–19.

Freund, David M. P. *Colored Property: State Policy and White Racial Politics in Suburban America*. Chicago: University of Chicago Press, 2007.

Harris, Dianne. *Little White Houses: How the Postwar Home Constructed Race in America*. Minneapolis: University of Minnesota Press, 2013.

Hayden, Dolores. *Building Suburbia: Green Fields and Urban Growth, 1820–2000*. New York: Vintage, 2003.

Jurca, Catherine. "Hollywood, the Dream House Factory." *Cinema Journal* 37, no. 4 (Summer 1998): 19–36.

Krajewski, Markus. *The Server: A Media History from the Present to the Baroque*. New Haven: Yale University Press, 2018.

"Movie Maids: Eight New Hollywood Films Backtrack to Hack Racial Stereotypes in Casting Negro Actors as Maids and Menials." *Ebony* 3 (August 1948): 56–59.

Regester, Charlene. "African American Extras in Hollywood during the 1920s and 1930s." *Film History* 9 (1997): 95–115.

Rhodes, John David. *Spectacle of Property: The House in American Film*. Minneapolis: University of Minnesota Press, 2017.

Schoonover, Karl. "The Cinema of Disposal: Max Ophuls and Accumulation in America." *differences: A Journal of Feminist Cultural Studies* 29, no. 1 (2018): 33–65.

Wilderson, Frank B. *Red, White, and Black: Cinema and the Structure of U.S. Antagonisms*. Durham, NC: Duke University Press, 2010.

2

Take a Giant Step

Racialized Spatial Ruptures in the Northern Cinematic Suburbs

MERRILL SCHLEIER

HE FILM *TAKE A GIANT STEP* (Philip Leacock, United Artists, 1959) explores the travails of the Scotts, the first African American family to move into an all-white neighborhood in a northeastern suburb. Experiencing what Michael Omi and Howard Winant refer to as various scales of racism—that is, racism is administered differently and unevenly in different contexts and spatial regimes—I argue that the fictional Scotts' experiences underscore the racialized ruptures between institutional, social, and private domestic spaces for African Americans in white suburban spaces after World War II. These unequal spatial divisions ensure their racial containment, prompting their feelings of isolation, entrapment, and placelessness.[1] *Take a Giant Step* also exposes the intrinsic relationship between race and real estate in the United States, created by the federal government's housing policies in collusion with private capital, which created segregation throughout the northeastern suburbs during this time. I take up George Lipsitz's challenge to assess the relationship between the spatial dynamics of racial segregation and racial representation—that is, "racism takes place"—and how production design, architectural style, and prop placement are redolent of such spatial and ideological values.[2] This chapter also focuses on how the spatialization of racism mediates the identities and circumscribed movement of the Scotts and middle-class suburban Blacks in general. Even though the boundaries of de jure segregation began to open some institutional and public spaces to Blacks in the northeastern United States after World War II, de facto segregation still affected African Americans and the Scotts' ability to enjoy their private suburban domestic abode and its concomitant social spaces, thus maintaining their racial containment. Despite their upstanding demeanor and economic advantages, their middle-class status does not mitigate the racism they must endure, notwithstanding their ardent desire to assimilate.

Based on the well-received, semiautobiographical play of 1953 by African American playwright Louis S. Peterson, who coauthored the film script with veteran screenwriter Julius J. Epstein, *Take a Giant Step* is also one of the earliest Hollywood postwar Black family dramas by a Black author (produced by the independent production company Lancaster-Hill-Hecht), which was designed primarily to appeal to Black urban audiences, predating the well-known theater production and subsequent film *Raisin in the Sun* (Petrie, 1961) by several years.[3] Unlike previous Hollywood social problem films in which an African American protagonist sets in motion a change in attitudes with the help of a white savior type, *Take a Giant Step* shifts agency squarely to the Scott family, especially confrontational teenager Spence Scott. The film stars rock'n'roll singer Johnny Nash, whose oppositional stance conforms to the alienated teen trope, initiated by *Rebel Without a Cause* (Ray, 1955), that was adopted in many suburb films; his character also challenges racist attitudes and their concomitant spatial regimes, prefiguring Black activist voices of subsequent decades.

The parameters of the plot also share much with other suburban dysfunction films in the Scotts' overconsumption of material goods and their embrace of the American Dream, which occurs to the detriment of their son's emotional development. Told from the dissatisfied teenager Spence's point of view, the narrative also exposes his racial trauma due to his white friends' social freeze, prompted by their parents' fears of miscegenation in the largely segregated neighborhood. In response to his challenge to a racist teacher that prompts a cigar-smoking episode in the school restroom, Spence is expelled from school. Coupled with his parent's workaholic behavior and failure to fully comprehend his isolation, this prompts him to run away from home to seek community with other African Americans and to discover his manhood. There is a constant tension in the film between Spence's quest for freedom and his racial containment, preventing him from realizing his masculine and racial identities, or even his personhood. Following the death of his sickly grandmother, Gram (Estelle Helmsley), Spence finally decides to attend college while fulfilling his parents' aspirational dreams of higher education for their son, marking his escape from the suburbs. Gram's literal imprisonment in the house acts as a parallel to Spence's metaphorical entrapment, thus her death serves as a liberating force in his quest for self-realization.

In accord with most midcentury suburb cycle films, such as *The Desperate Hours* (Wyler, 1955), *The Man in the Gray Flannel Suit* (Johnson, 1956), and *Crime of Passion* (Oswald, 1956), the Scotts' middle-class dwelling and possessions in *Take a Giant Step* act as both ciphers of the American Dream and consumer plenty and also its failures, serving as what sociologist Anthony M. Platt refers to as both "a refuge and a prison," especially for Blacks.[4] The Scotts suffer from double jeopardy by race and class—unmoored and alienated from one another and other African Americans because of their "Black flight" to a middle-class neighborhood and adherence to white suburban, consumerist values and placeless because of their detachment from whites and Blacks of any class. Indeed, the Scotts are trapped in what George Lipsitz has termed a "white spatial imaginary," which positioned "the properly gendered prosperous suburban home as the privileged moral geography of the nation."[5]

The aforementioned midcentury suburb cycle films concentrate ironically on the putative victimization of white middle-class denizens under siege—Hollywood's version of white fragility.[6] Such cinematic white suburbanites are intent on preserving or enhancing their property, which is often threatened by outside predation, thereby displacing the aggression and racial trauma perpetrated by whites against African Americans onto the whites themselves. Dianne Harris has shown that despite the largely homogeneous character of the emerging postwar suburbs, "the specter of the 'outsider'—an imagined figure who intended harm through invasion (scopic or actual), influence, or contamination via proximity—loomed large."[7] This is a common theme in such suburb films in which mental illness, exploitation, and criminality are represented as allegorized versions of the threat of "others" to the sanctity of suburban private property. Caucasian fears of the Black body are literally projected onto the Scotts in *Take a Giant Step*, especially their son, while the African American family becomes their neighbors' looming menace by ellipsis. The film also reverses the implicit racism of traditional suburb films by exploring the racial containment of the Scotts in public and private spaces alike.

Yet Hollywood's decision to adapt Louis S. Peterson's 1953 play about the tentative beginnings of integration of white suburban space is a whitewash of actual events in the United States. Even though the film closely followed Peterson's original text in that both chronicled his teenage experiences, the play was based in the 1930s. By contrast, the film takes place in the present and situates the Scotts in a homogeneous white suburb rather than in the diverse, open access neighborhood of the theatrical version. In both iterations, Spence and his parents suffer innumerable slights and microaggressions, but never the overt violence that characterized the majority of Black-white relations in the newly segregated suburbs of midcentury America. According to suburban studies scholars Becky Nicolaides and Andrew Wiese, "Contrary to popular stereotypes of placid consensus, the 1950s was a period of intensive, high stakes, sometimes violent conflict over suburban space that pivoted squarely around the issue of race."[8] More typical were the experiences of the African American Myers family who moved in 1957 into all-white Levittown Pennsylvania, and were subjected to months of twenty-four hour-a-day harassment and acts of vandalism. One of the more egregious cases in 1958 was that of noted scientist Percy Julian whose family was harassed and threatened in the Chicago suburb of Oak Park, before his house was finally bombed and set on fire.[9] As Carl Rowan reported in *Ebony* in that year, there was not a week that went by when a Negro family did not experience physical harm, property damage, or loss of employment for seeking to secure equal housing.[10]

Yet *Take a Giant Step* represses the pervasive acts of real suburban harassment and violence in favor of the numerous snubs and slights, experienced in Spence's school, the father's place of business, and in their neighborhood. We never see the elder Scotts subjected to overt confrontations, rather the paucity of social intercourse between the family and their invisible white neighbors compromises the former's full enjoyment of their private abode and neighborhood alike.[11] As one reviewer at the time noted, the Scotts are not "subjected to any virulent, Faubus-like white supremacism [sic]." They "live in the north where the prejudice is of a subtle, more corrosive kind."[12] In spite of their upstanding demeanor, gainful employment, and middle-class status, the Scotts do not inhabit common domestic or social spaces with their white middle-class peers. And even though Spence's white teenage friends visit the Scott residence, he is neither invited to their homes nor to their social get-togethers, although he is a valuable member of the school's baseball team. The Scotts are ensconced in their amply appointed bourgeois interior or gilded cage, which renders such private and social domains both psychologically and, at times, physically carceral.

Black in the White Cinematic Spatial Imaginary

The Scott family resides in a white Colonial Revival dwelling located in a cul-de-sac in an older northeastern suburb, a movie town shot on the Universal Studios' backlot, probably on Colonial Street. Serving as the setting for a number of films such as *All I Desire* (Sirk, 1953) and *Inherit the Wind* (Kramer, 1960) and midcentury television sitcoms such as *Leave It to Beaver* (1957–63), the backlot's old-fashioned architecture acts as a code for traditional middle-class Caucasian values and property ownership.[13] The style also retained its popular appeal because it echoed Neoclassicism or the "simple and honest housing of our forefathers, requirements that have not changed since Thomas Jefferson at Monticello and Washington at Mount Vernon," reported *Popular Mechanics* in 1946.[14] Thus, while the Scotts' dwelling evokes a sense of nostalgia and putative normality, it has been traditionally associated with upper- and middle-class whiteness. Yet it also serves an additional function for an African American family in the white spatial imaginary. Eric Hobsbawm argues that Colonial Revival monuments and public buildings, and I would suggest domestic dwellings, were rendered in classical idiom beginning in the late nineteenth century to ensure the assimilation and conformity of mostly heterogeneous immigrant populations to dominant white ideologies.[15] Dianne Harris concurs, claiming that the postwar "little white houses" served as homogenizing spaces that performed, administered, and modeled whiteness for its inhabitants.[16] Additionally, the Neoclassical style of Washington and Jefferson evokes the stain of the nation's foundational racist underpinnings, that is, slavery. In *Take a Giant Step*, the house's classically inspired white facade and pale inside decor serve to entrap the Scott family ontologically in such traditional Caucasian, middle-class beliefs while evoking past physical incarceration. The home's NeoColonial exterior, the exaggerated whiteness of its interior appurtenances, its Colonialist-inspired living room wallpaper, and the profile portrait of Thomas Jefferson that is affixed to the wall act as virtual reminders of African Americans' previously forced habitation on plantations.

Likewise, their son, seventeen-year-old Spence, is the only African American pupil in an imposing Jeffersonian, Neoclassical brick edifice, replete with multiple pediments, fluted columns, and an elevated stairwell, in which racist ideas on the Civil War are disseminated. In contrast to the house and neighborhood, the institutional space of the school serves more as a vehicle of racial containment and sociopolitical control. The traditional architecture's embedded meaning is echoed in the racist pronouncements that Spence encounters in his history class. In view of the Supreme Court's recent *Brown v. Board of Education* (1954) ruling to integrate public schools throughout the nation, the suburban school's architecture and the ensuing historical information espoused therein are in keeping with white resistance to Black attendance in the suburbs, forging the inextricable link between segregated housing and segregated schools. Surrounded by his all-white seated classmates who are rendered as a group, the singular, African American student faces down his white teacher because of her blatantly racist lesson. We learn afterward that the trigger for his challenging stance is the teacher's answer to a student's question, "Why didn't the slaves rebel during the Civil War?" Designed purposely to rile Spence, Miss Bailey (actress uncredited) replies that African Americans were too "backward," the first of the film's microaggressions, which prompts the laughter of the entire class. Indeed, the film opens with a close-up of an upright Spence before the camera pulls away showing him in a long shot, towering above his seated white classmates, while revealing a vast spatial chasm between him and the prim teacher (figure 2.1). The latter's retort is accompanied by a tracking shot, the terminus of which is a glaring Spence confronting her, thereby performing what bel hooks has referred to as a "Black oppositional gaze" to counter her racism and his fellow pupils' collusion with trying to cause his humiliation.[17] In confiding the incident to his grandmother later, he demonstrates his precociousness and antagonistic attitude, referring to the teacher and his classmates as "dumb jerks" and invoking Frederick Douglass and the uprising of enslaved people during the Civil War. The scene illustrates that despite his admission to the school's suburban institutional spaces, white authorities and white students alike try to make him feel inferior and unwanted, prompting Spence's rebellion against such racist architectural, spatial, and ideological confines.

For the fictional Scotts and middle-class African Americans, the white spatial suburban imaginary serves as an aspirational promise, in the form of private property, consumer goods, and social status, and a potential threat. When his parents hear about their son's expulsion from public school, the proper, conformist Mrs. Scott (Beah Richards)

Figure 2.1. Spence (Johnny Nash) confronts his racist teacher (actress uncredited) in *Take a Giant Step* (Philip Leacock, United Artists, 1959). Digital frame enlargement.

is more concerned about the reactions of her invisible white suburban neighbors, while chastising Spence for his oppositional behavior: "You have no business talking back to white women. . . ," she warns. "If you were in the South, you could be lynched for that. . . . So my advice to you is try and remember your place." She thereby transfers centuries of racial trauma and fear to both her son's public school and their domestic space alike. Later, his father (Frederick O'Neal) concurs, reporting on the humiliations he must bear daily in order to provide for Spence and the family's middle-class comforts: "I hear those crumbs, talking about niggers, making jokes about niggers. But I stay on because I need the job. So I can get the things that you need. What do you do?" For the elder Scotts, place means inhabiting a submissive position both physically and behaviorally to maintain their livelihoods and safety, in the face of the imminent violence that is still very present in white neighborhoods throughout the northeastern suburbs. Even though the audience never sees the Scotts' white neighbors, the latter's values have been internalized and are further administered through surveillance and northeastern Jim Crow behavior, functioning like spatial control and coercion over the parents' careful conduct in public spaces and in their private dwelling.

Spence further rebels against the white spatial imaginary and the acquiescent spatial position adopted by his parents, seen in his efforts to commandeer his own environment by expressing his wrath on the suburban abode, which also signals a challenge to their adopted assimilationist values. After contradicting his teacher's claims of Black passivity and subsequent to his expulsion from school, the rebellious teen strides through his almost evacuated suburban neighborhood. He removes a pointed garden stake from his front lawn, which he brings into the living room and angrily strikes the furniture and himself. Spence is seen at a proverbial crossroads: either accept the town's racism with its negative views of African Americans, which he later expresses in the comment "I hate being Black," a sign of his racial trauma, or stand up and resist. While Spence's parents might be viewed as the counterparts to the restrained Myers family who integrated Pennsylvania's Levittown in 1957, Spence chooses to challenge the white status quo more aggressively.

But despite Spence's fraught integration into a reluctant suburban public educational system and its athletic program, he soon learns that he is newly barred from most heteronormative suburban social spaces. The parent of one of Spence's friends has recently forbidden his son to accompany the Black teenager to school or to invite him to a coed party. The cowardly Bobby (Del Erickson) blames Spence's exclusion on his girlfriend's father, who "doesn't like colored people," hence introducing the white fear of miscegenation and its concomitant devaluation of the sexually mature Black body, attitudes that were prevalent in the northeastern suburbs. As Gunnar Myrdal reported in *An American Dilemma* (1944), his landmark study of race in America, the ban on intermarriage held a preeminent place in social segregation. "No other way of crossing the color line is so attended by the emotion commonly associated with violating a social taboo as intermarriage and extra-marital relations between a Negro man and a white woman."[18] Interracial marriage was illegal in the United States until 1967, when the Supreme Court struck down antimiscegenation laws, the same year as Stanley Kramer's film *Guess Who's Coming to Dinner*, which featured a mixed-race romance.[19] Spence previously reported glumly to the family's attractive maid Christine (Ruby Dee) that he lacked a girlfriend, meaning that his full sexual identity as a Black man in the largely segregated northeastern suburbs would never be realized.

The Jim Crow exclusion of Spence is further underscored spatially on suburban Main Street, where he glances longingly into the malt shop's picture window that is occupied exclusively by his homogeneous white male peers and their paramours, a place where he is denied entry by de facto segregation practices (figure 2.2). Historian Thomas Sugrue claims that the informal racialization of space in the North "excluded Blacks from restaurants, hotels, amusement parks, and swimming pools, and relegated them to separate sections of the theater," policies usually associated with de jure segregation in the South.[20] *Take a Giant Step*'s Spence recognizes himself as both part of and separated from the white world, hence signifying his nullibicity or placelessness. To emphasize his pain, the film's pressbook reported in emphatic terms:

> SPIT IT OUT! SNARL IT OUT. SCREAM IT OUT, SPENCE! TELL THEM YOU DON'T REALLY CARE IF YOU'RE ALWAYS ON THE OUTSIDE—LOOKING IN . . . THEN TRY TO TELL YOURSELF THAT LONE- LINESS AND LONGING HASN'T REALLY HURT YOU. DEEP DOWN IN THE PIT OF YOUR HEART.[21]

A reverse angle shot shows Spence viewing his visage in the window's reflective glass, which separates exterior and interior space, and for a fleeting moment the audience vicariously experiences what W. E. B.

Figure 2.2. Spence (Johnny Nash) stares longingly into the malt shop in *Take a Giant Step* (Philip Leacock, United Artists, 1959). Digital frame enlargement.

Du Bois referred to as the African American's double consciousness.[22] African American studies scholar Houston Baker argues that for a place to be recognized by one as an "actual PLACE, as a personally valued locale, one must set and maintain the boundaries. If one, however, is constituted and maintained within the boundaries set by a dominating authority, one is not a setter of place but a prisoner of another's desire." This sense of having no place, he argues, "travels and has the motility of a policing force."[23] Hence in Spence's home, school, and neighborhood, an all-encompassing whiteness and its concomitant exclusions in public and suburban social space prevail, a sign of his racial containment.

White hostility to miscegenation is similarly explored in the NAACP-financed, thirty-two-minute, educational documentary *Crisis in Levittown* (Bobker and Becker, 1957), which represents an effort to explore racial prejudice in suburban housing. Completed two years earlier than *Take a Giant Step*, it likewise chronicles the experiences of an African American family, the Myerses' move to Pennsylvania's segregated subdivision, here told from the perspective of its white inhabitants, which provides additional insight into the Scotts' invisible neighbors. Professor Dan Dodson of the NYU School of Education, who acts as both narrator and interlocutor, interviews the community's denizens while offering interpretative commentary, but interestingly he never asks Bill and Daisy Myers how they apprehended the controversy that accompanied their move to the segregated enclave; indeed, the T-shirted Mr. Myers is seen watering his lawn for less than two minutes at the film's end, deprived of his ability to speak. Dodson identifies several major causes for white Levittowners' exclusionary racial tactics, some of which are attributed to putatively nonracial factors such as the anxiety concerning declining property values, loss of status, and violence. But it is the "fear of intermarriage," or residents' trepidations about Black-white mixing, that seems the most volatile. Several women in the documentary that are seated on lawn chairs in front of their suburban homes underscore their surveillance and control. One of the typical homemakers opines: "Well, I am very much against mixed marriages. That's eventually what it is going to come to if children are raised together. They're not going to think anything of marrying together."[24] In accord with Levittown's suburban women, the unseen white residents in *Take a Giant Step* prefer that the Scotts leave their neighborhood, but unable to expel them, they resort to exclusionary tactics to separate the now sexually mature Spence from most forms of social intercourse and its concomitant spaces.

Housebound Gram, who acts as Spence's confidante and support system, is the only person who is aware of the neighbors' ire and his spatial and interpersonal isolation. She informs Mr. and Mrs. Scott in a previous scene of their insensitivity to their son's plight: "What have either of you done to get the boy's respect I'd like to know except bully the boy? . . . Do you know that that boy is absolutely alone? He hasn't got a friend in the world. You didn't know, did you? That all his little pals have taken up with the girls. And the little girls' mothers don't want them going around with a colored boy." In the foregoing scene, however, Spence expresses his anger toward his white friends by taking control of his domestic abode in an effort to maintain his dignity in light of their craven behavior at school and their adherence to their parents' segregationist practices. "If I'm not good enough for the little gathering then I'm not good enough to pitch for you," he declares, before ejecting them from his house, which serves to counterbalance his own spatial marginalization.

White Nooses around the Black Necks of the Cities[25]

The Scotts' upstanding suburban dwelling and neighborhood that convey their entrapment in white physical space and ideology is juxtaposed with the lower and working-class, segregated Black urban neighborhood, to which he flees to sow his wild oats and find communion with other African Americans, although both act as carceral spaces for the young Spence. Similar to the cinematic trope of the teen escape from the suburbs to the city to signify nonconformity, rejection of materialistic values, and the search for identity, Spence's journey also maps the racialization of space in America, "the two warring images of suburban abundance and urban decline" that "defined both popular discourse and certain realities of the postwar metropolis," a condition created by government policies in collusion with private capital. Despite the existence of postwar Black suburbs, they were few and far between.[26] Unlike his sedate, sequestered environment filled with single-family-owned homes, federal, state, and local governments practiced racial zoning, which meant that African American neighborhoods were often filled with honky-tonk bars, burlesque clubs, and pawnshops, which were not permitted in the white suburbs.[27] Thus the Black environs were often separated from the white suburbs by both race and class, according to Eric Avila, echoing the chocolate cities of danger, heterosociality, and unpredictability versus the vanilla suburbs of homogeneity, certainty, and containment.[28] The sense of entrapment felt by the Scotts in their private home was magnified exponentially for most African Americans, as *Ebony* reported in 1958: "The great mass of Negroes are crammed into swollen slums with more or less hostile white communities ringing them like the walls of Alcatraz."[29]

The conditions found in Black urban space are underscored in the numerous places Spence visits—several bars and the confined apartment of a prostitute. After passing a pawnshop, he enters a smoke-filled tavern that evening where a seminude dancer is performing to the accompaniment of jazz music, which lends the scene a risqué flavor, but he is thrown out for being underage. He persists and finds another lowbrow establishment, which acts as the African American equivalent of the wholesome suburban malt shop, an undesirable Black social space for a teenager where he is served beer despite his age, and before meeting an older married woman waiting for her illicit lover and several prostitutes who are using the premise's telephone to solicit rent money. One of the women, Violet (Pauline Myers), finally encourages Spence to sit at their table, before inviting him to her cramped kitchenette apartment, which exploitive landlords could rent at exorbitant prices because of the paucity of available housing occasioned by segregation. To underscore its makeshift construction, they hear commotion from the next unit, which emphasizes their lack of privacy and distinguishes it from his own upscale dwelling.

The disparity in their respective domestic arrangements and class allegiances are mitigated by their joint racial trauma, which is also informed by the dual specters of miscegenation and the effects of segregation. Adopting Caucasian standards of beauty, Violet decorates her bed with a white doll with flowing blonde hair, which she lifts up admiringly and places on a chair, subsequently occupied by Spence, serving as a transitional object between them (figure 2.3). The scene probably references Drs. Mamie Clark and Kenneth Clark's doll experiments of the 1940s, in which African American children were given both Black and white dolls and asked to identify the better ones. The Black youngsters' repeated selection of Caucasian over Black dolls convinced the Clarks that, at an early age, African Americans suffered a crisis in self-esteem as a result of racial apartheid, a conclusion that influenced the Supreme Court in their 1954 *Brown v. Board of Education* decision. Spence's proximity to the white effigy serves to further emphasize the prohibition against interracial unions that still haunts both the white and Black spatial imaginaries, and which

Figure 2.3. Spence, the prostitute Violet, and the blonde doll in *Take a Giant Step* (Philip Leacock, United Artists, 1959). Digital frame enlargement.

continued to enforce the segregation of social spaces. Spence rejects the prostitute's advances, realizing that he also doesn't belong in the African American neighborhood, and angrily leaves the premises, emphasizing his fear and inability to consummate his sexual yearnings.

The only character in the film that is left out of both the white and Black spatial imaginaries is Alan (Sherman Raskin), Spence's Jewish friend, who is even more marginalized in the suburbs than his African American schoolmate. According to Karen Brodkin, Jews were also not considered white until shortly after the postwar period when European ethnics were permitted to move to Levittowns around the country after 1947.[30] But they were still barred from most middle and upper class white American suburbs until the late 1960s.[31] In accord with Spence, Alan suffers a social freeze, barred from both the school's athletic coterie and the heteronormative social space of the malt shop—indeed, both run into each other near its windowed entrance. A tracking shot shows them both striding down the street, assuming a provisional, yet uneasy, alliance. Spence even admits, "I've always liked you, Alan, even if nobody else . . . ," thus identifying the Jew as even more reviled than his Black friend. At the film's denouement, both marshal their outcast statuses and intellectual acumen in the service of self-improvement, heading to college to escape the white suburbs and its exclusions.

Class, Race, and Placelessness

Hollywood rendered the Scott family as staunchly middle class and above reproach, representing the upstanding candidates typically selected to break suburban racial barriers, but who were often subjected to investigations and lengthy interviews in an effort to guarantee their successful assimilation. Mr. Scott is a bank teller; the well-dressed and mannered Mrs. Scott works at the Red Cross; Spence is a bright, precocious student who reads books on Sigmund Freud; and the upscale family has even secured a young, attractive maid to care for Mrs. Scott's ailing mother. But the Scotts are middle class not only because of their professional employment but also due to their belief in hard work, their steadfast morals, and their valuation of education. Acquiring a private home and plethora of bourgeois accouterments served as outward signifiers of their desire to project decency and uprightness. Evelyn Brooks Higginbotham referred to the adoption of such standards as the "politics of respectability," which began during the Jim Crow era, when Blacks had to prove to whites that they were decent enough to deserve the benefits of equality.[32] In her memoir, the college-educated Daisy Myers, a member of the first family to integrate Levittown in 1957, recalls that even the very supportive Quaker-led William Penn Center, which helped orchestrate the family's move to the segregated suburban community, put them through the "third degree" and a lengthy investigation to ensure that they were above reproach. "They pried into our lives so extensively that one would wonder whether if they were going to give us a house instead of having us buy it," she reported.[33]

Like the Myerses, the Scotts' unimpeachable characteristics do not guarantee their acceptance in the white suburbs; rather, they remain an anomaly and are excluded from normative social intercourse despite their efforts to integrate. Notwithstanding their upstanding demeanor, they do not interact with their neighbors, ever concerned with the latter's reactions to them; their son is the only one who is seen engaging with his peers. A *Saturday Evening Post* article "When a Negro Moves Next Door" (1959) reported that it was still a rarity for an African American family to reside in a segregated white, middle-class suburbia, let alone be included in its activities.[34] Although Black suburban ownership rose from 1.5 to 2.5 million from 1940 to 1960 (only 5% of the total suburban population), the process was frequently contentious. The exclusion of Blacks and other minorities from postwar, suburban white developments in the Northeast is well documented; they were barred by restrictive racial covenants; by the federal government's discriminatory loan practices, which began in the 1930s and metastasized in the postwar suburban expansion, and were supported by private banks, redlining, racial zoning, steering, and blockbusting, among other practices. Ta-Nehisi Coates has observed that even middle-class respectability and stature did not necessarily advantage the aspirational postwar Black home seeker; rather, their achievement was seen as an opportunity for further plunder of their resources in the secondary loan markets where they were charged more than whites for comparable homes.[35] Middle-class status and decency didn't guarantee acceptance or successful assimilation by Black suburbanites in white environs even if it was desired.

But the differences between the Scotts and other white cinematic suburban families is also telling—Mrs. Scott works outside the home during a time when white women and their suburban cinematic analogues were expected to be domestic helpmates and caretakers. Most white families could enjoy a middle-class life if they chose with a single breadwinner, a commentary on the lower socioeconomic status of middle-class Blacks who earned less than comparable whites in midcentury America. Even though the fictional Scotts' habitation of the suburbs was made possible by their middle-class status and ability to afford a private home, on average African Americans still earned only $2,544 to a white family's $4,613 in 1955.[36] The family is rendered differently than most white nuclear cinematic families of the era; indeed, they are seen as more fractured due to the parents' need to produce a dual income to accommodate their upscale expenses and to finance a maid to care for Gram.

Screenwriter Peterson was critical of the Scotts' adoption of middle-class, consumerist values and morality as much as the racial discrimination directed at them. This class critique accords with the depiction of white cinematic suburbanites in such films as *The Man in the Gray Flannel Suit*, *Rebel Without a Cause*, and *Bigger Than Life* (Ray, 1956), which were prompted by midcentury social critics such as William Whyte, Vance Packard, and David Riesman who advanced the idea of a suburban malaise, supposedly produced by the deadening conformity and the consumerist ethos of the white middle-class suburbs. In order to underscore the Scotts' adoption of these putative white ideals, production designer Edward Carrere filled their two-story home with a plethora of consumer objects, including a television set, which their son abjures, and a fully appointed kitchen with a host of shiny new, exaggeratedly white appliances.[37] In accord with the architecture of the house, Carrere employed traditional Colonial Revival furnishings for the living room, which featured an ample fireplace surmounted by a European-styled landscape painting, wingback chairs, and a matching skirted sofa. Curio cabinets line the walls and display numerous Rococo-inspired figurines and knick-knacks, which reflect their traditional values, meant to convey conservative whiteness and orthodoxy, while the plentiful display of books suggests success through educational uplift.

Mrs. Scott's internalized assimilationist values are evidenced especially at the end of the film, when she seeks to effect reconciliation between Scott and his white buddies. After Gram's death, she invites the three, previously rejected baseball team members and the Jewish Alan to the Scott residence for Gram's postfuneral get-together, where ice cream and cake will be served in the backyard. The same friends whose parents excluded Spence from their social gatherings now inhabit the Scotts' living room; but Mrs. Scott is unconcerned about these slights. Rather she informs Spence later that she planned the occasion because his schoolmates are still his friends, reflecting her desire for a rapprochement. But when Spence returns home and finds his white cohorts seated on the sofa (Alan is separated from the threesome), he remains standing, which underscores his stalwart, spatial detachment, echoing the film's initial scene. Spence informs the group that the get-together is not only a commemoration of his grandmother's death but his own farewell party, since he has decided to attend college elsewhere. The elder Scotts will remain in their white middle-class environs continuing to make compromises, while their son plans to leave the white suburbs to establish his racial and gender identities.

Peterson's evaluation of the Scotts' acquisitiveness accords with the views of African American sociologist E. Franklin Frazier in his award-winning book *Black Bourgeoisie* (1957), which provided a more nuanced, albeit blameworthy, reading of the effects of suburbanization upon middle-class African Americans. Frazier regarded their adoption of suburban values as a form of collusion with the white propertied classes, thus showcasing an overt consideration of race that was repressed in the aforementioned social critic's portrayal of the white middle-class suburbs.[38] But his book provoked criticism for portraying aspiring Black families as pathologized almost a decade before the *Moynihan Report* (1965), identifying middle-class

African Americans as materialists while impugning its matriarchs for their putative shortcomings. Rather than an in-depth analysis of the policies and institutions that created and perpetuated the structures of American racism, Frazier placed a disproportionate responsibility on its victims. Yet *Black Bourgeoisie* is still a useful tool for understanding how Peterson apprehended the Scott family's dilemma and their spatial experiences in the midcentury American suburbs.

Frazier believed that the Black bourgeoisie were in a double bind, both ideologically and spatially. Encouraged to succeed in business under the capitalist system, they had internalized white capitalist values of success and accomplishment. Educated at first by northern missionaries and later in Black colleges administered by white northern philanthropists who adhered to a segregationist model, African Americans like the fictional Scotts came to believe, according to Frazier, that the procurement of material goods guaranteed them status, serving as a compensation for, or an escape from, their subordination. Despite his tacit recognition that whites created the segregated, exclusionary environments in the first place, Frazier still claimed that most of the Black bourgeoisie's conflicts arose from "their constant striving for status within the Negro world as well as the estimation of whites," accepting unconditionally "the value of the white bourgeois world, its morals and its canons of respectability, its standards of beauty and consumption."[39] Borrowing from the sociologist and economist Thorstein Veblen in *The Theory of the Leisure Class* (1899), he accused the Black middle class of practicing "conspicuous consumption," or displaying their possessions as a means of advertising their social and economic class, which stemmed from their feelings of inferiority and internalized self-hatred.[40] He further reproached such popular Black magazines as *Ebony*, *Jet*, and *Hue* for reinforcing such a consumerist ethos in their celebration of rich and famous African Americans in business, sports, and entertainment and for featuring articles with copious illustrations that showcased their luxurious homes and possessions. In one particularly trenchant passage, Frazier painted a picture of middle-class African Americans' putative profligate waste and commodity fetishism: "They are constantly buying things—houses, automobiles, furniture and all sorts of gadgets, not to mention clothes. . . . The houses of many middle-class Negroes have the appearance of museums for the exhibition of American manufactures and spurious art objects. The objects which they are constantly buying are always on display."[41] Frazier's diatribes accord with those of playwright and screenwriter Louis Peterson in *Take a Giant Step*, which are articulated by Gram, who attributes some of the Scotts' familial problems to their collusion with white consumerism, reprimanding them particularly for overworking to maintain their middle-class standard of living, but which means leaving their son to his own resources. Granting that they have provided him with a glut of possessions or everything they lacked, Gram claims that their absentee parenting has instead deprived him of the requisite emotional support to become a well-adjusted man. And in spite of good intentions, their consumerist ethos is also practiced at the expense of Spence's racial identity and growth. In a poignant scene, after Spence runs away from home, Gram chastises her daughter and son-in-law for moving to the white suburbs in the first place, where their son is eventually marginalized because of his race: "When you decided to move down here, did you ever stop and take into consideration that something like this was bound to happen sooner or later? And the most important thing might have been just your love and comfort. You did not. Went right on working. And instead of your company, he got a book, a bicycle, an electric train. The stuff that came into this house was ridiculous."

Frazier recognized that the causes for African Americans' dilemmas were enacted spatially, and that space was ideologically laden. He argued that the Black bourgeoisie were in "the process of becoming NOBODY" precisely because "they were robbed of their cultural traditions and physically separated from most Blacks as they became more upwardly mobile." In the case of Spence, he is alienated from his parents, his white friends, and any hope of meeting African American cohorts. If one extends Frazier's logic, when the African American middle class detached themselves from their segregated communities, which included working and lower class Blacks, whether by moving to Black or to white middle-class suburban locations as "the system of rigid segregation" unraveled, they were situated *nowhere*, lacking any place.[42] Such is the case with the Scotts who neither socialize nor interact with their neighbors, but who fear their judgments, especially with regard to their son's misbehavior.

Conclusion

Take a Giant Step depicts an African American family in a white suburban town rife with covert racism rather than physical aggression, subjected to numerous microaggressions, which is at odds with the contentious suburban integration of the United States in the 1950s. The film underscores the scales of racialized space that the Scotts must negotiate—although allowed entrance to the suburbs and some public and institutional spaces, they are barred from most social spaces. Yet the specter of racial violence and racial trauma haunts the white suburban imaginary, while its invisible gaze lends multiple places in its domain a carceral dimension, even infiltrating the privacy of their home, which melds segregated public space and private domestic space. Despite Peterson's tacit acknowledgment that institutional racism troubles the middle-class white suburbs, his original play and its subsequent cinematic adaptation perpetuate the belief that individual accomplishment and meritorious behavior rather than collective action will counter the structural racism that continues to oppress the Scott family. Thus, in order to realize his manhood, rebellious, outlier Spence departs the carceral spaces of the middle-class white suburbs and the working-class, segregated Black urban neighborhood alike to attend college. The pressbook underscores the severity of the teen's placelessness, a narrative and spatial problem that the film never resolves: "Negro audiences will understand most deeply the story of Spence Scott caught between white and Negro worlds!"[43]

Notes

Appreciation is extended to Ned Comstock of the Film and Television Library at the University of Southern California for providing access to archival sources when travel was impossible.

1 Michael Omi and Howard Winant, *Racial Formation in the United States*, 3rd ed. (New York: Routledge, 2014), 128. The authors suggest that "racist projects exist in a dense matrix, operating in various scales, networked with each other in formally and informally organized ways, enveloping and penetrating contemporary social relations, institutions, identities, and experiences." Gunnar Myrdal differentiates between personal, social, and institutional spaces in *An American Dilemma: The Negro Problem and American Democracy*, vol. 2 (New York: Harper Brothers, 1944), 606.

2. George Lipsitz, *How Racism Takes Place* (Philadelphia: Temple University Press, 2011), 5.

3. Louis Peterson, "Take a Giant Step," in *Black Theater USA*, ed. James Hatch (New York: Free Press, 1974), 547–584; Marc A. Reid, *Redefining Black Film* (Berkeley: University of California Press, 1993). See also Mark A. Reid, "*Take a Giant Step. A Raisin in the Sun*: The Black Family Film," *Jump Cut*, no. 36 (May 1991): 81–88.

4. Anthony M. Platt, "Between Scorn and Longing—Frazier's Black Bourgeoisie," in *E. Franklin Frazier and the Black Bourgeoisie*, ed. James E. Teele (Columbia: University of Missouri Press, 2002), 71.

5. Lipsitz, *How Racism Takes Place*, 13.

6. Robin DiAngleo, *White Fragility: Why It's So Hard for White People to Talk about Racism* (Boston: Beacon Press, 2018).

7. Dianne Harris, *Little White Houses: How the Postwar Home Constructed Race in America* (Minneapolis: University of Minnesota Press, 2013), 117.

8. Becky Nicolaides and Andrew Wiese, eds., *The Suburban Reader*, 2nd ed. (New York: Routledge, 2016), 337.

9. Carl Rowan, "Why Negroes Move to White Neighborhoods," *Ebony* 13 (August 1958), 17–24.

10. Rowan, "Why Negroes Move to White Neighborhoods."

11. Arnold Hirsch, *Making the Second Ghetto: Race and Housing in Chicago* (Chicago: University of Chicago Press, 1998), 40, refers to the "hidden violence" that characterized this era, which was whitewashed in the media.

12. "*Take a Giant Step*," *Filmfacts*, January 6, 1961, 312. Orval Faubus, the governor of Arkansas from 1955 to 1967, refused to comply with the Supreme Court's 1954 decision to integrate the public schools, and called in the National Guard.

13. Stephen Rowley, *Movie Towns and Sitcom Suburbs: Building Hollywood's Ideal Communities* (New York: Palgrave, 2015), 63–64.

14. David Gerhard, "The American Colonial Revival in the 1930s," *Winterthur Portfolio* 22 (Summer–Autumn 1987): 109–110.

15. Eric Hobsbawm and Terence Ranger, eds., *The Invention of Tradition* (New York: Cambridge University Press, 1992), 1–14.

16. Harris, *Little White Houses*.

17. bell hooks, "The Black Oppositional Gaze: Black Female Spectators," in *Black Looks: Race and Representation* (Boston: South End Press, 1992), 115–131.

18. Myrdal, *An American Dilemma*, 606.

19. For a further discussion of the handling of miscegenation in American cinema, see Ellen C. Scott, *Cinema Civil Rights: Regulation, Repression, and Race in the Classical Hollywood Era* (New Brunswick, NJ: Rutgers University Press, 2015).

20. Thomas Sugrue, *Sweet Land of Liberty: The Forgotten Struggle for Civil Rights in the North* (New York: Random House, 2009), xv. There were few instances of friction in northern social space in the 1940s since civil rights activists were focused more on gaining entry to institutional spaces. See Hirsch, *Making the Second Ghetto*, 41.

21. *Take a Giant Step* pressbook, 2. Courtesy of Cinema and Television Library, University of Southern California, Los Angeles.

22. W. E. B. DuBois, *The Souls of Black Folk* (Chicago: A. C. McClurg & Co., 1903; reprint ed., Seattle: Createspace International Publishing Platform, 2014), 5.

23. Huston Baker, *Workings of the Spirit: The Poetics of Afro-American Women's Writings* (Chicago: University of Chicago Press, 1991), 6. See also Gershun Avilez, "Housing the Black Body: Value, Domestic Space, and Segregation Narratives," *African American Review* 42 (2008): 135–146.

24. *Crisis in Levittown* (Lee Bobker and Lester Becker, 1957), Dynamic Films, thirty-two minutes. See https://archive.org/details/crisis_in_levittown_1957.

25. The subhead is from Martin Luther King Jr., *Where Do We Go From Here: Chaos or Community?* (Boston: Beacon Press, 1967), 212: "The suburbs are white nooses around the black necks of the cities."

26. Nicolaides and Wiese, *Suburban Reader*, 372.

27. Richard Rothstein, *The Color of Law: A Forgotten History of How Our Government Segregated America* (New York: Liveright, 2017), 50.

28. Eric Avila, *Popular Culture in the Age of White Flight: Fear and Fantasy in Suburban Los Angeles* (Berkeley: University of California Press, 2006), 4–6.

29. Rowan, "Why Negroes Move to White Neighborhoods," 18.

30. Karen Brodkin, *How Jews Became White Folks and What That Says about Race in America* (New Brunswick, NJ: Rutgers University Press, 1998), 25–52.

31. Albert I. Gordon, *Jews in Suburbia* (Boston: Beacon Press, 1959), 167–168.

32. Evelyn Brooks Higginbotham, *Righteous Discontent: The Women's Movement in the Black Baptist Church, 1880–1920* (Boston: Harvard University Press, 1994), 185.

33. Daisy D. Myers, *Sticks and Stones: The Myers Family in Levittown* (New York: New York Heritage Trust, 2004), 24. See Michelle Alexander, *The New Jim Crow: Mass Incarceration in the Age of Colorblindness* (New York: New Press, 2010), 226.

34. "When a Negro Moves Next Door," *Saturday Evening Post* (April 4, 1959), 32–33.

35. Ta-Nehisi Coates, "The Case for Reparations," *Atlantic* (June 2014), 196.

36. https://nces.ed.gov/pubs98/yi/yi16.pdf.

37. George Lipsitz, *The Possessive Investment in Whiteness: How White People Profit from Identity Politics*, rev. and expanded ed. (Philadelphia: Temple University Press, 2006).

38. E. Franklin Frazier, *Black Bourgeoisie* (Glencoe, IL: Free Press, 1957).

39. Frazier, *Black Bourgeoisie*, 204.

40. Thorstein Veblen, *The Theory of the Leisure Class* (New York: Macmillan, 1899), 36.

41. Frazier, *Black Bourgeoisie*, 230.

42. Frazier, *Black Bourgeoisie*, 126. The italics are mine.

43. *Take a Giant Step* pressbook, 2.

References

Alexander, Michelle. *The New Jim Crow: Mass Incarceration in the Age of Colorblindness*. New York: New Press, 2010.

Avila, Eric. *Popular Culture in the Age of White Flight: Fear and Fantasy in Suburban Los Angeles*. Berkeley: University of California Press, 2006.

Avilez, Gershun. "Housing the Black Body: Value, Domestic Space, and Segregation Narratives." *African American Review* 42 (2008): 135–146.

Baker, Huston. *Workings of the Spirit: The Poetics of Afro-American Women's Writings.* Chicago: University of Chicago Press, 1991.

Brodkin, Karen. *How Jews Became White Folks and What That Says about Race in America.* New Brunswick, NJ: Rutgers University Press, 1998.

Coates, Ta-Nehisi. "The Case for Reparations." *Atlantic* (June 2014): 196. https://nces.ed.gov/pubs98/yi/yi16.pdf.

Crisis in Levittown. Lee Bobker and Lester Becker, 1957. Dynamic Films, thirty-two minutes. https://archive.org/details/crisis_in_levittown_1957.

DiAngleo, Robin. *White Fragility: Why It's So Hard for White People to Talk about Racism.* Boston: Beacon Press, 2018.

DuBois, W. E. B. *The Souls of Black Folk.* Chicago: A. C. McClurg & Co., 1903; reprint ed., Seattle: Createspace International Publishing Platform, 2014.

Frazier, E. Franklin. *Black Bourgeoisie.* Glencoe, IL: Free Press, 1957.

Gerhard, David. "The American Colonial Revival in the 1930s." *Winterthur Portfolio* 22 (Summer–Autumn 1987): 109–148.

Gordon, Albert I. *Jews in Suburbia.* Boston: Beacon Press, 1959.

Harris, Dianne. *Little White Houses: How the Postwar Home Constructed Race in America.* Minneapolis: University of Minnesota Press, 2013.

Higginbotham, Evelyn Brooks. *Righteous Discontent: The Women's Movement in the Black Baptist Church, 1880–1920.* Cambridge: Harvard University Press, 1994.

Hirsch, Arnold. *Making the Second Ghetto: Race and Housing in Chicago.* Chicago: University of Chicago Press, 1998.

Hobsbawm, Eric, and Terence Ranger, eds. *The Invention of Tradition.* New York: Cambridge University Press, 1992.

hooks, bell. "The Black Oppositional Gaze: Black Female Spectators." In *Black Looks: Race and Representation,* 115–131. Boston: South End Press, 1992.

King, Martin Luther, Jr. *Where Do We Go from Here: Chaos or Community?* Boston: Beacon Press, 1967.

Lipsitz, George. *How Racism Takes Place.* Philadelphia: Temple University Press, 2011.

———. *The Possessive Investment in Whiteness: How White People Profit from Identity Politics.* Rev. and expanded ed. Philadelphia: Temple University Press, 2006.

Myers, Daisy D. *Sticks and Stones: The Myers Family in Levittown.* New York: New York Heritage Trust, 2004.

Myrdal, Gunnar. *An American Dilemma: The Negro Problem and American Democracy.* Vol. 2. New York: Harper Brothers, 1944.

Nicolaides, Becky, and Andrew Wiese, eds. *The Suburban Reader.* 2nd ed. New York: Routledge, 2016.

Omi, Michael, and Howard Winant. *Racial Formation in the United States.* 3rd ed. New York: Routledge, 2014.

Peterson, Louis. "Take a Giant Step." In *Black Theater USA,* edited by James Hatch. New York: Free Press, 1974.

Platt, Anthony. "Between Scorn and Longing—Frazier's Black Bourgeoisie." In *E. Franklin Frazier and the Black Bourgeoisie,* edited by James E. Teele. Columbia: University of Missouri Press, 2002.

Reid, Marc A. *Redefining Black Film*. Berkeley: University of California Press, 1993.

————. "*Take a Giant Step. A Raisin in the Sun*: The Black Family Film." *Jump Cut*, no. 36 (May 1991): 81–88.

Rothstein, Richard. *The Color of Law: A Forgotten History of How Our Government Segregated America*. New York: Liveright, 2017.

Rowan, Carl. "Why Negroes Move to White Neighborhoods." *Ebony* 13 (August 1958), 17–24.

Rowley, Stephen. *Movie Towns and Sitcom Suburbs: Building Hollywood's Ideal Communities*. New York: Palgrave, 2015.

Scott, Ellen C. *Cinema Civil Rights: Regulation, Repression, and Race in the Classical Hollywood Era*. New Brunswick, NJ: Rutgers University Press, 2015.

Sugrue, Thomas. *Sweet Land of Liberty: The Forgotten Struggle for Civil Rights in the North*. New York: Random House, 2009.

"*Take a Giant Step*." *Filmfacts*, January 6, 1961, 312.

Take a Giant Step pressbook. Courtesy of Cinema and Television Library, University of Southern California, Los Angeles.

Veblen, Thorstein. *The Theory of the Leisure Class*. New York: Macmillan, 1899.

"When a Negro Moves Next Door." *Saturday Evening Post* (April 4, 1959), 32–33.

3

"Where Have You Been?"

Bill Gunn's Suburban Nightmares

ELLEN C. SCOTT

WHEN CONSIDERING RACE IN THE AMERICAN SUBURBS, we most often think of their constitutive integration battles: the Levittowns, restrictive covenants, and redlining that confined Black efforts to attain the American Dream in the 1950s and beyond. These were struggles that while they sometimes made news, were largely omitted from 1950s Hollywood cinema—which was racially squeamish at best. In truth, however, both silent and first-wave 1970s Black independent features hosted an as yet underheralded figuration of the suburbs, a space often cast in opposition to the city and as curiously important to African Americans and Latinos.

This chapter will consider the place of the suburbs in Bill Gunn's 1973 film *Ganja and Hess*. Gunn, who was part of a wave of Black New York independent filmmaking in the 1970s and 1980s that included William Greaves, Jessie Maple, and Kathleen Collins, among others, began something in *The Angel Levine* (Kadar, 1970) and *The Landlord* (Ashby, 1970) (both of which he wrote) and *Stop!* (1970) (which he wrote and directed)—an interrogation of the difference space makes—that reaches fruition in *Ganja and Hess* (1973). In the opening of *The Landlord*, Gunn

77

sets up a juxtaposition between the wealthy, white Long Island suburb where the film's main character, Elgar (Beau Bridges), was raised and the Brooklyn brownstone he buys as an early gentrifier and in which he and his African American tenants reside. However, in most of Gunn's films the suburbs are Black and brown places that are less a locus of racial exclusion than a place of mystical expansion—diffusing the spatially constricted urban drama, providing room for an extended consideration of tangled domestic and familial concerns, and offering grounds for psychic, spiritual, sexual, and subjective experimentation that the urban milieu, with its claustrophobic architecture, forecloses.[1] But Gunn also uses the suburbs to unsettle the image of the Black bourgeoisie and, further, to link the gothic-tinged suburban landscapes to histories of colonial entanglements and Black migrations—forced and otherwise.

Gunn was raised in Philadelphia but lived much of his adult life in the New York suburb of Nyack, along the Hudson River. Producer Chiz Schultz has commented on the similarity between Hess's house in *Ganja and Hess* and Gunn's home, noting that both were layered with antique art and were marked by the obsessive energies of the collector.[2] The suburbs were more than simply a cheaper shooting location. The upstate locales Gunn chose—Nyack, Ossining, and Spring Valley—each had a long history of Black and brown residence and labor that challenge the narrative of suburban white flight as the only genesis for the suburbs. Spring Valley, one *New York Times* article noted with obvious racism, had by the 1970s increasingly become marked by "typical urban problems" and had "lost allure as a vacation destination beginning in the 1960s as suburbanization and the advent of modern highways and the Tappan Zee Bridge made Rockland County more accessible to New York City and Westchester commuters."[3] But Black and brown habitation of Rockland County predated the 1960s. It is important to note that former African American slaves and free Blacks founded Rockland County, both imbuing the setting with the stain of slavery and the empowerment of Blacks.[4] Part of the aim, then, in Gunn's films, was to make visible a kind of suburb other than the one built for the white middle classes—a Black and brown suburb that did not require integration into whiteness but which was nevertheless haunted by whiteness.[5]

Gunn uses the suburbs to refigure the locale's cinematic norms, not only reclaiming the untethered essence of Black migratory subjectivity through nonurban spaces but also, crucially, rendering their whiteness strange and introducing to the suburban landscape a Black queer sensibility. In turn, the suburbs represented in the film are not middle-class, tract-laden communities but rather the lush, green-gardened, semirural expanses of the country home; they are wild and overgrown; wooded not wooden. The notion of the suburbs as a site of horror is not new. George Romero's *Dead* trilogy, whose initial installment *The Night of the Living Dead* (1969) was a crucial pretext for Gunn's film and also starred Duane Jones, is also set in the rural suburbs of post–civil rights America. And as Richard Dyer notes, Romero's trilogy suggests whiteness as death—"that whites are the living dead."[6] Gunn's film builds upon these provocative tenets of Romero's film in refiguring Black/white relations. Yet Gunn's conceptualization of the suburbs expands our notions of the suburb beyond its figuration in the *Dead* trilogy, figuring it as a web-laden attic of Black subjectivity—an annexable space that gives room for the Black performative self to grow, if with deadly complications. If Romero's films insisted that the postapocalyptic suburban home or mall would rely upon human Black action heroes for its survival, Gunn's film insists that the undead Black antihero is crucial to the suburb's living death. Gunn further denaturalizes the suburb's racial and architectural connotations, disassociating it from its prefab look and postulating the New York suburb as a postwhite, ancient ethnic zone where whiteness survives only as the uncanny.

In *Ganja and Hess*, Hess (Duane Jones), a Black anthropologist living in the Rockland County suburbs of New York, studies the Myrthians, an ancient, pre-Egyptian, pre-Christian African civilization whose effort to save their anemic queen by transfusing the blood of slaves and later consuming their bodies results in a collective addiction to blood. In the course of his research he is pierced with a carved bone that initiates the blood thirst. He becomes addicted to blood—afflicted with the ailment he studies. The scripts reveal that Gunn developed an elaborate storyline and mythology of the Myrthians, a culture where it was "less of a sacrilege to spill blood than to drink it."[7] However, the finished film reveals the narrative obliquely and the actors improvise over the script's general tenets rather than reading lines. The Myrthians, though Hess's obsession, rarely come up in the finished film. Instead the origin story of the blood curse is borne in a nondiegetic echoic song that Sam Waymon (arguably the film's griot) chants in the credit sequence.[8]

In the film's early scenes, Hess meets a white museum archeologist who introduces him to George Meda (Bill Gunn) who will assist him in studying the Myrthians. Hess drives Meda back to his country home and Meda, loosened by the lavish, decadent feast and wine, unwinds and unburdens himself, revealing his suicidal tendencies; Meda not only rehearses hanging or drowning himself on Hess's property but attacks Hess with an axe, leaves him for dead, and shoots himself. Hess, immortal, wakes after being attacked and finds Meda's dead, naked body. Compulsively Hess leans over Meda and licks his blood off the bathroom floor. Feeling remorse, he prays for his own soul's redemption. He attempts a victimless appeasement of his blood addiction by stealing from a local blood bank. He absently hosts a garden party, spending time with his adolescent, French-speaking son (Enrico Fales) who has been at a boarding school. But he is so distracted by his blood lust and haunted by the chanting voices of the Myrthians that he cannot attend to his guests and wanders away into the expanses of his property, while we viewers are made to linger on images of a Black woman with cornrows attending his party and an aged, paint-stripped blackamoor in the attic. Drifting, he descends on a local dive bar, and lets a Black prostitute (Candece Tarpley) take him home. His desire ignites when she removes her blonde wig, revealing her natural hair. However, in the midst of their lovemaking, her pimp (Tommy Lane), attempting to rob Hess, emerges from behind a curtain and stabs him. Realizing Hess's strength and invulnerability, the panicked prostitute calls on the pimp to kill him. As happened earlier with Meda, Hess finds himself victim of a bedroom murder attempt at the hands the very folk he is studiously avoiding making his prey. He kills the couple and turns them into undead predators. In one of the film's most graphic scenes, Hess cuts the pimp's throat and watches the sparkling, grotesque blood pump out.

Several days later, he receives a call from a person he did not know existed: Meda's wife, Ganja (Marlene Clark). She is looking for her husband. Speechless, Hess hangs up on her. But when she calls back, and he tersely reveals that Meda is not there, Ganja admits estrangement from her husband and to being short of money and asks if she can stay at Hess's place. Ganja, it turns out, is not really seeking Meda but rather needs a place to be. He agrees to her strange request. Ganja, like her husband before, is immediately relaxed with Hess and the two, in short order, begin a love affair. Hess's sexual desire for Ganja provokes his desire for blood. He goes to a nearby urban haunt and engages a prostitute (a white woman holding an infant), comes up to her room, and consumes her. Meanwhile, back at home, Ganja searches for a bottle of wine for the dinner she plans to make for Hess and finds her husband's dead body in the basement freezer. When she confronts Hess, he is stoic and unresponsive. Initially Ganja is angry but after a long, one-sided talk with the apathetic Hess about her troubled relationship with her mother, she gets over his apparent murder of her husband, reasoning that "everyone is into something." In a seeming parody of the home makeover scene, the sequence of Ganja and Hess dragging Meda's body out to the field is with humorous irony crosscut with Luther, Hess's chauffer and stable boy (who is also a pastor), marrying Hess and Ganja in Hess's backyard to the tune of *Jesu, Joy of Man's Desiring*. Hess decides to make Ganja immortal so they will be together forever. But after he drinks her blood, she is disoriented, weak, sick, and hungry. Hess has Richard (Richard Harrow), an athletic coach at the community center, over for dinner, and eventually Ganja beds and consumes him. Disgusted with herself, she turns to Hess. The two bury his body in the high grass (presumably near Meda), although Ganja, disturbed, protests that Richard is still breathing.

Hess decides to seek salvation and end his vampiric life.[9] He flirts with the dreadful power of the cross that can end his life in a lengthy documentary-style sequence at Luther's church. Feeling the cross's power, he returns home to set the scene for his own death and redemption by hanging a cross from his ceiling, allowing its shadow to fall on him, killing him. He beckons Ganja to join him but she does not. The film ends as athletic coach Richard, resurrected, emerges from the pool in the yard and runs nude, penis dangling, to the house, jumping over a butler's corpse to Ganja who is poised in the window of the home she now owns. She smiles.

Bill Gunn's Working-Class Suburb

Through its spatial politics, Gunn's film maps the Black upper class's predatory relationship to the Black working class. This may derive, in part, from the changing demographics of the Rockland County suburb where the film takes place. The upstate locales Gunn chose for his film (Nyack, Ossining, and Spring Valley) each had a long history of Black and brown residence and labor that challenge the narrative of suburban white flight as the only genesis for the suburbs. Set in Rockland County, which was an early free Black community that had recently become a site of migration for the urban poor, Hess stands at the intersection of these histories: both bound by his blackness and his predatory relationship with those Blacks to whom he, in his wealth and ancientness, gives work and shelter. Though Hess is the film's protagonist, the opening voice-over is given through the working-class preacher Luther, who doubles as Hess's driver and who ultimately sets him on the course toward ecstasy and salvation. By contrast with Luther, who works and lives with the working poor, the upper-class Hess descends on suburban space in his Rolls Royce primarily for blood, embodying economic exploitation. But the very class system that grants Black men like Hess status is a trap, making them into predators, victims of their own lusts. Hess, in the film's logic and as Luther tells us, "is not a criminal. He's a victim."[10] Further, Hess is a doctor who is addicted to blood. Through this conceit, Gunn redresses the medical metaphor of the civil rights era, which constructed racism as a disease. The ambiguity around what blood addiction figures (drug addiction, sex addiction, homosexuality, or blackness itself?) indicates a steep prognosis since the disease has ceased to be legible or dissectible. In one sense, the film is about Hess's obvious addiction/predation. Even though Hess is a predator, however, he is preyed upon repeatedly by those in the community whose real social ills are somehow deeper than his spiritual curse. The social horrors of poverty outstrip the horror film's monstrosity.

Central in the class paradox at the film's core is the country home and its expanses, which hide the perversities of the rich, giving ground to addiction and avoidance. Hess tells Ganja "your home is supposed to shelter and contain you. . . . I fill it, and I love it. . . . I mean, I really love it. . . . The way it would be possible for one to love you (he smiles)." This line, one bearing a notable resemblance to bell hooks's formulation of the value of the home for Black women in her essay "Homeplace," suggests Hess's passionate—even avowedly amorous—relationship to his home.[11] But Hess's utterance also suggests a certain self-conscious perversion of the traditional African American home space, one perhaps linked to Hess's identity as a feminized, elite male: Hess's slippage between human and object in this statement is symptomatic of the film's larger point about the fluidity between these categories in upper class life. One of the script's central axioms, strongly rooted in the class-conscious underpinnings of Gunn's film, is "we are all junkies of one sort or another . . . what decides if you are a criminal or not is which side of the law your fix is on."[12] Gunn even penned a line where a character critiques the middle class as "addicted" to "society," which it has "taken in large doses."[13] For Hess the suburban expanses provide obscurity, cover for his addiction. His museum-like home, which is filled with art and often resounds with classical music, allows him to play the role of civilized anthropologist in denial of his baser connections to blackness, flesh, and blood. But even these succumb to the baser instincts he avoids: the white museum archeologist almost always conjures for Hess the image of the Myrthian queen; the classical record gives way to Myrthian chanting inside his head; dignified dinner guests end up as the main course.

Place Out of Time:
Afro (Near) Futurism and Suburban Portals

Both Hess's home and the fifty-acre plot on which it sits are filled with portals—openings to the past and future. The home in which Hess lives bears more in common with the haunted castle than with the tracts of the middle class burbs. It is an old, Victorian suburb with links to the landed aristocracy rather than the aspiring middle classes. Though the film avoids *blaming* Hess for his predatory relationship to other Black people, his adoption of material values and upper-class pleasures is obvious. In this sense Hess is both a proxy for whiteness and its victim. In Hess's attics (where Hess retreats to drink blood in secret), bathrooms (where Hess drinks blood from a glass like wine), bedrooms (where he is haunted by his blood lust), and basements (where Hess hides the dead body of Meda on which he feeds) creep the melancholy powers of desire and perversion as eternal and universal as life itself. Though the film was shot in 16mm and in realist style by Black documentary cinematographer James E. Hinton, the house captures its inhabitants in a series of still lifes or tableaus. Unlike the cinema's unified mansions—Tara of *Gone with the Wind* (1939), for example—Gunn's mansion is a layered mesh of spaces, deeply pocketed with relics of history and trauma from Africa to slavery to the noose, to the rugged wooden cross, to the European religious paintings, sculptures, nudes, and still lifes.

In some ritualistic sequences, the film takes on the aesthetics of the stage and the space of the home seems to fade away into blackness, invoking a portal effect. These theatrical sequences use chiaroscuro lighting, prominent symbolic props, and, seemingly, the intense energy of the scene's happenings and psychic resonances to dissolve the realist spatial arrangements that prevail in most other sequences. For example, in one sequence Hess, overcome by his desire for Ganja's blood, retreats to the attic to drink some from a glass. Ganja searches for him and finally finds him. The sex scene that follows mingles their interaction with images of works of art. But more importantly, the dimensions of the attic seem to fade into darkness, giving place to the characters and their actions. This same chiaroscuro, stage-like effect accompanies the scene of Hess's final descent into the shadow of the cross, Meda's time in the tree, and the dinner scene before Richard is consumed.

Still Life: Whites Aghast

The art lends the suburban home a monastic, cloistered quality. Further, Hinton's shooting style, coupled with the mansion set's bric-a-brac aesthetic, makes it difficult to know where the narrative begins and the suburban home's art ends. Indeed, the visual art of the museum and home (mostly European) and sonic art (mostly of African descent) are so interposed with the narrative through crosscutting and semidiegetic sound that the art seems to participate affectually in the scene's happening. The artwork bleeds into the narrative. Works of art witness the acts from the scene's margins, chiming in as ministering angels and building the scene's aesthetic qualities through their presence. Thus, the artwork's mythic past mingles uncomfortably with the present.

But the statuesque, stoic Hess is relentlessly associated with works of art not just in his home but also throughout the film. When we first see him, it is in the Metropolitan Museum of Art. The camera catches him meeting the museum archeologist in businesslike poise, but the film's soundtrack belies the everydayness of the encounter, opening up the cavernous dimensions of the space. As he passes through the museum not only do their footsteps echo in the corridors but also the words of the Bible echo on the soundtrack. The words "Whosoever drinketh my blood . . ." catch Hess leaving the frame as the camera focuses on the shrinking, terrified white androgyne in *Woman Overtaken by a Storm*, a 1799 painting by Chevalier Féréol de Bonnemaison that was done in the wake of the French Revolution. The camera slowly tracks in on the scared, cold, cowering figure whose frail, white body and weak hair are being blown in an inexorable, dwarfing wind (figure 3.1).

This is but the first of a number of emoting, frozen white artistic figures that Gunn inserts into the narrative. In film editor Victor Kanefsky's stylized approach to crosscutting, these works of art—both painting and statuary—seem to be reacting to the scene's happenings. The art, ancient and alive, stands witness to the film's horrific embryonic struggles. For example, not only does a white, robed figure sit behind Meda as he tells his story to Hess on his first night in the house, but later that evening, a gray, seemingly horned figure looks on after Meda

Figure 3.1. Death as frozen whiteness in *Ganja and Hess* (Bill Gunn, Kelly/Jordan Enterprises, 1973). Digital frame enlargement.

stabs Hess. Similarly, when Ganja tells Hess of a childhood struggle with her mother, a grotesquely smiling golden angel, seemingly looking on, repeatedly catches the camera's gaze. Are these frozen figures, like Hess, humans with the blood sucked out of them? Or are they ancient white people? Or is the film suggesting a homology between bloodless humans and whiteness? Crosscutting works of art with the film's most emotionally climactic scenes has the effect of confusing the line between objects and beings, living and dead affect. The title sequence's statuary and the opening scene's ponderous zoom in on Bonnemaison's painting join with shots of a staring, frost-whitened Meda in the freezer in indicating that whiteness in *Ganja and Hess* is not a position of privileged invisibility but rather a state of terrifying exposure, naked isolation, and epic frigidity. It is an undead frozenness of both time and temperature.

Gunn casts the white (suburban) zombie as object of horror, by subversively suggesting white people are lifeless and obsolete—frozen in time. In the opening sequence, for example, the camera captures the stillness of the museum's white statues cast in poses intimating doom, like the dismal figures of Pompeii. These figures are some of the only "whites" in the film, most of which are museum-bound. The only other white characters are the employees at the blood clinic, the museum archeologist, the white prostitute and her child, and significantly, the whitened, frozen Meda in Hess's basement. Through largely relegating whites to the reactive artwork, whiteness is moved out of the spectral center—and white figures act as witnesses rather than as full-fledged participants in the main drama. The dead, frozen white subject is given attention and life only in reaction to the infinite, cosmic, immortal Ganja and Hess. In a film where "the blood of the thing is the truth of the thing," the plaster body is, by definition, a lie and an abomination robbed of its truth. Thus, in *Ganja and Hess*, whiteness—pictured primarily as deadened statuary—signifies death and *pastness* in frozen form.

The suburb thus becomes a space where animacy is given to the ancient inert; it is a haunted space. On the one hand, the suburban home and its contents come increasingly into the narrative life of the characters, participating in watching and listening and to the building of the characters into a more expansive historical frame. However, Ganja, Meda, and Hess also become part of the art that surrounds them, mixing with the ancients it invokes: after Hess has killed Ganja and transformed her into a vampire, he poses in stillness, marking the ritualized moment through his posture and either imitating or making art (figure 3.2). The

Figure 3.2. Hess (Duane Jones) nude after having killed Ganja and seen as a still artistic object and extension of the home in *Ganja and Hess* (Bill Gunn, Kelly/Jordan Enterprises, 1973). Digital frame enlargement.

link between Hess's own artistic and vulnerable pose and the art of the bedroom is highlighted when Hess hides himself behind the bronzed angel on the bed frame, seemingly deferring to a figure as much caught in time as he is. It is as if the souls of history are witnesses to the Ganja and Hess drama, frozen in time and in reaction to them. Thus, through the halls of this suburban home with its peculiar, haphazard, lived-in luxury and its opulent spreads of wine, cheese, books, and art, Ganja and Hess's narrative becomes greater than their own—linked to both European and African expressive histories and the histories of blood-wrought decadence.[14]

Victim or Criminal?
Scenes of Subjection and the Black Suburban Nude

Gunn penned in one script draft:

> Black today is nature's hiding place. Where she stores her loot. This is what she enjoys in her hours away from labor. When she partakes of black . . . nature believes she is sinning. She falls peacefully into sleep among her dark hours . . . and wakes suspicious to the sun's white rays. At night she dares to lie naked among the dark folds of her very own desires. She speaks to no one of night, but gives it generously to anyone that has the profoundness to hunger for it.

Here, in Gunn's words, by contrast with whiteness's deadly frozenness, blackness is equated with the night's soft pleasures in its density and beauty. It is "nature's secret" hidden in plain sight. Hess, in this voice-over, ascribes to Ganja this blackness, calling her "black as all things secret."[15] In the finished film, even though this line of dialogue does not appear, Gunn actualizes this theory through the way the scenes of Black characters are shot. James E. Hinton, one of American cinema's first known Black cinematographers, developed a mode of shooting Black bodies, often against a cavernous black backdrop, that made these bodies legible, desirable, and preeminently human, despite the pathologies historically attached to them.

Throughout *Ganja and Hess*, Gunn insists on the vulnerability and innocence of the Black man, reversing white cinema's racial cosmology. He suggests this through the prevalence of prostrate Black male figures and Black male nude figures often frozen in poses of subjection—and of the blood-soaked Black male body (in the first scene and later in the scenes where Richard and Meda die and are then buried), a visual reminder of the vulnerability of the Black male form. The chiaroscuro scene of Meda in the tree, playfully kicking his legs like a child next to a noose, points to the polarity between the innocent victim and the murderer that Meda lays out in the next scene. All the film's essential innocents, and particularly the "boyish" recreation center social worker Richard and Rev. Luther Williams, are Black men, rather than the white victims that populate both cinematic and news media narratives. Through them, Gunn complicates significantly the association between Black masculinity and criminality, insisting on the Black male working-class figure as one of essential innocence despite the social pathologies foisted upon them. Gunn, perhaps masochistically, asserts this vulnerability most clearly through his own character, Meda, who writes a suicide poem addressed "to the Black male children":

> Philosophy is a prison. It disregards the uncustomary things about you. . . . You are the despised of the earth. That is as if you were water in the desert. To be adored on this planet is to be a symbol of success. And you must not succeed on any terms because life is endless. You are as nameless as a flower. You are the child of Venus and her natural affection is lust. She will touch your belly with her tongue but you must not suffer in it. For love is all there is and you are cannon fodder in its defense.

This missive, which Meda pens to himself as much as to the Black boys of the future, articulates the foreclosed possibility of Black male survival. It bespeaks the marginality of the "uncustomary" Black child, but also defines him as Venus's illegitimate child (and lover), thus caught in a natural love that is socially shunned as perverse. In Meda, Luther, Richard, and even the vampiric yet vulnerable Hess, Black men who have historically been cast as bucks in the camera's eye are revealed with naked vulnerability.

The suburban landscape provides both possibilities and traps for this Black male innocent. If the suburban expanses become a space where the Black male figure is given the temporary luxury of exposition (Luther's inaugural self-narration) and vulnerability (Meda's on-screen monologue and missive), it also is the place where men become subject to controlling forces, whether embodied in Hess or in a broader madness.

Further, in Gunn the suburbs are a space of expression of (Black male) queerness. The film even arguably represents, in a protean way, one of the earliest cinematic considerations of Black "bottoming," as Darieck Scott has put it.[16] Several of those writing about Gunn's legacy have noted his status as a gay man who struggled with his sexuality and his mother.[17] Many of *Ganja and Hess*'s images of vulnerable Black men, many frontally nude, are plainly homoerotic. The fight scene between Meda and Hess, both naked from the waist up, takes place in the bedroom. And when Hess discovers Meda's naked body, he leans down over him from behind and licks his blood off the floor, a clearly homoerotic gesture. In the script, this homoeroticism is even more pointed: Hess also offers a charged invitation to Richard to come to dinner, one that implies a sexual invite[18] and after Ganja has finished consuming Richard, Hess asks, "his eyes afire": "Did you save any for me?" In the script, Ganja even directly asks Hess if he's gay and he avoids the question jitterily, retorting "Because I am not married?" but never answering. Together, these script elements confirm the homoerotic tension latent in the finished film's Black male nudes. Further, though Luther, reverend, chauffer, and *stable boy*, is never explicitly made an erotic figure, in real life the actor who played Luther, Sam Waymon (who was also Nina Simone's brother and the film's composer) and Gunn lived together in a mansion in Nyack, leaving the nature of both their on- and off-screen connection mysterious.[19] Accordingly and by extension, Hess's suburban home is at worst an expanded closet replete with queer desire but perhaps legible also as a place of queer visibility and vulnerability—of exploration and sexual experimentation, a theme further pursued in *Stop!* (1970). Through their approach to the suburban home, Gunn and Hinton repurpose the European artist's veneer—making it grounds for intersectional commentary on race relations, vulnerability, queer relationality, and human empathy.

Fields of Transformation: Wading through the High Grass

If the suburban home is a chiaroscuro, darkness-dabbled space knotted with portals to other worlds, pasts, and destinies, the land around the home is similarly and perhaps even more intensely a space of afro-futurist transfiguration and time fissures between past, present, and future. Instead of a manicured suburban lawn that often served as a place of recreation and surveillance in the white suburbs, Gunn purposely invokes the fields, which have traditionally been a space of Black labor. The high grass acreage outside Hess's home is a gateway and site of radical uncertainty—shot so as to maximize their obscuring effects and to suggest them as a primordial hiding place and a place animated by forces outside of standard temporalities or spatial dynamics. Indeed, the film's most pivotal scenes happen in these fields, which become a staging space for ritual and for psychic and spiritual transformation. Gunn uses these unplanned, vernacular spaces to morph the suburbs into the bush. The high grass becomes a place where Hess can, as so many slaves once longed to, conjure and return to Africa and home. The "backyard" fields are, indeed, the only space where the Myrthian queen appears to Hess. In the wedding scene, in magical realist style, the Myrthian past, embodied in the full figure of the half-naked queen lingering in the back of the frame, is layered into Ganja and Hess's present, as white, Black, and brown bourgeoisie guests gather around the swimming pool, a symbol of the suburban mundane. The fields are also a space of Hess's destiny. After Hess's first act of preying in the film, the fields are the place where Hess prays for his salvation. It is also here that Gunn/Hinton situates the ritual scene of Hess's stabbing of Ganja to make her into a vampire (figure 3.3). In this sequence, the two are garbed only in large, wrapped cloths like early humans or an African king and queen in Afro-centric iconography, furthering the association between the suburban reaches

Figure 3.3. Ganja (Marlene Clark) and Hess (Duane Jones) returned to the moment of the fall in the primordial and African-inspired Garden of Eden in *Ganja and Hess* (Bill Gunn, Kelly/Jordan Enterprises, 1973). Digital frame enlargement.

and Africa. When Hess finally falls into the cross's shadows, the suburban home is crosscut with shots of Lebanon, where Jesus performed his first miracle and Christian salvation arguably began, thus suggesting that his vampiric death ends in salvation.

The fields are a place that is also associated with death. Ganja and Hess drag the plastic-covered, bloody bodies of their human prey into the field when they are done with them. It is, in this sense, a space essentially linked to the (open) grave—a final resting place. But it is also a space the cinematographer and editor return to repeatedly as a place of symbolic representation, loosely commenting on the narrative. For instance, in slow motion, Ganja, in a white nightgown and with a blood-soaked face, runs through the field and falls down, symbolizing her descent into vampirism and addiction. Likewise, after Hess visits the church and decides to give himself over to the shadow of the cross, he runs in slow motion through the field in a kind of billowy freedom dance. The lawn and pool also become the sites for resurrection when Richard, also in slow motion cinematography, ascends in full-frontal nudity from the pool, resurrected and poised to be reunited with Ganja. Though Richard is not a major character, the script begins and ends with him. And this symbolic closing scene seals his centrality to the film's message: Richard is the only character with a life driven by social purpose—its only conscious brother. When Hess asks him what he would do if given the secret to eternal life, he says that he would "teach it to the children." Why? His incendiary response: "Because they'll need to be indestructible."[20] Richard's status as representative of the working class and advocate of social reform, though more obvious in the script than in the finished film, allows us to read Richard's suburban ascension in the film's final frames as not only resurrection of his body but of a distinctly Black revolutionary spirit that the film never directly addresses and that Hess, in all his repression and upper-class hedonism, cannot embody. In Richard, the working class repressed returns—and the effete Hess (who has repressed himself) is roundly replaced. As Romero's *Night of the Living Dead* ended with the destruction of Duane Jones's living Black male body on the suburban lawn, *Ganja and Hess* ends with the resurrected Black male body, indestructible, rebounding on the same suburban grass. Further, as Richard leaps over the dead body of Archie (Leonard Jackson), the butler, Gunn seems to suggest a rejection of the stereotypical servant in favor of the working-class revolutionary. In sum, the suburban estate, through its art, its deep spaces, and expansive grounds, becomes a repository for a wealth of past lives and future possibilities, allowing the characters to move through death and life, past and present, conscious and unconscious urges, and to discover the inner recesses of their timeless being.

The Suburban Talking Cure

In *Ganja and Hess*, the suburban home and its surroundings become a confessional space. In his book *The Sovereignty of Quiet: Beyond Resistance in Black Culture*, Kevin Quashie argues the constitutive nature of quiet in Black cultural life. "Quietness is a metaphor for the full range of one's inner life—one's desires, ambitions, hungers, vulnerability, fears . . . the interior—dynamic and ravishing—is a stay against the dominance of the social world; it has its own sovereignty. It is hard to see, even harder to describe, but no less potent in effability."[21] In *Ganja and Hess*, the quiet suburbs provide the interior space for the characters to reflect in ways typically denied Black urban characters who are driven by action, noise, and dialogue. They are places of the talking, writing, and resting cure linked, ultimately, to the patchy history of the sanatorium in their relationship of isolation to the health of their subjects. They are not a place of permanent dwelling but of temporary respite, transcendence, and expanse. Thus they become linked to the need to find and mine one's interior self. Within these spaces the Black and brown subjects socially defined as "urban" can unravel and let their problems breathe. *Ganja and Hess* contains metadiscursive suburban scenes of the main characters writing out their troubles. More than the writing cure, the suburbs give ground in Gunn's work for the talking cure. Bill Gunn makes the suburb's stillness an open site—one available for the telling of Black truths—the unraveling of lives that have undergone trauma. "Dinner," at Hess's home, is an elaborate affair—a meaty metaphor that cuts many ways. Hess provides an opulent spread to his guests partly to seek connection, partly to resurrect his humanity through rituals and gestures of suburban, civilized life, and partly as an unavoidable, compulsive prelude to their becoming his dinner. Both Meda and Ganja try to connect with and warm Hess with their wild stories—humorous punchlines about drugs, movies, and sex. Hess is at first cold with and unmoved by either guest, refusing to say a word let alone laugh at their opening gambit, seemingly waiting for something that cuts deeper—to the bone. Throughout the course of the dinner, enjoyed not at the table but in front of the fire, Meda, who was dressed in a stiff suit when he arrived, undresses and unwinds, drinking and perhaps drugging in excess. The scene cuts midstream from suicidal

Meda in the tree to him discussing with Hess his ideas about suicide. Snot runs down his moustache as he talks his way through his trauma to an off-screen Hess, as if to a therapist:

> I got into this very heavy idea about suicide and I tried it once. . . . this was in New York and I really had this idea, it was a very schizophrenic idea because I was . . . you know . . . that I was a victim on one hand and on the other hand I was a murderer. Do you understand? And it's very complicated but that's what I was going through. . . . And I was in the kitchen and I took a knife and put it right to my neck. . . . I couldn't do anything . . . I just couldn't do it. It was like . . . what am I saying? It was like the murderer let the victim cut. It was like a cat and mouse game, you understand that?

Using what actress Marlene Clarke, the actress who plays Ganja, remembers as an intensely personal style, influenced by method acting, Meda unfurls himself before a statuesque, unmovable Dr. Hess. Untrammeled by the urban pressures of time, space, and industrial drive, Meda can finally unwind. But the results are tragic. Suicide bleeds into murder when Meda, ironically dressed in clothes matching his host, attempts to kill Hess by essentially splitting him in half with an axe, literalizing the schizophrenic metaphor. Thinking he has killed Hess, Meda gives himself a final baptismal wash in the bathtub and then, in front of the mirror, fully nude and with a rustic cross behind him, shoots himself in the chest. Thus the talking has not produced the cure but rather an ecstatic magnification of the ill. The suburbs have not given the Black subject a place to cast off his troubles but have only given him more room to grow—a longer rope. The murderer wins.

Quite a similar scene unfolds in Ganja's initial hours in Hess's home. Her opening gambit about a male ballerina friend who muled drugs into the country in his rear end, one rife with homoerotic motifs, fails to amuse Hess, who drinks water and sweats without breaking a smile. However, a compulsive self-emptying similar to her husband's comes after she realizes her husband is in Hess's basement in the freezer. At first Ganja makes a scene, interrupting their candlelit dinner, where they sit on opposite ends of a long dinner table, by coolly revealing her knowledge of her husband's whereabouts. Her revelation fails again to move Hess, whose emotionlessness is a recurrent theme, and she madly tears up the living room, in a scene replicating the suburban wife's temper tantrum—wrought to the teeth with melodrama. Then, lulled by the muted surroundings, her host's impassivity to her rage, and the house's unusual hold, she begins to talk—and talk deeply—while a ministering golden angel literally comes out of the house's woodwork to listen:

> When I was about ten or twelve years old my favorite time of the year was winter because of the snow. And I made the best snowballs in all of Boston. I was in the best snowball fights and I always won. This particular day, there were just snowballs flying; it was all you could see, it was all you could feel. Some hit hard, some hit soft, and fell down all over—fell behind your collar. You could feel it in your muffler and I got home about 6:30 or 7:00 because I had been fighting since 3 o'clock in the afternoon. And she said, "Where have you been?" And I said, "I have been having this tremendous snowball fight and it was really fun. And I beat everybody and everybody beat me and it was a tremendous day." And she slapped my face and said, "Where have you been? Someone said they saw you being chased by a boy." And I said we were all chasing each other because we were having a snowball fight. And she said, "You are a liar and a slut." And I said to her, "I swear to you that I was having a snowball fight," and she didn't believe me. She never believed me. It was as though I was a disease. . . . It was "I came down with Ganja" and I think that day I decided that I was a disease—and I was going to give her a full case of it.

Through this cinematic talking cure—the theatrical, autobiographical, and semidocumentary style monologue—Ganja tells the story of her conversion from child into disease, from innocent, powerful snowball fighter into, through her mother's eyes and projections, a sexual being—available to become both predator and prey. The memory is a traumatic tale of her mother's (first?) slap but also one of her formative moments. The sensory detail about the snow and the distanced look in Ganja's eyes bespeak a kind of trancelike depth to her utterance—an active, talk-induced reversion to her past. The suburb, with its attendant liberation of the tensions of space and time, has produced in Ganja an almost drug-like freedom. Ganja's figuration of herself, a Black woman, as disease fits with the film's refiguration of vampirism and addiction as a kind of disease. In one sense, Hess has "caught" Ganja but by the end of the film Ganja has also caught Hess's disease, his addiction to blood. In the center is the talking through trauma. In the script, Ganja accepts Hess's consumption of her husband because she doesn't love Meda, a fact that cements her status as a money-focused femme fatale destined to also abandon Hess. But in the finished film, Ganja's acceptance emerges as less mercenary. Instead, the peculiar cast of the suburban home allows Ganja to break with the melodrama and traditional social relations—to unwind and get past the death of her husband and Hess's apparent role in it, pushing into a mental place in which death and its perversities can be explained by reference to her own traumatic relationship to her mother and outside of the immediacies of direct causality. Haunted by their pasts and their quest to restore their lost innocence, Ganja and Meda both reckon with themselves in the silence of Hess's catacombs, which turn out to be a profound, echoing inner space. For Ganja, unlike Meda, the talking cure seems to work in that the truths—both of their interior selves and of the deathly circumstances that surround them—have united them. She has experienced pure joy and release. The gothic suburbs have made their psychotic match.

Conclusion

In *Ganja and Hess*, the suburbs emerge as a place of hauntings, ironies, and perversities where the problems of Black upper and middle-class life reveal themselves. On the one hand, the suburbs provide an expanse: problems can be spread across different grounds, remapped and reconfigured to be solved or reaestheticized in settings and garbs that are other than urban. It is also a place of dramatization where the encrypted urban soul can uncurl itself to discover its hidden dimensions, traumas, and fears and the histories to which it is linked. This is not a direct process but a complex one that involves engagement with fantasy, costume, and a kind of layering of the real onto the unreal. These cinematic suburbs thicken, layer, and unpack baggage. But despite their expansiveness and hidden dimensions, the suburbs provide no enduring shelter. Gunn's characters are successful but unmoored and unhappy: haunted and lonely. Suburbs don't provide an escape, only a larger labyrinth for the pathology to play itself out in—as the case of Meda suggests, a larger, more dramatic noose. Suburban space is where the film's characters are consistently involved in experiments of selfhood that often prove deadly—at least to their relationships and, at worst, to their souls. Further, the suburban mansion emerges as a place that contains the trauma of its Black subjects—as represented in blackamoor statues and African relics that mix with jazz records and with treatises on Black culture. It is a place where obsessions, with deep roots, take hold but also where mortality gives death to Black dreaming. "Personal problems," to use a phrase Gunn liked, are also ancient, blood-bound, and filled with racial history. Thus, the suburbs offer not only the space of boredom and social containment that they often become in cinema but also, in relation to the city, provide a wide open space, one in which the characters can find or lose themselves, develop, or disintegrate. Though the film's would-be monster, Hess, is a Black man, it is whiteness that is the inhuman force animating the film's eeriest moments of horror. Even death takes on new meanings in the haunted suburbs. It is less of an anguished demise and more of a fade to black.

Notes

1. For more on the ways that segregation rendered Blacks "invisible," see Craig E. Barton, *Sites of Memory: Perspectives on Architecture and Race* (Princeton, NJ: Princeton Architectural Press, 2001).

2. "Bill's own house was a house of real beauty and everything was chosen carefully." *Ganja and Hess* commentary track. New York: Image Entertainment, 2006.

3. Earl Caldwell, "Negroes Astir in Spring Valley," *New York Times*, August 11, 1967; https://www.nytimes.com/1967/08/11/archives/negroes-astir-in-spring-valley-and-black-power-cry-is-heard.html; Raymond Hernandez, "Once a Resort Village Struggles with Urban Problems," *New York Times*, June 15, 1994, https://www.nytimes.com/1994/06/15/nyregion/once-a-resort-village-struggles-with-urban-problems.html. According to Hernandez, "The village became a magnet for struggling families. Landlords began converting vacation houses into cheap rentals. In a county where most people own their homes, Spring Valley has the highest number of rental units, and 59 percent of the village's residents are renters."

4. See A. J. Wilson, *Long Hammering: Essays on the Forging of an African American Presence in the Hudson River Valley to the Early 20th Century* (Trenton, NJ: Africa World Press, 1994). See also Edythe Ann Quinn, "The Kinship System in the Hills," in *Mighty Change, Tall Within: Black Identity in the Hudson Valley*, ed. Myra B. Young Armstead (Albany: State University of New York Press, 2003).

5. The definitive history of African Americans in the suburbs is Andrew Wiese's *Places of Their Own: African American Suburbanization in the Twentieth Century* (Chicago: University of Chicago Press, 2004), 5. As Wiese writes, "Between 1960 and 2000, the number of African Americans living in the suburbs grew by approximately 9 million, representing a migration as large as the exodus of African Americans from the rural South in the mid-twentieth century."

6. Richard Dyer, "White," *Screen* (Autumn 1988), 44–65, https://doi. org/10.1093/screen/29.4.44. *Ganja and Hess* further reconfigures horror by allowing viewers, as Richard Dyer has identified as occurring with a narrow group of films, "to see whiteness as whiteness," to perceive white dependency on blackness, and, further, to demonstrate that "whites are the living dead" or at least that whites "have more death" than Black people.

7. Bill Gunn, *Ganja and Hess "Original Script,"* on *Ganja and Hess*, DVD (New York: Image Entertainment, 2006), 19. (Throughout, I will refer to the screenplay that appears on this DVD.) One sequence clarified the parameters of the blood lust:

HESS: The Myrthians thought they had a passion for blood, not a need for it. But it was a need . . . like needing a job.

MEDA: Hunger.

HESS: It's more of a perversion than that. Something one would feel guilty about needing. After all, blood has a dreadful connotation. Like a passion for soiled underwear or urine. Drinking blood is a very anti-social act.

MEDA: Unless you happen to exist in a blood society.

HESS: We do exist in a blood society. . . . But even so, if it ever caught on here, it would be considered a perversion, and a bloodsucker a degenerate." (9)

8. "By the Christians it is written that in the Black Myrthian age. Thousands of slaves were bled to death but murdered in such a way that slaves could not die. There was visited upon them a curse that they should live forever unless the shadow of the cross, an implement of torture touched their darkened hearts. . . . The blood of the thang is the truth of the thing. . . . They had come to be addicted to truth till the Christians came" (transcribed from the finished film). Harkening back to an age of Black ascendancy and linking the narrative also to the history of slavery, the slaves of song exist in a kind of undead state. However, the song suggests that the coming of the Christians, presumably white, not only removed the darkness from their hearts but also severed their relationship to a kind of blood-soaked human truth. Through the subtle, aural revelation of this cosmology, the film resists narrative, instead giving us scenes less serialized than symbolically drenched. The film also in this way forces the spectator to appreciate the aural/oral tradition as one of the text's many African retentions. Gunn, who was first a screenwriter, allows the aural to be the foundation on which the image riffs. It is a horror film that gives up on the tropes of explaining itself. What results is a far more meta and meditative, indirect film style, one that in many ways takes on the subjective isolation of Hess, its main character.

9. In the finished film, the reasons that Hess seeks mortality and salvation—giving himself over to the shadow of the cross that will surely kill him—remains unclear. In the script, this decision is explained through Hess's chance encounter with the white prostitute he earlier consumed: upon seeing her dismal fate and realizing that she has preyed upon her own child who is wrapped in a sling around her neck and shoulder, Hess seeks redemption.

10. This theme would later be explored in Octavia E. Butler's novel *The Fledgling* (New York: Grand Central Publishing, 2005) where the Black vampire, like Hess, is not predatory but seeks symbiosis.

11. bell hooks, "Homeplace," in *Yearning: Race, Gender, and Cultural Politics* (Boston: South End Press, 1990), 41–49.

12. *Ganja and Hess*, screenplay, 28.

13. *Ganja and Hess*, screenplay, 28.

14. The home and its art also extend the critique of whiteness in George Romero's zombie franchise. *Night of the Living Dead* replaced the white male hero with a Black one.

15. *Ganja and Hess*, screenplay, 50.

16. He writes, "In [Amiri] Baraka and [Eldridge] Cleaver by implication—against their intention—and in [Samuel] Delany explicitly, *bottoming* thus becomes a metaphor and model for one of the black powers we are seeking in abjection: among its many inflections of meaning, it evokes the willed enactment of powerlessness that encodes a power of its own, in which pain or discomfort are put to multifarious uses." Darieck Scott, *Extravagant Abjections: Blackness, Power, and Sexuality in the African American Literary Imagination* (New York: NYU Press, 2010), 165.

17. Hilton Als, "The Year in Theater and Farewell to a Friend," *New Yorker*, January 2, 2016; Hilton Als, "Three's Company: A Family's Secrets Are Revealed in 'The First Breeze of Summer,'" *New Yorker*, August 25, 2008. Als suggests that Gunn died of AIDS in 1989 and not encephalitis, as most sources claim. See also Steve Ryfle, "The Eclipsed Vision of Bill Gunn: An African-American Auteur's Genius, from *Ganga & Hess* to *Personal Problems*," *Cineaste*, Fall 2018, https://www.cineaste.com/fall2018/the-eclipsed-visions-of-bill-gunn.

18. "I've got a house guest . . . a young lady . . . she's been living . . . in Holland for a while and she's a bit at odds as far as friends are concerned. . . . I thought you might like to come to dinner tonight." *Ganja and Hess*, script, 85.

19. Bill Batson, "Nyack Sketch Log: Sam Waymon Lived Here," *Nyack News and Views*, February 12, 2013. https://nyacknewsandviews.com/2013/02/bb_samwaymon/.

20. *Ganja and Hess*, script, 88.

21. Kevin Quashie, *The Sovereignty of Quiet: Beyond Resistance in Black Culture* (New Brunswick, NJ: Rutgers University Press, 2014), 6.

References

Als, Hilton. "Three's Company: A Family's Secrets Are Revealed in 'The First Breeze of Summer.'" *New Yorker*, August 25, 2008, https://www.newyorker.com/magazine/2008/09/01/threes-company.

———. "The Year in Theater and Farewell to a Friend." *New Yorker*, January 2, 2016, https://www.newyorker.com/culture/culture-desk/the-year-in-theatre-and-farewell-to-a-friend.

Barton, Craig Evan. *Sites of Memory: Perspectives on Architecture and Race*. Princeton, NJ: Princeton Architectural Press, 2001.

Batson, Bill. "Nyack Sketch Log: Sam Waymon Lived Here." *Nyack News and Views*, February 12, 2013. https://nyacknewsandviews.com/2013/02/bb_samwaymon/.

Caldwell, Earl. "Negroes Astir in Spring Valley." *New York Times*, August 11, 1967. https://www.nytimes.com/1967/08/11/archives/negroes-astir-in-spring-valley-and-black-power-cry-is-heard.html.

Dyer, Richard. "White." *Screen* 29 (Autumn 1988): 44–65.

Gunn, Bill. *Ganja and Hess "Original Script."* On *Ganja and Hess* DVD. New York: Image Entertainment, 2006.

Hernandez, Raymond. "Once a Resort Village Struggles with Urban Problems." *New York Times*, June 15, 1994. https://www.nytimes.com/1994/06/15/nyregion/once-a-resort-village-struggles-with-urban-problems.html.

hooks, bell. "Homeplace." In *Yearning: Race, Gender, and Cultural Politics*, 41–49. Boston: South End Press, 1990.

Quashie, Kevin. *The Sovereignty of Quiet: Beyond Resistance in Black Culture*. New Brunswick, NJ: Rutgers University Press, 2014.

Quinn, Edythe Ann. "The Kinship System in the Hills." In *Mighty Change, Tall Within: Black Identity in the Hudson Valley*, edited by Myra B. Young Armstead. Albany: State University of New York Press, 2003.

Ryfle, Steve. "The Eclipsed Vision of Bill Gunn: An African-American Auteur's Elusive Genius, from *Ganja & Hess* to *Personal Problems*." *Cineaste*, Fall 2018. https://www.cineaste.com/fall2018/the-eclipsed-visions-of-bill-gunn.

Scott, Darieck. *Extravagant Abjections: Blackness, Power, and Sexuality in the African American Literary Imagination*. New York: NYU Press, 2010.

Wiese, Andrew. *Places of Their Own: African American Suburbanization in the Twentieth Century*. Chicago: University of Chicago Press, 2004.

Wilson, A. J. *Long Hammering: Essays on the Forging of an African American Presence in the Hudson River Valley to the Early 20th Century*. Trenton, NJ: Africa World Press, 1994.

4

The House They Live In

Charles Burnett, Indie Hollywood, and the Politics of Black Suburbia

JOSHUA GLICK

A house constitutes a body of images that give mankind proofs or illusions of stability.

—Gaston Bachelard[1]

≈

THE UNEXPECTED ARRIVAL OF HARRY (Danny Glover) at the Los Angeles bungalow of Gideon and Suzie (Paul Butler and Mary Alice) begins as a joyous reunion. Harry is an old friend and workmate from the couple's hometown in Mississippi and appears to be in desperate need of a short rest on his Greyhound journey from Detroit to Oakland (figure 4.1). Occurring toward the beginning of Charles Burnett's third and most ambitious feature, *To Sleep With Anger* (1990), Harry's arrival is initially a festive occasion for reminiscing.

Figure 4.1. Harry (Danny Glover) arrives at the doorstep of Gideon (Paul Butler) and Suzie (Mary Alice) in *To Sleep With Anger* (Charles Burnett, Samuel Goldwyn Company, 1990). Digital frame enlargement.

Gideon and Suzie are charmed by his ingratiating demeanor and the ways in which he pleasantly reminds them of close family and friends from their southern Black community; however, early signs show that Harry will be more of a disturbance than a welcome guest. When Harry opts to sleep in and stay home the next morning rather than accompany the family to Sunday church, he takes the opportunity to rummage through their belongings, skulking about the house as if mischievously investigating their collective psyche. He subtly moves furniture, opens cabinet drawers, reads mail, and fidgets with heirlooms and pieces of memorabilia. As Gideon, Suzie, and their children will soon find, Harry is at once a familiar face from their Mississippi past and, on a more symbolic level, a folkloric trickster emanating from their shared heritage in the Jim Crow South.[2] Bringing aspects of their past into the present and suppressing the persistence of others, Harry amplifies interpersonal frictions and exploits their vulnerabilities. Burnett's textured portrait of the suburban family's struggle to survive their guest signals both the fragility of familial bonds and their importance as a source of material and moral support.

While *To Sleep With Anger* was awarded prestigious accolades throughout the 2010s, it occupied a more precarious position within film culture during its premiere and commercial rollout.[3] *To Sleep With Anger* was heavily praised on the festival circuit, but was dismissed by many critics and egregiously mismanaged by distributors. Like Burnett's peers in the late 1980s, he aimed to advance a new cinematic language for depicting Black life on-screen at a time when Hollywood was in a financially weak position and more amenable to independent minority voices.[4] *To Sleep With Anger* captures how folkways can constitute a useable past. At the same time, the film demonstrates the limits of Hollywood to engage with challenging forms of art and a broader society's resistance to a more full and complex representation of the Black family in America. In order to understand the sociopolitical stakes of *To Sleep With Anger*, it is important to analyze the film's contentious relationship to the late 1980s-'90s media industries as well as how it portrays the crucial role of the suburbs in the formation of Black identity.

Visions of Indie Hollywood

To Sleep With Anger was to expand on Burnett's past films and be the largest project of his career; and yet he headed toward the end of the 1980s with uneven momentum. The international prizes bestowed on his debut feature, *Killer of Sheep* (1977), at the start of the decade had begun to resonate at home. Critics and curators offered high praise for his lyrical, observational portrait of a working-class African American family in South Central Los Angeles.[5] Burnett's next film, *My Brother's Wedding* (1983), was panned by the news and trade industry press following its premiere at the New Directors/New Films series at the Museum of Modern Art. *My Brother's Wedding* was also set in the Watts suburb of Los Angeles. It concentrates on contentious interactions between a young African American man and his family and close friends, each of whom pressure him to follow a different path. He feels torn between a strained sense of obligation to continue his parents' dry cleaning business, a desire to help his wayward childhood buddy secure steady employment, and a guilt-ridden anxiety to live up to his older brother, a successful "buppie" attorney who recently married into an affluent family. Critics could more easily relate *Killer of Sheep* to the language of Euro-American art cinema. *My Brother's Wedding* emphasized patient listening to a cross section of Black subjects, each occupying a different class position. The *New York Times's* Janet Maslin characterized Burnett's directorial approach as "innocent," the acting "amateurish," and the filmic form "stiff" and "rudimentary."[6]

Undeterred, Burnett began a new project that would focus more on how an African American family reconciles their contemporary experiences in Los Angeles with their past life in the South. This meant engaging the story worlds he was surrounded by growing up in Vicksburg, New Orleans (to visit relatives), and Los Angeles. As Burnett later told an interviewer, "I think that it is the artist's job to establish links with the past, to give some self-respect to the people. . . . I think the erosion of memory is the design of the establishment."[7]

After a prospective deal with public television fell through, Burnett found willing collaborators in the emerging sector of indie Hollywood. The sense that the media industries offered an opportunity for socially progressive projects around the turn of the decade stemmed from a severe economic downturn, the declining appeal of big-budget, star-driven blockbusters, and a climate of cultural opposition to Reagan-era conservatism. As a vulnerable film and television infrastructure turned to fresh voices and bolder subject matter, the success of Steven Soderbergh, Jim Jarmusch, Susan Seidelman, Richard Linklater, and Spike Lee fueled the notion that a rebooted auteurist cinema—featuring topical projects "authored" by filmmakers with strong personal vision—could appeal to viewers across age, race, and gender lines.[8] Producers Caldecot Chubb and Ed Pressman (*Sisters* [1973], *Badlands* [1974], *Wall Street* [1987]) expressed enthusiasm for *To Sleep With Anger*.[9] The fact that the MacArthur Foundation awarded Burnett their coveted "Genius Grant" in 1988, and the Library of Congress selected *Killer of Sheep* to be included in its National Film Registry shortly after, added to his cultural capital.[10] As the film began to take shape, the participation of Danny Glover, who agreed to play the part of Harry as well as serve as coproducer, raised its public profile. With major roles in *The Color Purple* (Spielberg, 1985) and *Lethal Weapon 2* (Donner, 1989), Glover was one of the most well-known and beloved African American actors in the country. His family was from rural Georgia and he saw the film as being of keen personal interest: "I wanted to do this movie because I could smell and hear it in a different way. Some of [this film] reminds me of people I met as a kid on my grandparents' farm . . . their past is not expository; they live it. They wear their pasts in their gestures, in their smiles or just shifts in their body movements."[11] Walt Lloyd, the director of photography for the Sundance-winning *sex, lies, and videotape* (Soderbergh, 1989), signed on as director of photography. His sharp eye for filming intimate conversations dovetailed with Burnett's own aesthetic taste and further elevated the project's artistic cachet. Even as the film grew in scale, Burnett followed his artisanal method of working with a small, local group. He believed that building camaraderie for an on-location shoot was important for depicting a fine-grained account of family life. Burnett's wife, Gaye Shannon-Burnett, designed the costumes and their son played the trumpet-practicing child living next door to Gideon and Suzie. As crew members would recall, production felt like a family gathering, where members of the surrounding community (including gangs) were respectful and supportive of a Black crew making a film in a Black neighborhood.[12]

LA's Southern Folkways

To Sleep With Anger centers on the pension-earning Gideon, a former railway laborer who then worked a public service job in Los Angeles, and his wife Suzie, who still works as a midwife. They live together in the suburban Sugar Hill enclave southwest of downtown. One of their sons, Junior (Carl Lumbly), is family-oriented and industrious (his exact profession is unspecified). Junior's wife, Pat (Vonetta McGee), is a social worker, providing aid to the city's homeless population. The other son, Samuel (Richard Brooks), is a loan officer who is both more materially driven than his sibling and frustrated by his family's adherence to folk tradition and hierarchical structure, including their calling him by the diminutive nickname "Babe Brother." His wife, Linda (Sheryl Lee Ralph), is a real estate agent who also feels a slight sense of alienation from some of Gideon and Suzie's rural customs.

The family made the midcentury journey to Southern California as part of the second wave of the Great Migration. As journalist Isabel Wilkerson writes in her incisive account of the Great Migration, *The Warmth of Other Suns*, the urgent need to escape widespread racial violence, as well as the desire to realize professional and educational opportunities, propelled African Americans from Arkansas, Mississippi, Tennessee, and Texas toward the industrial sectors of northern and West Coast cities. Individuals and families fled a southern socioeconomic system that repressively constricted every aspect of daily experience; however, "receiving stations" such as Washington, DC, Pittsburgh, New York, Chicago, and Los Angeles did not simply welcome them with open arms.[13] Minority migration to Los Angeles in the 1940s and 1950s involved having to contend with the harsh realities of segregation. The city's political and business elite enforced racial exclusion and privatism, cultivating what cultural studies scholar George Lipsitz calls a "white spatial imaginary" that led to inequitable access to a better life. Discriminatory housing policies confined minority families to downtown as well as South Central and eastern pockets of the city—areas with underserved housing stock, schools, and limited public utilities.[14]

Sugar Hill was the epicenter of the battle for racial integration in Los Angeles. The neighborhood was white and affluent for much of the early twentieth century. When these families began to move west to emerging developments in Brentwood, Beverly Hills, and Bel-Air during the Great Depression, prominent African Americans moved in. Golden State Mutual Life Insurance Company cofounder Norman Houston, producer Sidney P. Dones, and actress Hattie McDaniel acquired properties in Sugar Hill, but were met with severe opposition from homeowner associations, local businesses, and the police. The NAACP along with the National Urban League challenged the very premise of discriminatory housing policies in the courts.[15] The case went to the California Supreme Court, where restrictive covenants were found to be unconstitutional according to the Fourteenth Amendment. The ruling paved the way for the landmark Supreme Court case *Shelley v. Kraemer* (1948).[16] The legislation did not by any means eliminate discriminatory housing in Los Angeles. It did limit its systematic abuse and provided the legal grounds by which minorities could more freely move in the city.

Given the racial politics of metropolitan development, home ownership meant something distinct to African Americans. Historian Andrew Wiese notes that many Black families viewed their house as more than a material possession or an appreciating asset, but as "evidence of permanence, a marker of achievement, and the satisfaction of a long-deferred dream in the Black South."[17] It was a social space, integral to what urban studies scholar Dolores Hayden calls the process of "self-building," and could help provide a refuge from the hostility of white supremacy.[18] As one of the quintessential Los Angeles domestic building types, the bungalow's low-hanging eaves and open, interconnected rooms drew on a wide variety of historical styles. They were mass-produced, but also gave the owners agency to accent the structure and make it their own.[19] In *To Sleep With Anger*, Gideon and Suzie's residence symbolizes a sense of economic achievement and inclusion in the metropolitan polity. Their family also appears to be part of Los Angeles's African American middle class who benefitted from the initiatives of Tom Bradley, the city's first Black mayor. Following Bradley's historic election in 1973, his administration increased affirmative action programs for city hiring as well as minority participation in clerical, legal, business, and public service sectors.[20] Nonetheless, Pat's reflections on the challenges she faces as a social worker indirectly acknowledge the Bradley administration's role in the growing distance between the city's "haves" and "have-nots." Her lament about the city's homeless population growing each year and hurting from diminishing public funds points to Bradley's terrible track record on affordable housing and public health outreach to the city's most underserved inhabitants.

While Gideon and Suzie's family doesn't seem to face the prospects of unemployment, physical harm, or homelessness, they struggle to reconcile their rural past with their suburban present. On the one hand, Southern folkways are meaningfully integrated into their daily life. Gideon and Suzie's backyard serves as a practical source of food cultivation rather than just existing as leisure space. As urban historian Becky Nicolaides claims, this process of "self-provisioning" was often practiced by Black and white rural migrants to Los Angeles. Raising livestock and planting vegetables were done out of pride and economic necessity.[21] As a midwife, Suzie's birthing practice draws on both Senegambian traditions and the more contemporary Lamaze method. Additionally, Gideon and Suzie retain their dual investment in Christian faith and mysticism. Attending church offers spiritual nourishment and connects the family with a larger community through the shared practice of prayer. Gideon also believes in the power of his "toby," a handcrafted charm used to ward off evil spirits that was passed down to him by his great-grandmother.

Still, the film's opening dream sequence emphasizes that the past can conjure ambivalent feelings. The scene begins with a suit-clad Gideon sitting next to a large portrait of a regally dressed elderly woman. Sister Rosetta Tharpe's 1956 rendition of the hymn "Precious Memories" plays on the soundtrack. The song's lyrics along with the duo's cream-colored attire and similar tilt of their hats encourages their close association, suggesting that she is Gideon's mother or relative: "Precious memories how they linger / How they ever flood my soul / In the stillness of the midnight / Precious sacred scenes unfold." As Tharpe's resounding voice plays against the plodding guitar, piano, and organ chords, both people and objects begin to catch flame, before a quick dissolve transitions to an awakening Gideon, who had fallen asleep in his backyard. The unsettling imagery reveals how memories, like dreams, can be fragile and fleeting. The dream is also portentous of deep disruption, anticipating the loss of Gideon's toby and then the more profound threat of Harry.

Haunted House

Harry is not simply a provocateur, but a spectral figure, haunting the family in ways that recall past socio-racial traumas, challenge their sense of middle-class suburban piety, and force them to recalibrate their relationship to one another.[22] After goading Gideon to throw a party reminiscent of "an old fashioned fish fry," he asserts himself in boisterous fashion throughout the evening. He convenes a group of raffish friends (many of whom grew up together in Mississippi) to noisily drink home-made corn liquor, which, as he proclaims, is a taste of "the *real* South" and contains a "fight in every bottle." Harry also takes aim at organized religion as a misguided waste of time and energy. He cheers on Percy's (Jimmy Witherspoon) emotional performance of the blues ballad "See See Rider," while he scoffs at Hattie's (Ethel Ayler) gospel standard "Stand by Me." Both songs are styles of vernacular musicking that derive from what Black arts poet LeRoi Jones called the "social and music[al] fabric" of the deep South.[23] However, the cultural forms diverge in their embrace of secular desire and lament on the one hand, and the expression of deep spiritual faith on the other. Harry bristles at the sight of Hattie, once a lively performer in Delta juke joints, proudly declaring herself a "saved" woman. So, too, does he mock how her sanctified praise song suggests that a higher power somehow helps people to confront and work through worldly conflicts. Aspects of Harry's rebellious character could be interpreted in terms of a survivalist response to the trauma of living in the Jim Crow South, albeit a quite different one than that of Gideon and Suzie's attempts to achieve socioeconomic stability. Harry's rejection of organized religion and investment in a nomadic existence is part of a broader resistance to institutional authority, a resistance to those figures, systems of belief, and organizations that seek to limit both sensory pleasure and uphold the status quo.

Harry's alignment of free movement and expression with personal agency makes him particularly alluring to Babe Brother, who feels constrained by a sense of dutiful obligation to Linda and Sunny along with his parents and brother's morally upstanding lifestyle. However, following Harry goes beyond skipping church and a couple late nights out on the town. It involves shirking all social responsibilities. Indeed, Harry reveals the depths of his ethical corruption in a conversation with his old acquaintance, Marsh, in the kitchen at the fish fry. Discussing people they knew from back home in Mississippi, Marsh references how one friend was murdered, his death made to look like a lynching, and another friend was dragged behind a car after accusing a white man of owing him money. In a series of intense, tightly framed shot-reverse-shots, the cryptic exchange reveals that Harry might have had a hand in the killing.

Harry's hurricane-like force gathers strength as the film progresses, causing the family to fracture. He draws Babe Brother away from Linda and Sunny, encouraging in him an irreverent demeanor that escalates to verbal and physical abuse. Contemporaneously, Harry tries to marginalize all the women in the family, attempting to instill a misogynistic patriarchy that recalls a much more conservative, pre–women's liberation era social reality. He challenges the ethical commitments of Pat, whose work with the city's poor and homeless he considers an insurmountable challenge, and thus foolish to even try to alleviate the suffering. When all of Harry's friends descend on Samuel and Linda's house for a big dinner, Harry treats Linda like a dutiful housewife, expecting her to prepare and serve a feast and tend to their every need. Furthermore, Harry's slovenly habits consign Suzie to the role of maid, demanding that she clean up after him as he lounges about the kitchen, living room, and bedroom.

Harry's direct interactions with Gideon for the most part stay on the level of quick conversations, but they end up taking a mystical, intensely deleterious turn. An aimless, seemingly innocent walk that the two take along tracks in a rail yard results in a painful stroll down memory lane. Pausing for a moment, they gaze out at the steel rails extending out into a dirt-filled landscape. Harry comments on the fact that both men laid tracks back in Mississippi. Doubled over with exhaustion, Gideon has a hallucinatory vision of Black laborers, hammering the rails in a plodding, percussive rhythm. It is as if Harry casts a spell, forcing Gideon to relive the kind of backbreaking and soul-sucking labor he was forced to perform in the past. Upon arriving back at his house, Gideon is barely able to walk he is so weak. In a successive sequence of shots, the repetition of the color red seems to suggest that Gideon is in great danger, perhaps that he is now marked for dead. When he stumbles into bed, Harry stands quiet in the living room covered in a demonic red glow. The next morning, Suzie leans over the stove in the kitchen holding a whistling red teakettle, Gideon wears red pajamas in his bedroom, and Harry sits in a rocking chair in the living room methodically carving the bright red skin off an apple. Moments later, Gideon suffers a stroke.

It is after this incident that Suzie instructs Harry to leave, asserting control over the family that she had been denied by way of his bombastic presence. Harry agrees, but threatens to take Babe Brother with him, who he has all but convinced to join his entourage on an extended road trip through the Delta. These tensions come to a head in a late-night altercation in Gideon and Suzie's kitchen. With a thunderstorm raging outside, Junior scolds his younger sibling for shirking his responsibilities and disrespecting the family, who then snaps back that nobody respects his standing as an individual, free to make his own decisions, and that his real name is Samuel. What begins as a verbal altercation escalates to a physical fight that brings their respective wives and mother into the fray to intervene. At the moment that Suzie—preventing the brothers from stabbing each other—gets badly cut, the two brothers realize the consequences of their squabbling and the damage that Harry has caused. Like a fever breaking, their aggression dissipates as the family members coordinate the rush to the hospital to get their mother medical care. The waiting room becomes a contemplative space for the brothers and their wives to reconnect. They even bond in their frustration with the slow speed of the hospital bureaucracy, the implication being that their race keeps them lower on the waiting list.

The familial convening triggers a reverse energy flow within the house. Harry accidentally slips on marbles scattered on the kitchen floor, has a heart attack, and seconds later dies. Drawing strength from the family's vigil at his bedside during his illness, Gideon subsequently awakens from his coma reinvigorated (figure 4.2). Nonetheless, the delay of the coroner to collect the corpse ensures that Harry remains an "unwelcomed guest." His lifeless body is at once a tragicomic disturbance "beyond the grave" and a reminder of the inadequate access to public utilities and prejudice that Black Angelenos continue to suffer. One friend comments, "If this was a white person, they would have had him on his feet, marching on out of here." Even with Harry's body lying prostrate on the kitchen floor, the family relishes a newfound stability. Gathered together in the suburban living room, they talk about the course of events. Gideon appears to be on the mend, Babe Brother resolves to fix the roof with his older sibling and also expresses regret for drifting so far from his wife and son. They speak less about Harry and more about their sense of mutual support for one another, their shared past, and the struggles that they must endure together. The house itself serves as a unifying agent, a structure that physically frames the conversation and evokes their renewed sense of togetherness. In the film's closing scene, friendly residents from across the street, aware of the bizarre and morbid situation of Harry's corpse, invite the family over for a picnic. As Gideon and Suzie's family begin to file out of the front door, it is as if they are crossing a symbolic threshold, not the liminal domestic portal separating "civilization" from "wilderness" depicted in the films of John Ford, but a transitional space that situates the family within a broader social collectivity—the neighborhood.

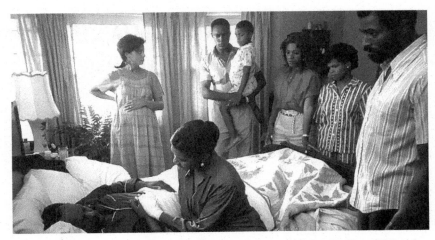

Figure 4.2. The family gathered around Gideon's bedside in *To Sleep With Anger* (Charles Burnett, Samuel Goldwyn Company, 1990). Digital frame enlargement.

Family Values and a New Black Cinema

To Sleep With Anger won a Special Jury Prize when it premiered at Sundance in the winter of 1990, which led to the Samuel Goldwyn Company acquiring it for distribution. The film was well received on the international festival circuit. Regrettably, it had a more difficult time connecting with a nationwide crossover demographic of Black and white viewers during the course of its theatrical run.[24] In the *New York Times* article, "An All-Black Film (Except the Audience)," Goldwyn's head of production, Tom Rothman, asserted: "The numbers and the pattern have been the same everywhere, regardless of how we use television, radio, newsprint and public appearances to support [*To Sleep With Anger*]. . . . this picture has performed well in specialty houses, but in so-called black theaters across the country, the performance has been significantly less."[25] Despite Goldwyn's claims to taking the rollout seriously, it pursued a public relations strategy that deemphasized the film's attention to geography and race, ultimately curbing its resonance.[26] Advertisements and press releases announced Burnett as an auteur, Glover as the star, and dressed the film in vague superlatives: "Unique, "Unforgettable," "Magical," and "Brilliant"[27] (figure 4.3). The film was called an entertaining generic hybrid, full of humor and suspense. But *To Sleep With Anger* was not a star vehicle for Glover, nor did it offer the dynamic story beats of Hollywood cinema.[28] Also,

Figure 4.3. Advertisement, *Los Angeles Times*, October 24, 1990, F5.

minority members of the media industries critiqued Goldwyn's resistance to cultivating meaningful ties with Black publications and to devoting far less money to the project than was regularly being spent on indie and mainstream studio films alike. The president of the Black Public Relations Society, Patricia Tobin, said that Hollywood studios can't simply reach out to *Ebony* and *Essence* "once in a while and expect them to rally around upcoming projects. There needs to be a sustained relationship and respect for the Black viewers as a complex community."[29] Additionally, even though Goldwyn may have contacted particular newspaper editors and faith leaders shortly before the film's release, it failed to cultivate meaningful connections with Black institutions. "It's not that the black community is not responding," Burnett told the *New York Times*. "It's that they don't know anything about it. The problem has really been trying to communicate with black audiences."[30]

What further complicated *To Sleep With Anger*'s release and long-term ability to reach viewers were contiguous cycles of Black cinema. It was not the benign melodramas—what critic Caryn James called the "suffocating genteelism" of *Driving Miss Daisy* (Beresford, 1989) and *Mr. & Mrs. Bridge* (Ivory, 1990)—that overshadowed Burnett's film.[31] It was the hype surrounding the so-called hood films. As film scholar Paula Massood writes, *Boyz n the Hood* (Singleton, 1991) and *Menace II Society* (Hughes, 1993) concentrated on Black working-class intercommunity violence in Los Angeles and the struggle to survive amid the rising presence of gangs, municipal neglect, police brutality, and the drug trade.[32] *To Sleep With Anger* did share some characteristics with these films; for example, a relatively low budget, on-location shooting, a Black cast, and an emphasis on daily experiences. Still, Burnett's magical realist, methodically paced film contrasted the ways in which these other films were youth focused, engaged with hip-hop culture, and featured tighter narrative arcs and propulsive action.[33] Burnett acknowledged how these projects involved above-the-line Black talent to bring urgent, personal stories to the big screen. At the same time, he bristled at how they attracted attention from money-hungry studio heads, eager to capitalize on the screen violence, and led to an overdetermination concerning what audiences considered to be a "black film."[34] As urban historian Benjamin Wiggins argues, the publicity surrounding this subgenre was a deliberate marketing ploy that reflected the complicity between racism and capitalism in the media industries. While publicity for *To Sleep With Anger* often obscured the central position of place and race within the narrative, for the "hood films" advertising sensationalized tales of inner city conflict. Hollywood promoted these films in such a way that "crime," "drugs," and "violence" were seen as problems confined to a pathologized, minority inner city rather than as the result of structural racism, political corruption, and predatory economic policies, all of which extended to the suburbs and were in fact addressed directly by the films themselves.[35]

The socio-spatial dimensions of *To Sleep With Anger* ultimately transcended the common grammar by which Black families were represented and discussed in the mainstream media. This was not lost on all critics. Writing in *DoubleTake*, Ray Carney noted that *To Sleep With*

Anger "violated virtually every cinematic convention about the depiction of African Americans on-screen. There are no drugs, no gangs, no guns, no policemen, no hookers, no hoops, no high fives, and no rap or hip-hop scoring on the soundtrack." Burnett depicted "middle-class mothers and fathers who head stable families, living in well-kept houses in suburban neighborhoods, and care as much about their jobs, their marriages, their children and their relationships with their neighbors as any white suburbanite does."[36] *To Sleep With Anger* also challenged the saccharin idealism of the exceptional African American family as portrayed in *The Cosby Show* (1984–92). It was not the fact that the series took as its focus an upper class Black family that caused the friction. Burnett and scholar-critics such as Henry Louis Gates Jr. noted at the time that such images were definitely needed in a televisual landscape that sensationalized acts of Black-on-Black violence. It was the fact that the humanist charge of *The Cosby Show* shied away from complex questions of history, cultural geography, and racial identity that were so crucial to understanding the politics of social location for late twentieth-century African American communities.[37] Like many other popular sitcoms, the series felt isolated from the world beyond its confined interiors. In his nuanced analysis of *To Sleep With Anger*, critic David Wallace called it no "*Cosby Show* clone," noting that viewers should not expect "comic one-liners," that the film "offers a complex and poetic look at what could happen to a family when an outsider meddles with relationships, loyalties and traditions, already brought close to the breaking point by the stress of everyday living."[38] *To Sleep With Anger*'s depiction of an African American family talking to itself about itself modeled compassionate social relations that Burnett believed provided "a sense of direction, an example" for Black communities.[39] Reflecting on how intergenerational interaction constituted a form of vernacular wisdom and activated a useable past, Burnett wrote that "Negro folklore" was a "source of symbolic knowledge that allowed one to comprehend life."[40]

Questions surrounding what Americans in general and youth in particular should know about the past were indeed highly politicized around the turn of the decade. They were at the center of what sociologist James Davison Hunter and others described as "the culture wars," the sphere of heated debate between liberals and conservatives about "different conceptions of moral authority, over different ideas and beliefs about truth, the good, obligation to one another, the nature of community . . ."[41] In the best-selling book *What Do Our 17-Year-Olds Know?* (1987), authors Diane Ravitch and Chester E. Finn Jr. rightly point out that "history" was low on the agenda of school boards; however, they placed the blame on the demise of the Western canon and the rise of ethnic studies and cultural studies.[42] In response to Ravitch and Finn, George Lipsitz argued that their position amounted to an "uncritical glorification" and "institutionalized cheerleading" of white, male "heroes" of great wars.[43] Burnett answered widespread top-down nostalgia with *To Sleep With Anger*'s affirmation of experiential knowledge from below. He recalled that in school all forms of history were strictly told from the white, European perspective. When there was any mention of Black history or culture, "it was all just negative. . . . Hollywood insists on perpetuating these myths about blacks, dangerous myths, and this is going to destroy black people."[44]

To Sleep With Anger offers an alternative understanding of Black history and its relationship to present-day middle-class suburbia. The blustering trumpet playing of the child who lives next door, a surrogate for Burnett (who grew up playing the instrument), helps to frame this understanding. Throughout the film, the child does not so much practice music as sound off a seemingly random selection of notes, as if trying in vain to learn the correct embouchure and finger configuration to play a song only he can hear. His bursts quite literally stop narrative action, compelling characters to repeat themselves, speak slower and louder, and rethink what they were doing. Certainly, the cacophony serves as a metaphor for the increasingly discordant atmosphere within a Harry-occupied home, but the sonic interruption also forces characters (and, in turn, the viewer) to constantly take stock of, reorient themselves to, and reflect on what is unfolding. It is a playful gesture whereby Burnett, a much different kind of trickster figure than Harry, encourages the audience to pay heightened attention to what the characters say and do. As the family leaves the house at the film's conclusion, the discordant diegetic trumpet blasts morph into a sonorous nondiegetic jazz melody, shifting the tenor of the mood toward familial harmony.

Burnett was never a didactic filmmaker in the sense of outlining clear problems and arguing for solutions. Nonetheless, a cinema that addressed "family values" offered a rhetorical stance against the simultaneous withering of the welfare state and the aggressive expansion of the media industries, which together contributed to the fragmentation of Black communities and collective amnesia. In *To Sleep With Anger*, the family's successful challenge to Harry involves confronting forces that threaten to drive them apart and trying to reconfigure their relationship to one another. In exploring these issues, Burnett, like contemporaries

Julie Dash, John Singleton, and Reginald Hudlin, was striving for new forms of cinema that reframed how Black communities understood themselves and how Americans perceived the relationship between space, race, and power.

Unfortunately, studio Hollywood neutralized their endeavors. Burnett was quickly shunned following *To Sleep With Anger*'s low box office returns. While some of his colleagues found ready employment in the immediate years to come, they soon discovered their agency within the United States' commercial film, television, and information industries severely limited or their ideas appropriated, packaged, and exploited. By mid-decade, *Don't Be a Menace to South Central While Drinking Your Juice in the Hood* (Barclay, 1996) proved that the geography and themes of New Black Cinema could be the stuff of profitable slapstick comedy for the crossover youth audience.[45]

It would not be until the 2010s that Black cinema would once again move to the center of American culture. The shifting political economy of the media industries, combined with the emerging Black Lives Matter movement, reinvigorated the sense of possibility for moving images made by and about Black subjects. Drawing on new streaming services and distribution networks, insurgent filmmakers such as Barry Jenkins, Donald Glover, Jordan Peele, and Ava DuVernay created films that examine the ways in which the politics of "home-making" shapes Black identity. Their films capture how an increasing number of Black families have come to call the suburbs home and depict the prospects of class mobility as falling in tension with everyday race prejudice. The suburbs are not simply a backdrop for social life in this new wave of Black cinema, but a central battleground where the struggle for racial and economic justice is imagined and waged.

Notes

1. Gaston Bachelard, *The Poetics of Space* (Boston: Beacon Press, 1964), 17.

2. Harry's name echoes the soul-stealing "Hairy Man" of the folktale "Wiley and the Hairy Man." Ayana Smith, "Blues, Criticism, and the Signifying Trickster," *Popular Music* 24, no. 2 (May 2005): 179–191; Jeannine King, "Memory and the Phantom South in African American Migration Film," *Mississippi Quarterly* 63, nos. 3–4 (Summer 2010): 4.

3. The Library of Congress's National Film Registry selected the film for inclusion in its 2017 lineup, which coincided with a Criterion Collection treatment. The Academy of Motion Picture Arts and Sciences also awarded Burnett with a Governor's Award in 2018. David Sims, "*To Sleep With Anger*

Is a Masterpiece from an Overlooked Film Pioneer," *Atlantic*, March 7, 2019. https://www.theatlantic.com/entertainment/archive/2019/03/sleep-anger-criterion-collection-charles-burnett/584239/.

4. Burnett was a core member of the LA Rebellion, a loose formation of Black filmmakers who came together at UCLA's Ethno-Communications Program in 1969. While their artistic and political aims were certainly not monolithic, they endeavored to create a formally experimental, socially engaged cinema. Ntongela Masilela, "The Los Angeles School of Black Filmmakers," in *Black American Cinema*, ed. Manthia Diawara (New York: Routledge, 1993), 107–117; James Naremore, *Charles Burnett: A Cinema of Symbolic Knowledge* (Los Angeles: University of California Press, 2017); Allyson Nadia Field, Jan-Christopher Horak, and Jacqueline Najuma Stewart, eds., *L.A. Rebellion: Creating a New Black Cinema* (Berkeley: University of California Press, 2015).

5. Janet Maslin, "Screen: 'Killer of Sheep' Is Shown at the Whitney," *New York Times*, November 14, 1978, C10; "Filmmaker Presents, Discusses, His Films," *Philadelphia Tribune*, October 5, 1979, A6; "Films Depicting Life in California Slated," *Los Angeles Times*, March 2, 1981, SD_A5; "Black Directors Get U.K. Hail," *Variety*, January 20, 1982, 6; Kevin Thomas, "Black Film Series Begins with 'Sheep,'" *Los Angeles Times*, October 12, 1987, OC_F4.

6. Janet Maslin, "'My Brother's Wedding' from Coast," *New York Times*, March 30, 1984, C7. See Amy Corbin's insightful article, "Charles Burnett's Dialogic Aesthetics: *My Brother's Wedding* as a Bridge between *Killer of Sheep* and *To Sleep With Anger*," *Black Camera* 6, no. 1 (2014): 34–56.

7. Charles Burnett, interviewed by Aida Hozic, "The House I Live In: An Interview with Charles Burnett," *Callaloo* 17, no. 2 (Spring 1994): 475; Charles Burnett, quoted in Sojin Kim and R. Mark Livengood, "Talking with Charles Burnett," *Journal of American Folklore* 111, no. 439 (Winter 1998): 70.

8. See, for example, Geoff King, ed., *American Independent Cinema* (New York: Routledge, 2012); Yannis Tzioumakis, *American Independent Cinema* (Edinburgh: Edinburgh University Press, 2017), 192–277.

9. Chubb and Pressman brought on board associates Thomas Byrnes and Harris Tulchin, who convinced Sony subsidiary SVC to contribute $1 million. The Corporation for Public Broadcasting was initially interested, but Burnett ended the deal: "They didn't like its blackness, the mysticism, the references to the South." Charles Burnett, interviewed by Bérénice Reynaud, "An Interview with Charles Burnett," *Black American Literature Forum* 25, no. 2 (Summer 1991): 325; Charles Burnett, interviewed by Aida Hozic, "The House I Live In: An Interview with Charles Burnett," *Callaloo* 17, no. 2 (Spring 1994): 479; Charles Burnett, quoted in Bruce McCabe, "A Filmmaker with Serious Concerns," *Boston Globe*, June 9, 1979, 7.

10. Al Young, "Charles Burnett Spellbinds Viewers with His Personal Vision," *American Visions* 5, no. 6 (December 1990): 36; Kathleen Teltsch, "MacArthur Foundation Names 31 Recipients of 1988 Awards," *New York Times*, July 19, 1988, A23; David Ferrell, "Puppeteer, Film Maker Win MacArthur Grants," *Los Angeles Times*, July 19, 1988, D1.

11. Danny Glover, quoted in Al Young, "Charles Burnett Spellbinds Viewers with His Personal Vision," *American Visions* 5, no. 6 (December 1990): 36; Naremore, *Cinema of Symbolic Knowledge*, 66–91.

12. While *To Sleep With Anger*'s $1.4 budget far exceeded the costs of *Killer of Sheep* and *My Brother's Wedding* ($10,000 and $80,000, respectfully), the expenses were quite low for a commercial production. Danny Glover, quoted in David Wallace, "Burnett—Telling a Story on a Shoestring," *Los Angeles Times*, October 24, 1990, F1; Charles Burnett, quoted in Samir Hachem, "The House of Spirits," *Village Voice*, August 12, 1989, in Robert E. Kapsis, ed., *Charles Burnett Interviews* (Jackson: University Press of Mississippi), 27.

13. Isabel Wilkerson, *The Warmth of Other Suns: The Epic Story of America's Great Migration* (New York: Random House, 2010), 36–46, 95–122, and 205–221.

14. George Lipsitz, *How Racism Takes Place* (Philadelphia: Temple University Press, 2011), 28–29.

15. Hadley Meares, "The Thrill of Sugar Hill," *Curbed Los Angeles*, February 22, 2018.

16. Becky M. Nicolaides, *My Blue Heaven: Life and Politics in the Working-Class Suburbs of Los Angeles, 1920–1965* (Chicago: University of Chicago Press, 2002), 26–38. See also Josh Sides, *L.A. City Limits: African American Los Angeles from the Great Depression to the Present* (Berkeley: University of California Press, 2003), 98–108; Carey McWilliams, "The Evolution of Sugar Hill," *Script: The California Magazine*, March 1949, 25.

17. Andrew Wiese, *Places of Their Own: African American Suburbanization in the Twentieth Century* (Chicago: University of Chicago Press, 2005), 8, 37–70.

18. Dolores Hayden, *Building Suburbia: Green Fields and Urban Growth, 1820–2000* (New York: Random House, 2003), 110–115.

19. John David Rhodes, *Spectacle of Property: The House in American Film* (Minneapolis: University of Minnesota Press, 2017), 55–103.

20. Raphael J. Sonenshein, *Politics in Black and White: Race and Power in Los Angeles* (Princeton: Princeton University Press, 1993), 39–209.

21. Nicolaides, *My Blue Heaven*, 26–38.

22. For a broader discussion of the haunted house in cinema, see Barry Curtis, *Dark Places: The Haunted House in Film* (London: Reaktion Books, 2008), 31–75, 167–204.

23. LeRoi Jones, *Blues People: The Negro Experience in White America and the Music That Developed from It* (New York: Morrow Quill Paperbacks, 1963), 63; see also Christopher Small, *Music of the Common Tongue: Survival and Celebration in African American Music* (Hanover, NH: Wesleyan University Press, 1998), 81–222.

24. "Goldwyn Picks Up Rights to 'Anger,'" *Variety*, May 16, 1990, 7; Will Tusher, "Anger Grabs 4 Indie Awards," *Variety*, April 1, 1991, 10; Janet Maslin, "Cannes and the Sudden Limelight," *New York Times*, May 18, 1990, C3; Sheila Benson, "Black Film Makers Carry Sundance Festival," *Los Angeles Times*, January 29, 1990, F2.

25. Larry Rohter, "An All-Black Film (Except the Audience)," *New York Times*, November 20, 1990, C15; Tom Rothman, quoted in Larry Rohter, "Blacks Shun Film Made by Blacks," *Globe and Mail*, November 23, 1990, C3; Anne Thompson, "Goldwyn's 'Anger': Artfilm or Black Film?," *Variety*, November 12, 1990, 5.

26. Ed Guerrero, *Framing Blackness: The African American Image in Film* (Philadelphia: Temple University Press, 1993), 168–169. Julie Dash recounted how *Daughters of the Dust* experienced similar struggles. She was often told that her film about three generations of Gullah women of the Sea Islands didn't fit within recognizable genres. Recounting a typical conversation with studio execs, she told the *Washington Post*, "People kept saying, 'well, what is it like? Is it like '*Sounder*?' Is it like *The Color Purple*?' 'We can't see it . . .'" Julie Dash, quoted in David Mills, "A Dash of Difference," *Washington Post*, February 28, 1992, C1.

27. "Advertisement," *Los Angeles Times*, October 24, 1990, F5; "Advertisement," *Globe and Mail*, November 9, 1990, D5; "Advertisement," *Los Angeles Sentinel*, October 25, 1990, B8; "Advertisement," *New York Times*, October 14, 1990, 22; "Advertisement," *Chicago Tribune*, October 26, 1990, 176.

28. David Sterritt, "Making Movies That Fill a Vacuum," *Christian Science Monitor*, October 2, 1990, 11; Roger Ebert, "*To Sleep With Anger*," October 26, 1990, RogerEbert.com; Caryn James, "After Pizza and Polite Squabbling, a Film Wins," *New York Times*, January 29, 1990, C17; Charles E. Belle, "Business in the Black," *Atlanta Daily World*, November 30, 1990, 4; Sheila Benson, "A Magical, Mystical Tour of South-Central Los Angeles," *Los Angeles Times*, November 2, 1990, SDF8.

29. Larry Rohter, "An All-Black Film (Except the Audience)," *New York Times*, November 20, 1990, C15; Patricia Tobin and Tom Rothman, quoted in Larry Rohter, "Blacks Shun Film Made by Blacks," *Globe and Mail*, November 23, 1990, C3; David Fox, "NAACP Chapter Seeks to Boost 'Sleep' at the Box Office," *Los Angeles Times*, October 27, 1990, 80.

30. Rohter, "An All-Black Film," C15; Anne Thompson, "Goldwyn's 'Anger': Artfilm or Black Film?," *Variety*, November 12, 1990, 5.

31. Caryn James, "Hold the Hype! It's Only a Middling Movie," *New York Times*, December 9, 1990, H11.

32. Paula J. Massood, *Black City Cinema: African American Urban Experiences in Film* (Philadelphia: Temple University Press, 2003), 145–170.

33. Michael Fleming, "Youthful Black Helmers Fear a Hollywood Whitewash," *Variety*, February 21, 1990, 1.

34. Charles Burnett, in Johanna Steinmetz, "One Man's Families: Director Charles Burnett Focuses on Urban Blacks," *Chicago Tribune*, December 8, 1991, M16; Nelson George, "Black Indies: The Wave beyond Spike," *Emerge* 1, no. 3 (January 1990).

35. Benjamin Wiggins, "Race and Place at the City Limits: Imaginative Geographies of South Central Los Angeles," *Ethnic and Racial Studies* 39, no. 14 (March 2016): 2585–2586.

36. Ray Carney, "Forgotten Films: Charles Burnett's *To Sleep With Anger,*" *DoubleTake* 1, no. 2 (Fall 1995): 123, 128.

37. See, for example, Henry Louis Gates Jr., "TV's Black World Turns—but Stays Unreal," *New York Times*, November 12, 1989.

38. David Wallace, "Burnett—Telling a Story on a Shoestring," *Los Angeles Times*, October 24, 1990, F1.

39. Charles Burnett, interviewed by Bérénice Reynaud, "An Interview with Charles Burnett," *Black American Literature Forum*, 25 no. 2 (Summer 1991): 329–331; Charles Burnett, quoted in Daniel Cerone, "Awakening to the Realities of Black Life," *Los Angeles Times*, August 12, 1989, 65.

40. Charles Burnett, "Inner City Blues," in *Questions of Third Cinema*, ed. Jim Pines and Paul Willeman (London: BFI, 1990), 225.

41. James Davison Hunter, *Culture Wars: The Struggle to Define America* (New York: Basic Books, 1990), 49, 234.

42. Diane Ravitch and Chester E. Finn Jr., *What Do Our 17-Year-Olds Know? A Report on the First National Assessment of History and Literature* (New York: Harper and Row, 1987), 10–11.

43. George Lipsitz, *Time Passages: Collective Memory and American Popular Culture* (Minneapolis: University of Minnesota Press, 2001), 27.

44. Burnett, interviewed by Aida A. Hozic, "The House I Live In: An Interview with Charles Burnett," *Callaloo* 17, no. 2 (Spring 1994): 475; Charles Burnett and Charles Lane, "Charles Burnett and Charles Lane," *American Film*, August 1, 1991, 40–43.

45. For a recent reflection on the challenges faced by Black filmmakers in the 1990s, see Reggie Ugwu, "'They Set Us Up to Fail': Black Directors of the '90s Speak Out," *New York Times*, July 3, 2019.

References

Bachelard, Gaston. *The Poetics of Space*. Boston: Beacon Press, 1964.

Burnett, Charles. "Inner City Blues." In *Questions of Third Cinema*, edited by Jim Pines and Paul Willeman. London: BFI, 1990.

———. Interviewed by Bérénice Reynaud. "An Interview with Charles Burnett." *Black American Literature Forum* 25, no. 2 (Summer 1991): 324–334.

———. Interview in Robert E. Kapsis, ed., *Charles Burnett Interviews*. Jackson: University Press of Mississippi, 2011.

Corbin, Amy. "Charles Burnett's Dialogic Aesthetics: *My Brother's Wedding* as a Bridge between *Killer of Sheep* and *To Sleep With Anger*." *Black Camera* 6, no. 1 (2014): 34–56.

Field, Allyson Nadia, Jan-Christopher Horak, and Jacqueline Najuma Stewart, eds. *L.A. Rebellion: Creating a New Black Cinema*. Berkeley: University of California Press, 2015.

Gates, Henry Louis, Jr. "TV's Black World Turns—but Stays Unreal." *New York Times*, November 12, 1989, B1.

Guerrero, Ed. *Framing Blackness: The African American Image in Film*. Philadelphia: Temple University Press, 1993.

Hayden, Dolores. *Building Suburbia: Green Fields and Urban Growth, 1820–2000*. New York: Random House, 2003.

Hunter, James Davison. *Culture Wars: The Struggle to Define America*. New York: Basic Books, 1990.

Jones, LeRoi. *Blues People: The Negro Experience in White America and the Music That Developed from It*. New York: Morrow Quill Paperbacks, 1963.

King, Geoff, ed. *American Independent Cinema*. New York: Routledge, 2012.

King, Jeannine. "Memory and the Phantom South in African American Migration Film." *Mississippi Quarterly* 63, nos. 3–4 (Summer 2010): 477–491.

Lipsitz, George. *How Racism Takes Place*. Philadelphia: Temple University Press, 2011.

———. *Time Passages: Collective Memory and American Popular Culture*. Minneapolis: University of Minnesota Press, 2001.

Masilela, Ntongela. "The Los Angeles School of Black Filmmakers." In *Black American Cinema*, edited by Manthia Diawara. New York: Routledge, 1993.

Massood, Paula. *Black City Cinema: African American Urban Experiences in Film*. Philadelphia: Temple University Press, 2003.

Naremore, James. *Charles Burnett: A Cinema of Symbolic Knowledge*. Los Angeles: University of California Press, 2017.

Nicolaides, Becky M. *My Blue Heaven: Life and Politics in the Working-Class Suburbs of Los Angeles, 1920–1965*. Chicago: University of Chicago Press, 2002.

O'Brien, Ellen L. "Charles Burnett's *To Sleep With Anger*: An Anthropological Perspective." *Journal of Popular Culture* 35, no. 4 (Spring 2002).

Ravitch, Diane, and Chester E. Finn Jr. *What Do Our 17-Year-Olds Know? A Report on the First National Assessment of History and Literature*. New York: Harper and Row, 1987.

Rhodes, John David. *Spectacle of Property: The House in American Film*. Minneapolis: University of Minnesota Press, 2017.

Sides, Josh. *L.A. City Limits: African American Los Angeles from the Great Depression to the Present*. Berkeley: University of California Press, 2003.

Sims, David. "*To Sleep With Anger* Is a Masterpiece from an Overlooked Film Pioneer." *Atlantic*, March 7, 2019.

Smith, Ayana. "Blues, Criticism, and the Signifying Trickster." *Popular Music* 24, no. 2 (May 2005), 179–191.

Tzioumakis, Yannis. *American Independent Cinema*. Edinburgh: Edinburgh University Press, 2017.

Uguwu, Reggie. "'They Set Us Up to Fail': Black Directors of the '90s Speak Out." *New York Times*, July 3, 2019.

Wiese, Andrew. *Places of Their Own: African American Suburbanization in the Twentieth Century*. Chicago: University of Chicago Press, 2005.

Wiggins, Benjamin. "Race and Place at the City Limits: Imaginative Geographies of South Central Los Angeles." *Ethnic and Racial Studies* 39, no. 14 (March 2016): 2585–2586.

Wilkerson, Isabel. *The Warmth of Other Suns: The Epic Story of America's Great Migration* (New York: Random House, 2010).

5

Guess Who Doesn't Belong Here?

The Interracial Couple in Suburban Cinema

Timotheus Vermeulen

I F, INCREDIBLY YET UNSURPRISINGLY, interracial romance today remains a rare phenomenon in Hollywood cinema, reserved for societal dramas and family comedies and little in between, it is particularly underrepresented in the variety of films set in the suburbs.[1] The reason that such portrayals are so far and few between, or so it appears, is that according to the film industry the people inhabiting these environments— The Oranges and New Canaan, Lakewood and Levittown—are almost exclusively white. So common is this myth—as scholars like Becky Nico- laides,[2] Andrew Wiese,[3] Kevin M. Kruse and Thomas Sugrue,[4] and many others associated with the "New Suburban History" have demonstrated, it is a gross misconception about suburbs present or past—that one of the most important studies of cultural representations of the suburbs is ironically titled *White Diaspora*.[5] It isn't entirely surprising, in this sense, that the few interracial couples—where in this case at least one person isn't "white"—that we do see in the cinematic suburbs are strangers:

they happen to pass through, they visit family, or, most often, have just moved there from the city.[6] It is a strangeness, moreover, that few of the films in question pass up the opportunity to problematize. Recent interesting examples of this type include *The Watermelon Woman* (Dunye, 1996), *Crazy/Beautiful* (Stockwell, 2001), *Far from Heaven* (Haynes, 2002), *Lakeview Terrace* (LaBute, 2008), *Little Boxes* (Meyer, 2016), and of course *Get Out* (Peele, 2017). Interracial coupling, in other words, is principally considered in opposition to home—to belonging. Suburban couples are supposed to be as bland and uniform as the houses they inhabit are often purported to be.

In this chapter I examine the portrayal of one such trope: the interracial couple visiting their (obviously not interracial) family in the suburbs. My focus lies with Kevin Rodney Sullivan's 2005 feature *Guess Who*. I am interested in this film for two reasons. *Guess Who* is, as the title suggests, adapted from Stanley Kramer's 1967 popular *Guess Who's Coming to Dinner*. However, it isn't a domestic melodrama, as the original was, but a comedy of errors. This suggests a rather different view of race relations: apparently, sometime between the 1960s and the 1990s, societal tragedy has evolved to family comedy. The second reason I am interested in *Guess Who* is that it ostensibly expands the cinematic demography of the suburbs to include, and indeed stay with, Black families. In the inverse of Kramer's film, the daughter returning home—the photographer Theresa (Zoe Saldana)—is Black while the fiancée—recently unemployed banker Simon (Ashton Kutcher)—is white. Theresa's African American family, moreover, is so at home in the suburbs that they are called the Joneses, a name evoking the blandness and uniformity of the suburbs if there ever was one. I should state from the outset, however, that if this dual take on the trope seems like a critical commentary on the cinematic tradition of the suburbs, turning tragedy into comedy and positing a white man as the "other," I do not think it is. First, interracial relations are still configured in opposition to notions of belonging—Simon and Theresa do not fit in the suburban house as long as they are together. There is, as I will show, quite literally no room for them there. Second, Kutcher's supposed "other" demands more close-ups, point-of-view, and over-the shoulder shots than any other character in the film, encouraging the viewer to experience his side of the story. What I mean is that if he is "other," so is the viewer, paradoxically making the Joneses strangers in their own home. Third, and most poignantly, the film's take on the trope of the interracial couple visiting a Black family in the suburbs at no point problematizes the very idea of race itself as a historical social construction, or hegemonic "doctrine," in the words of Karen and Barbara Fields.[7]

Concepts like ideology, imbalance, or inequality are noticeably absent. In *Guess Who*, as I will show, race is conceived of as a set of natural or inborn traits that distinguishes one group of people from other groups of people: what the one is, the other is not, and vice versa.

Drawing on close textual analysis of the film's treatment of the interracial couple and spatial and social theory I develop a cultural topology of the Jones's home, which I take as a synecdoche for the suburb. It is introduced as such by way of a crane shot panning down from a long view of the New York skyline to downtown Cranford, New Jersey, a short cab ride passing through tree-lined streets, and, most significantly, a white picket fenced Neoclassical bungalow; through its repeated mention as "suburban" or "Jersey" by characters; as well as the private home's centrality in suburban culture more generally.[8] My argument is that the suburban house, for all its spaciousness, is narrow-minded in its patriarchy and racism, treating both gender and race in essentialized, oppositional terms. This argument is structured around three recurrent spatial dialectics, or what Edward Soja[9] has called "spatialities"—articulations of space as condition for and consequence of social action: *spaces of disavowal*, where there is a pretense that race is of no consequence; *spaces of exchange*, where race relations are negotiated; and *spaces of conflict*, where perceived racial difference polarizes. This is to say: much if not all of the Jones home is defined in terms of either disavowal, oppositional negotiation, or conflict. As the mention of the concepts of dialectics, spatiality, and space as opposed to place suggests, these relationships are dynamic rather than static: they can be performed in various locations in the house and aren't exclusive to any particular room, even if they are more likely to take place in one spot than another. The space of exchange moves from the kitchen to the lounge while the front porch accommodates both scenes of disavowal and a significant conflict. I argue that there is no resolution for the interracial couple in *Guess Who*—even if or especially if it contradicts and undermines the film's narrative trajectory—partly as a result of this patriarchal and racial inconsistency, this "how-to-behave-oppositionally-where?" *Guess Who* suggests that interracial kinship is not just a contested topos in the suburbs but that it has no place there at all.

"This Is My House, My Rules"

Early on in *Guess Who*, Simon and Theresa are frolicking around in her childhood bedroom at her parents' home, which they visit for the weekend. He jokingly puts on her lingerie after which she jumps him on the bed. It is at that moment that the door opens and her father, Percy (played by Bernie Mac), peeks in (figure 5.1). The couple's banter is innocent, playful more than erotic, but as reverse shots cut between the couple's stupefied embarrassment—they have literally stopped moving—and Percy's unnerved look—his forehead wrinkling, eyes glaring, jaw stiffening, gradually turning the other cheek—the sentiment that prevails is that of an indecent exposure. The incident communicates at least three rules of the house. First, it informs the viewer that in this house the boundaries between private and communal spaces are porous, if they exist at all. Doors are there to be opened. Indeed, what is so telling about the scene's staging is that it suggests that the transgression is Simon and Theresa's rather than Percy's: they, rather than he, show a disrespect for the house rules—they should have known Percy could come in. Second, this scene suggests this is a strict socio-normative house. As subsequently becomes apparent in exchanges with Simon and Theresa but also in uncomfortable interactions with a sexually ambiguous wedding planner, it is not just the frolicking that irks Percy but also the fact that a man was dressed up in lingerie. In this house, you behave your (pick your social category). Third, the scene implies that space is

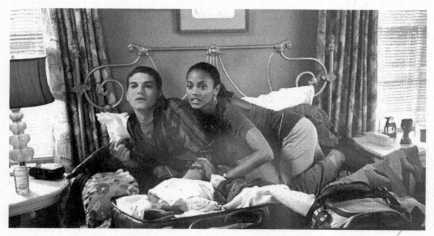

Figure 5.1. Theresa (Zoe Saldana) and Simon (Ashton Kutcher) caught in the act by Percy (Bernie Mac) in *Guess Who* (Kevin Rodney Sullivan, Columbia Pictures, 2005). Digital frame enlargement.

hierarchical: Simon and Theresa need to obey Percy's rules. Their use of this space—and, one must therefore assume, all other spaces in the house, since this would appear to be the most private one—is regulated by him, to the point that Simon is subsequently evicted from the room and asked to find alternative sleeping arrangements.

The film explicitly frames this exposition of space as porous yet hierarchical in terms of both patriarchy and race. Patriarchy is as common a trope in depictions of the suburbs as racism is. As Catherine Jurca writes, "at its center are men who desperately want the promises of home fulfilled."[10] Accounts of these men range from the controlling fathers who think they know best to anxious men in gray flannel suits driven onto the streets and out of the suburbs for fear of emasculation,[11] but what they tend to have in common is a tension between the strict socio-spatial hierarchies of the nuclear family and the transparency of the picture windows, the democracy of the open floor plan, and the perceived femininity of the décor.[12] Indeed, Percy follows in the unsteady footsteps of a long line of fictive white suburban dads by imposing control as a means to preserve a masculinity that otherwise seems lost from the house's interior—all expressions of his love of NASCAR are banished to the basement.[13] The scene is set up in its entirety to posit Percy in the role of authoritarian father: the camera views him from below, making the viewer look up at him, whereas it shoots Theresa and Simon from above; Percy is wearing a coordinated pressed shirt, suspenders, and tie, while his daughter and her fiancée are dressed casually in slacks; and, most tellingly, the scene is located in Theresa's childhood bedroom. So as to press the point, Simon later explicates that this is Theresa's "father's house" and so he will "play by his rules" while Theresa in a whining voice complains to her mother—who isn't, like the maternal figure in so many other romantic comedies, absent but is mostly passive and silent, a witness to events rather than a participant. Percy further remarks that "this house can't handle no more testosterone." Simon and Theresa's symbolic castration, Percy's omnipresent phallic order, and a silenced wife: one does not have to be the staunchest of Lacanians to assume this house is ruled by the "name of the father."

At the same time, this scene is also contextualized by the preceding sequences—and should to my mind be considered—along the lines of race. Mere seconds earlier, Percy's confession to his wife Marilyn (Judith Scott) that he doesn't like Simon is explained by reference to race—an unconvincing "it's not that he is white" explicitly questioned by Marilyn's incredulous "it's not?" followed by a close-up of Percy looking away and biting his lip uncomfortably. Meanwhile, the scene where the parents first meet their daughter's new partner sees Percy mistaking Simon for the cab driver and the cab driver, who is Black, for Theresa's beau, the implication being that he is incapable of even imagining his daughter dating someone who isn't Black. This is to say that Simon's very presence in the house is destabilizing not just because he is a man, but because he is a white man.

The scene's introduction of the house rules along such conflicted patriarchal and racial lines provides the blueprint for the movie's treatment of space and race. Throughout the film, all behavior is dictated by (or opposed to) the law of the father, to the extent that Simon and Theresa both break up and ultimately get back together as a result of Percy's interference. In fact, it seems the entire house pivots around Percy, for there is no other familial center other than him. Family events take place all across the Jones home: family introductions are done in the kitchen, a father-daughter heart-to-heart is set in the conservatory, and the reiteration of Percy and Marilyn's wedding vows takes place in the garden while couples argue on the front porch and so on. The single place that seems underserved, narratively, is the place that so often functions as the center of the home: the living room. Instead, the house contracts and expands depending on Percy's movements and moods: a wide angle shot on the front porch exposes his public discomfort with the color of Simon's skin; tightly framed doorway shots in the low, cluttered kitchen provide a momentary refuge for his doubts and worries about interracial love; a mobile camera moves through open doors into the garden to accommodate Percy's expansion of his essentialist ideas about race. It is telling that the one time the house provides for the needs of others—Simon and Theresa sneaking out the window to spend some time together outdoors—is when Percy is fast asleep. The sense that prevails, however, a sense found so often in depictions of the suburb, is that this hyperbolic control is compensation for the lack of power Percy increasingly experiences: his wife sets the agenda, his daughters sneak out whenever he is not looking, a young white man sleeps in his basement.

The image of Percy barging in on another person's assumed private space is not an exception either. There is no space in the house that is off bounds, which cannot be at any point entered. A cliché of the cinematic depiction of the suburban home, the most prominent architectural feature in the house is the open doorway, which is visible in just about every other shot. Even Percy himself is at various instances exposed. During a fitting session with the wedding planner, for instance, construction workers putting up the wedding tent come in at the very moment he is in his underwear. Similarly, his plagiarized wedding vows are found in the basement by Simon. We don't see others entering the master bedroom, but at one point Simon remarks that he doesn't want to go upstairs to talk to Percy, which suggests that this, too, would have been a possibility. Presumably because there is no privacy to be found anywhere, intimate conversations take place everywhere regardless of a place's distinct qualities. Sensitive discussions—including those about race—move from the bedroom to the hallway to the kitchen out onto the front porch. Simon and Theresa, for instance, explicitly negotiate racial relations together in the bedroom, the kitchen, and on the front porch, which is also the place that they—citing racial difference—break up, the film cutting to a long shot of the two exiting the image in opposite directions separated by the white picket fence to explicate to the viewer that their lost love is a consequence exclusively of the suburban home (figure 5.2).

Hélène Charlery has noted that, in spite of appearances, *Guess Who* does not tell the story of Simon and Theresa's romantic involvement as much as that it recounts Simon and Percy's relationship.[14] Indeed, I would argue that this comedy of errors finds both its heart—the surprisingly melodramatic romance between Simon and Theresa—and its humor—the

Figure 5.2. Simon (Ashton Kutcher) walking away from the home as Theresa (Zoe Saldana) enters it, the two separated by a white picket fence in *Guess Who* (Kevin Rodney Sullivan, Columbia Pictures, 2005). Digital frame enlargement.

play with patriarchal and racial prejudice—in the men's conflict over suburban space. Simon and Theresa's troubles begin with Simon and Percy's standoff over who can do what and where, while their reunion comes on the heels of the men coming to a mutual understanding about what their positions are. This is visualized through a shared reterritorialization of the house's various indoor and outdoor spaces: finding and drinking a vodka bottle Marilyn had stashed away in the kitchen; teaching Simon sports in the living room, the furniture moved to the side to make way; and teaching Percy how to dance in the garden. Tellingly, as Charlery remarks, during all this, we learn almost nothing about Theresa other than that she is Simon's girlfriend and Percy's daughter—nor do we, to be sure, find out anything about her mother or her sister.

Comedies of errors traditionally concentrate on class, family, and sexuality yet it isn't an exaggeration to say that in *Guess Who* nearly every interaction in the Jones's household addresses race or ethnicity. Race is defined here along two axes. As Hernan Vera and Andrew Gordon have remarked, the film tends to address race through depoliticized stereotypes, disavowing sociohistorical discourses of inequality and oppression while enjoying the offensive caricatures they engender.[15] Race is also oppositional: white is defined in opposition to Black and vice versa. Simon is a stiff, thin, socially awkward slacker without hair gel or a sense of fashion. The single attribute missing from his Silicon Valley costume is a pair of white socks. Keisha instantly mistakes him for a tax auditor. Percy, by contrast, walks around with swagger, his movements as overstated as they are expressive. He is dressed in tailored suits and wears an oversized golden wristwatch. Similarly, while Simon speaks standard English as a marker of middle-class, unlocalizable whiteness,[16] avoiding much of Kutcher's usual frat boy slang, Percy's racial identity is articulated predominantly—and, to my admittedly foreign (i.e., non-Anglophone) ears, problematically—through the exaggerated use of what Lisa Green has described as "African American English" vernacular, voice, and gesture, elongating his vowels as if he is from the South, contracting words, dropping the auxiliary verb, and mixing grammatical modes, presumably in recognition of his inner city, working-class origins, and occasionally orating from deep in his chest, emphasizing his masculinity.[17] In other words: Mark Zuckerberg meets, well, Bernie Mac of Def Jam fame. Percy assumes—correctly—that "Whitey McWhiteman" has no athletic abilities while Keisha wonders about his sexual prowess. Simon instantly takes it—wrongly, as it turns out—that Percy doesn't like NASCAR. Race is perceived as caricatural opposition—which is the single reason Percy and Keisha's prejudice and

Simon's offensive mistake can be communicated to the viewer as a joke. As Percy explains at one point, talking about Simon and Theresa: "You ain't got nothing in common. For example: You don't like sports. Theresa loooves sports. You're a businessman. She's an artist. You're white. She's Black. Did I miss anything?" Simon responds: "No, that's just it. She's everything I'm not." Black is everything white is not and vice versa—and there is no gray. In other words, in *Guess Who*, the suburban home is represented as a fluid but rigid, patriarchal, and racialized space, which encourages, ultimately, oppositional relations.

"It's Not That He's White"

Guess Who's positioning of the home in these distinct terms sets the scene for three distinct racial dialectics, which is what I want to focus on for the remainder of this chapter: disavowal, in which everyone remains on "opposite" sides but pretends not to see the apparent distance, that is, color; conflict, in which the opposition is further polarized, the distance between being white and being Black becomes unbridgeable; and exchange, where characters attempt an interaction that acknowledges racial or ethnic difference—but without problematizing it. In one sense, these dialectics follow a conventional narrative trajectory: disavowal is the dominant modality early on in the film, conflict takes center stage midway through the plot, while exchange structures the final interactions. In another sense, however, I would argue that though each dialectic is sublated by another, it isn't suggested, necessarily, that any one of them is resolved. Indeed, the dualism between white and Black is as marked in the first scene on the front porch as it is in the penultimate scene in the garden.

As I suggested above, the three dialectics produce and are produced by suburban space but are not exclusive to a place. I take space here to be a continual cycle, a process, while place is its (momentary) materialization. This conceptualization follows Henri Lefebvre's canonical study of the social production of space.[18] Space, Lefebvre asserts, is at once the product of social processes and produces them. Lefebvre distinguishes between three dynamics: the "conceived," the "perceived," and the "lived." The first is the organization of, say, a room in a house, by architects, planners, or even, if you are a teenager, your parents. It's a top down, rationalized process. The perceived is the performance of space, how you use a place. "Spatial practice" is another label Lefebvre suggests for this. Lived is the label for the emotional register associated with par-

ticular locales—you may, for instance, have had a traumatic experience
somewhere, or, alternatively, shared a first kiss. It determines how you
feel and what you feel is possible. Every dialectic, that is, every space, is
produced, in other words, by a dynamic between three competing social
processes; but it's only in place that we see them in action, as it were.

In *Guess Who* the dialectics of disavowal, conflict, and exchange
are each made manifest by the particularities of a place but they are not
exclusive to one—no dialectic has its "proper" place. Sure, the explication
of race in caricatural, oppositional terms is local in the sense that it is
produced, or in any case prompted, by the space of the suburban home:
Simon begins to worry about race in the cab to the Joneses (i.e., lived),
he and Theresa are increasingly separated during their visit, sleeping in
separate bedrooms, going on different trips, and gradually exchanging
romantic two-shots for antagonistic shot-reverse-shot setups (perceived),
while as aforementioned the breakup is visualized by the white picket
fence splitting the image into halves, with Simon walking away from the
home in the bottom right while Theresa returns indoors on the top left
(conceived). What I mean when I say that these dialectics do not have a
proper place is that they move from room to room—often without resolution. They might manifest because of the particularities of one room
but influence interaction in another. Early on in the film, Simon tries
to impress Percy—for whom "a man who don't play sport is not a real
man"—by saying he used to be a NASCAR racer. It is a lie he thinks
will not be exposed because, as he later informs Theresa, he associates
NASCAR with white culture. Midway through the film, Simon admits
to Percy—who as it turns out is an avid fan—that he lied. Narratively
speaking, Simon's disavowal of race is sublated into conflict, since this
admission initiates another form of interaction in which both increasingly articulate their racial biases. Tellingly, however, while the lie was
encouraged by the particularities of one place—the bright and expansive
kitchen, with Simon on one end and Percy at the other, a kitchen table
separating them—it isn't dissuaded there. Instead, the lie is challenged
elsewhere entirely, in the one place, in fact, where it cannot be maintained: in a tiny go-kart on a downtown go-kart track, where the two
men are set to race one another. This is to say: if the dialectic has been
sublated, it has been accomplished by means not of resolution but of
displacement: the dialectic has been assimilated into another, but at least
two of the elements by which it was defined—Simon's lived experience of
the suburban home, the conceived space of the kitchen—have not been

resolved at all. It appears in this sense that race is as antagonistic as it is, in this home without closed doors, decentered, a persistent presence nowhere in particular and everywhere in general.

As Eduardo Bonila-Silva has noted, disavowal, the simultaneous registration of reality and the refusal to accept it for what it is in its entirety because of the trauma the ignored detail might prompt, often implies a concern with sociability.[19] After all, disavowal, of one's own reality or the one you share with someone else, may well be what makes an interaction possible at all. Indeed, I would argue that *Guess Who* suggests that as long as color is considered to be of no consequence, social interactions are contrived but tenable—a "colorblindness" that Michael Omi and Howard Winant have brilliantly exposed as opportunistically neoliberal[20] and that in a sense may be said to afford the film at all, since the fictional suburb of Cranford is suggested to be unproblematically multicultural and multiracial whereas, according to census data, its counterpart in reality is almost entirely white. The moment race is explicated, discourse is complicated—as a scene at the dinner table where the memory of the Ku Klux Klan is invoked demonstrates, the relationship between Simon and Percy is simultaneously one of historical subordination, where white hegemony imposes its will on (and by means of) Black lives, and local subordination, since Simon here is subject to Percy's law. In the cab to the Jones house, Simon and Theresa are chatting away carelessly until the moment he asks her whether she has told her parents that he is white. Theresa responds by mock shouting: "You're white? Stop the car!" The cab halts so abruptly that Simon bumps his head against the front seat. Race, in other words, is not to be talked about if you don't want anyone to get hurt. They soon after change the subject. Similarly, in the scene where Simon meets the Joneses, he jokingly remarks: "Wow. I wish Theresa would have told me you guys are Black. That would've saved an awkward moment." The response, however, is not laughter but silence, interrupted only by Marilyn's dismissive "kind of like this one." *Guess Who* implies that disavowal sustains a paper-thin surface level of sociability—with, as Italo Calvino once remarked, two sides and nothing in between—that is otherwise torn to pieces.

Guess Who articulates disavowal spatially as an equidistancing tool, suggesting it contracts space where it is used to establish sociability and expands space in those instances it seeks to salvage sociability. The scene where Percy and Marilyn welcome Simon in their kitchen described above is exemplary of this dynamic—inwards and outwards—and I will analyze it in detail. The scene is divided, narratively and aesthetically, into three parts, a division that is marked spatially. The first part sees Simon and Theresa standing in the doorway, exchanging polite pleasantries with her parents, who are positioned on the room's opposite side. "You have a very beautiful home, Mrs. Jones," Simon proffers nervously, hands behind his back, to which Marilyn replies, "Thank you, Simon. You can call me Marilyn." He continues, "You, too, Mr. Jones." Percy retorts, jokingly but defensively, asserting his authority, his head cocked back, chest forward, arms crossed: "Thanks. You can call me Mr. Jones." The interaction between Simon and Marilyn is presented through shot-reverse-shot wide-angle mid shots, which at once suggest a distance and an equal relation between the two. The first two shots frame them both from the knees up, but after Marilyn's reassuring words it cuts to a shot of Simon framed from the waist up so as to suggest slightly more intimacy. Interestingly, the cinematography shifts once Percy joins the conversation, filming him in a medium close-up, the emphasis on his bullish physical presence, while it backs away from Simon, returning to the initial mise-en-scène to suggest a deterioration in racial relations. If Marilyn's generous, egalitarian behavior here draws the room together, Percy's defensive insistence on his authority pushes Simon away. All images throughout are in deep focus, which situates the characters in the kitchen, amid its features, rather than in front of it, which emphasizes the sheer size of the room—indeed, Simon and Theresa are separated from her parents not just by distance but also by one of two (!) tables.

The second part of the scene is marked by Marilyn's invitation to Simon and Theresa to take a seat. The couple sit down at the table that previously separated the four, still on the other side but part of a different socio-spatial interaction that implies more proximity than before. Discussing Simon's work and family background, the cinematography gradually exchanges the shot-reverse-shot two-shot setup for a wide-angle medium shots of the four of them together and—after Theresa and Marilyn stand up to make lemonade on the other side of the table—shot-reverse-shot medium close-ups of Simon and Percy. The nature of the discussion and the cinematography follow each other closely with moments of tentative togetherness shown through wide-angle four-shots, the two men on either side of the image but related to one another through the two women in the middle; and the increasingly aggressive questioning by Percy—"Simon, you play any sports? . . . I don't understand why you don't play sports. It don't make sense. A man who don't play sports is not a real man"—depicted exclusively through shot-reverse-shot medium close-ups, drawing attention to Percy's confrontational body language and Simon's gestures of nervousness—his dropped shoulders, restless eyes, fidgety, sweaty hands. The film turns the conceived space of the kitchen into a battleground, quite literally, between the lived space of Marilyn, who associates it with family in an inclusive sense, Percy, for whom family is exclusive, and Simon, who as a child of a single parent home is unfamiliar with a unit like this.

The last part of the scene settles the fight between these opposing ideas about the racial makeup of family, as it were, since Percy physically closes in on Simon while Simon struggles for a satisfactory reply, finally deciding on the unconvincing lie that he drove in NASCAR races (figure 5.3). There are no more four shots from here on. Instead, the film cuts between shot-reverse-shot medium close-ups and close-ups of Simon and Percy from over one another's shoulder, two-shots of Theresa and Marilyn listening in silence, one stunned by the lie she hears, the other moved by what she takes for the truth; and medium close-ups of Simon seen from behind and between the profiles of Theresa and Marilyn, framed in a narrow space. Simon looks increasingly withdrawn, his face pale, shifting around on his chair, physically edging toward the open doorway so as to back away from Percy, return to his initial position, his

Figure 5.3. Percy (Bernie Mac) intrudes on Simon's (Ashton Kutcher) personal space in *Guess Who* (Kevin Rodney Sullivan, Columbia Pictures, 2005). Digital frame enlargement.

striped brown shirt disappearing against the matching hallway wallpaper as Percy corners him, standing over him, leaning forward, hands firmly on the table, his eyes looking Simon over from head to toe as he wonders whether Simon might have run steeple-chase. In other words, in a single scene, the kitchen is transformed from an expansive, open space to a communal space to an uneven, antagonistic space that is increasingly tight, increasingly restrictive—limited to the table—and, indeed, increasingly dualist, stretching from one opposite to the other. It is the first space that affords Simon's lie but the final space that necessitates it, one that responds to Percy's latently racial interrogation by articulating a racial bias but disavowing both so as to salvage sociability.

"It Doesn't Matter What I Say, You People Are Gonna Think I'm Racist"

Georg Simmel once stated that "conflict is . . . designed to resolve divergent dualisms; it is a way of achieving some kind of unity, even if it be through the annihilation of one of the conflicting parties. . . . Conflict itself resolves the tension between contrasts."[21] *Guess Who*'s narrative suggests, indeed, that the sublation of disavowal into conflict and subsequently of conflict into exchange achieves this harmony. Visually and spatially, however, the opposite is implied: the patriarchal and racial dualisms are not resolved but maintained, even polarized. During a dinner conversation where Percy's elderly father, too, is present, Percy bullies Simon into entertaining the family with racist jokes. The conversation, which takes place at the tall dining table, in the spacious dining room, follows Simon's admission of guilt at the racetrack. This means, in other words, that Percy is aware of Simon's racial bias. Percy's provocation aims at exposing this to the family just as Simon's acceptance of the challenge is an attempt on his behalf to prove he hasn't been disavowing any prejudice. Indeed, he prefaces his jokes by saying: "You know what. I'll tell the joke. . . . I'll tell you why: because by not telling the joke, I'm empowering it, right? . . . The only way to break down barriers is to have everything out in the open, right?" Upon Simon's attempt at racist comedy, however, the family's laughter soon turns into anguish and finally anger. Percy leaves the table disgusted while his father is outraged—the women once again remain silent.

In stark contrast to the scene in the kitchen, which changes its stylistic patterns to communicate the changing organization of space, this scene maintains a single pattern throughout, cutting between medium shots of the table and all those seated at it, two shots of Simon and Theresa and Percy and his dad, and close-ups, at times from over someone's shoulders, of each of the characters individually. Indeed, the opening shot and the closing shot are the same, so as to make manifest what is different: in the former Marilyn arrives with the food while in the latter Percy leaves, having lost his appetite. What the film's stylistic register suggests, I would argue, is a rigid spatiality that cannot, for all the size of this room, accommodate these polar opposites—Black and white. That this scene is set, once again, at a table, conventionally a place where family comes together but where in films set in the suburbs the dysfunction is often played out,[22] is indicative. This setup is repeated in the other conflicts, with alternatively Theresa leaving the scene, Marilyn departing, or Simon exiting. Indeed, spaces of conflict do not articulate race by means of distance at all—in some of the later scenes Simon and Percy are shouting at one another from up close, in two shots suggesting intimacy if not love. Instead, they mark racial difference through rigidity: "You people," Simon shouts. Conflict here doesn't "resolve divergent dualisms"; it pits them against each other to such an extent that they cannot occupy the same place. As Simon remarks to Theresa as they break up: "Oh, okay, I'm always gonna be the white boy." "And I," she replies, "will always be the Black girl, but I'm willing to deal with it," only to say seconds later, "the engagement is off."

There are two reasons I have chosen to call the third spatial dialectics prevalent in the film, particularly in its final twenty minutes, spaces of exchange and not, for instance, spaces of negotiation or, indeed, spaces of resolution. The first is that exchange, like conflict and sociability, is one of the four forms of social interaction distinguished by Simmel. Here it is defined as reciprocity, often but not necessarily economic: in interacting you give something while you expect to get something in return. The second reason for this choice is that in the Netherlands, where I am from originally, a more specific use has been proposed in recent years. Exchange is increasingly contrasted with compromise, especially politically. The latter—associated with, among others, New Labor and the multiculturalism of the 1990s—is a politics where the involved parties abandon their ideal positions to meet their opponents halfway. In the former, which has become the dominant model recently, everyone remains rooted on their spot exchanging particular, often opposed, or even incompatible program points from afar.

I would suggest that *Guess Who*'s treatment of race and racial relations resembles this distinct dialectics of exchange. Toward the end of the film,

Simon and Percy supposedly find common ground. Certainly, the scene in which they make up, alone in the house after their partners have left, consists almost exclusively of two shots, the two men engaged in shared physical activities—looking for vodka in the kitchen, playing football in the living room, dancing in the garden. Yet, contrary to appearances, they haven't abandoned their polarized positions as much as they exchange a set of caricatural and to my mind offensive qualities: Percy shares his athleticism teaching Simon sports, Simon his cultivation teaching Percy how to dance the tango; Percy communicates his experience with "Black women," Simon his way with words—Percy will go on to borrow Simon's speech to convince Marilyn to return home, leaving Simon bereft of words and, for a short while, of his girlfriend. All the while, the film does not deconstruct race. Percy's newly acquired skills, just like his fondness for NASCAR earlier, do not so much problematize his Black identity as that they apparently appropriate a white man's characteristics. Similarly, Simon at no point deterritorializes white identity, instead annexing supposedly Black male qualities—remember also Theresa and Keisha's conversation about Simon's sexual prowess alluded to earlier, where Theresa doesn't just answer Keisha's question about what it is like to be with a white guy, saying that Simon is sensual and that white guys in general have "huge" johnsons. Indeed, the dialogue cited at the end of this chapter's first section—where Black and white are contrasted—takes place in this very scene. Simon concludes with another statement, which in the context of exchange is even more indicative: "You know, she's my other half. Without her, I'm not whole." What this suggests, after all, is that interracial love isn't so much a resolution, or, indeed, a compromise where the qualities of the distinct individuals dissolve into that of the couple, but a bond between two people who remain as isolated as ever. I realize I might be accused of reading too much into this, since marriage in general often is discussed in these clichés. But given that it comes on the back not just of a film that suggests that race is oppositional, that white and Black stretch a space to the point that it snaps, like an elastic band, and either a white or a Black person has to exit a place, but as the conclusion to a scene where the characters themselves explicitly pit Black and white against one another, I think it is this reading that is encouraged here.

Knock, Knock. Who's There? The Other.

If *Guess Who* suggests that the interracial couple visiting the suburbs in 2005 can find happiness there, as much of the film's narrative implies, it is exclusively as visitors, that is to say, as people who come but also leave, people who cannot live there, who do not belong there. It is a harmony that isn't possible in any one place in particular but has to be situated in between spaces, in passing, on the go—and, ultimately, out. Indeed, the film's development of the suburban home as porous yet hierarchical, patriarchal and racialized through the dialectics of disavowal, conflict, and exchange and their respective productions of opposition makes manifest that interaction between races or ethnicities here is stretched out between essentialist polarities, polarities that in many senses lie well beyond the borders of the house, in history as much as in uneven practices of geography.

I have not had the time or space in this chapter to consider the spatial politics of *Guess Who* in relation to its source text, *Guess Who's Coming to Dinner*. I would like, however, to make one final observation that might seem counterintuitive given *Guess Who*'s reconsideration of genre—turning a drama into a comedy—and reversal of roles—making the lead character white and the family Black, while in the original the lead character is Black and the family white—but which I hope makes sense in the context of the above argument. *Guess Who* not only focuses on racial difference itself where *Guess Who's Coming to Dinner* concentrated on society's preconceptions about race, but it also, in contrast to the 1967 film, essentializes race, asserting that race *is* rather than *becomes*. It suggests as much, moreover, precisely by articulating race in exclusively oppositional terms. White is whatever Black isn't, and vice versa. An observant reader of an earlier draft of this text asked me how Percy's patriarchy and racial bias were related to Matt Drayton's (Spencer Tracy) authoritarian prejudice toward his daughter Joanna's (Katherine Houghton) relationship with Dr. John Prentice (Sidney Poitier). I think it is this distinction—between race as essence and race as social construct—that sets them apart. Both fathers feel they have the right—and are shown to have the power—to decide who their children should love; both worry about their daughter's choices in love because of the color of their partner's skin. However, Percy distrusts Simon, as he states at one point, because he *is* white, whereas Matt worries, by his own account at least, about Dr. Prentice because of how others might feel or come to feel about interracial marriage. In the first, race is what you are; in the latter, it is what others perceive you to be. I am sure there is more to be said about this relationship, but it seems to me striking that in this sense the trope of the interracial couple visiting the suburbs has, over a time span of thirty-eight years, not only not progressed, but in many senses has regressed.

Notes

1. I use the term "interracial"—and by extension race—throughout this essay, as opposed to, for instance, "interethnic," since it appears to be, in both relevant film reviews and discourse at large, the most commonly used term in accounts of romantic relationships between people who self-identify as one of the following social groups distinguished by the 2019 United States Census: "White, Black or African American, Asian, American Indian and Alaska Native, Native Hawaiian and Other Pacific Islander." It should be noted, however, that this terminology is not at all unproblematic. As, among others, Bonila-Silva (2017) and Fields and Fields (2012) have noted, race is not just an arbitrary concept, selecting from the billions of cultural, social, behavioral, physiological, psychological, and emotional qualities that characterize each individual person—in the process, moreover, ossifying qualities that are entirely gelatinous, context dependent, and can differ from day to day—a few to distinguish between "groups" of people. It is an ideological doctrine that propagates that "nature produced humankind in distinct groups, each defined by inborn traits that its members share and that differentiate them from the members of other distinct groups of the same kind but of unequal rank" (Fields and Fields 2012, 16). See also Essed and Goldberg 2002.

2. Becky Nicolaides, *My Blue Heaven: Life and Politics in the Working-Class Suburbs of Los Angeles* (Chicago: University of Chicago Press, 2002).

3. Andrew Wiese, *Places of Their Own: African American Suburbanization in the Twentieth Century* (Chicago: University of Chicago Press, 2005).

4. Kevin M. Kruse and Thomas J. Sugrue, "Introduction: The New Suburban History," in *The New Suburban History*, ed. Kevin M. Kruse and Thomas J. Sugrue (Chicago: University of Chicago Press, 2005), 1–10.

5. Catherine Jurca, *White Diaspora: The Suburb and the Twentieth-Century American Novel* (Princeton: Princeton University Press, 2001). It might be suggested that recent television has been more attentive to the diversity of actual suburbs, since there have been shows concentrating on Black, Indian, or Asian American families living in the suburbs since at least the seventies, but here, too, there is very little room for interracial couples.

6. See Robert Beuka, *SuburbiaNation: Reading Suburban Landscape in Twentieth-Century American Fiction and Film* (New York: Palgrave Macmillan, 2004).

7. Karen E. Fields and Barbara J. Fields, *Racecraft: The Soul of Inequality in American Life* (London: Verso, 2012): 16.

8. John Archer, *Architecture and Suburbia: From English Villa to American Dream House, 1690–2000* (Minneapolis: University of Minnesota Press, 2005).

9. Edward Soja, *Postmodern Geographies: The Reassertion of Space in Critical Social Theory* (London: Verso, 1989).

10. Catherine Jurca, *White Diaspora*, 11.

11. See Robert Beuka, *SuburbiaNation*.

12. Timotheus Vermeulen, *Scenes from the Suburbs: The Suburb in Contemporary US Film and Television* (Edinburgh: Edinburgh University Press, 2014).

13. The film is generically conservative in repeating the trope of the suburban patriarch. It might simultaneously be said to be historically quite progressive, or in any case innovative, in affording this role to a Black man, given that African American men have traditionally been culturally emasculated—first through the mythologies engendering and engendered by slavery, and later through narratives of Black matriarchs.

14. Hélène Charlery, "Interracial Romance as a Staged Spectacle in *Made in America, Bringing Down the House,* and *Guess Who,*" *South Atlantic Review* 76, no. 4 (Fall 2011): 85–100.

15. Hernan Vera and Andrew Gordon, "On How to Resolve Racial Taboos," *Contexts* 4, no. 4 (Fall 2005): 68–69.

16. Rosina Lippi-Green, *English with an Accent: Language, Ideology and Discrimination in the United States* (London: Routledge, 2012).

17. Lisa Green, *African-American English: A Linguistic Introduction* (Cambridge: Cambridge University Press, 2002).

18. Henri Lefebvre, *The Production of Space* (Oxford: Blackwell, 1991). See also Andrew Merrifield, "Place and Space: A Lefebvrian Reconciliation," *Transactions of the Institute of British Geographers,* n.s., 18, no. 4 (1993): 516–531.

19. Eduardo Bonila-Silva, *Racism without Racists: Color-Blind Racism and the Persistence of Racial Inequality in the United States* (Lanham, MD: Rowman and Littlefield, 2006). My own conceptualization of disavowal is derived, of course, from those psychoanalytic discussions about denial initiated a century ago by Sigmund Freud. Here disavowal is understood as the simultaneous registration of reality and the refusal to accept it for what it is in its entirety so as to suspend the trauma the ignored detail could otherwise cause (cf. E. E. Trunnell and W. E. Holt, "The Concept of Denial or Disavowal," *Journal of the American Psychoanalytic Association* 22 [1974]: 769–784). My use, however, relies on sociology, in particular Georg Simmel's categorization of social interactions and sociability: the impulse to be social, to interact with others—the other two labels, too, draw on Simmel's categorization.

20. Michael Omi and Howard Winant, *Racial Formation in the United States,* 3rd ed (New York: Routledge, 2014).

21. Georg Simmel, *On Individuality and Social Forms,* edited by Donald N. Levine (Chicago: University of Chicago Press, 1971): 70.

22. See Susanne Cowan, "The Gendered Architecture of the Home in Cinematic Space," *Built Environment* 26, no. 4 (2000): 303–315.

References

Archer, John. *Architecture and Suburbia: From English Villa to American Dream House, 1690–2000.* Minneapolis: University of Minnesota Press, 2005.

Beuka, Robert. *SuburbiaNation: Reading Suburban Landscape in Twentieth-Century American Fiction and Film.* New York: Palgrave Macmillan, 2004.

Bonila-Silva, Eduardo. *Racism without Racists: Color-Blind Racism and the Persistence of Racial Inequality in the United States*. 2nd ed. Lanham, MD: Rowman and Littlefield, 2006.

Charlery, Hélène. "Interracial Romance as a Staged Spectacle in *Made in America, Bringing Down the House*, and *Guess Who*." *South Atlantic Review* 76, no. 4 (Fall 2011): 85–100.

Cowan, Susanne. "The Gendered Architecture of the Home in Cinematic Space." *Built Environment* 26, no. 4 (2000): 303–315.

Essed, Philomena, and Theo Goldberg, eds. *Race Critical Theories: Text and Context*. Oxford: Blackwell, 2002.

Fields, Karen E., and Barbara J. Fields. *Racecraft: The Soul of Inequality in American Life*. London: Verso, 2012.

Green, Lisa. *African-American English: A Linguistic Introduction*. Cambridge: Cambridge University Press, 2002.

Jurca, Catherine. *White Diaspora: The Suburb and the Twentieth-Century American Novel*. Princeton: Princeton University Press, 2001.

Kruse, Kevin M., and Thomas J. Sugrue. "Introduction: The New Suburban History." In *The New Suburban History*, edited by Kevin M. Kruse and Thomas J. Sugrue, 1–10. Chicago: University of Chicago Press, 2005.

Lefebvre, Henri. *The Production of Space*. Oxford: Blackwell, (1974) 1991.

Lippi-Green, Rosina. *English with an Accent: Language, Ideology and Discrimination in the United States*. London: Routledge, 2012.

Merrifield, Andrew. "Place and Space: A Lefebvrian Reconciliation." *Transactions of the Institute of British Geographers*, n.s., 18, no. 4 (1993): 516–531.

Nicolaides, Becky. *My Blue Heaven: Life and Politics in the Working-Class Suburbs of Los Angeles*. Chicago: University of Chicago Press, 2002.

Omi, Michael, and Howard Winant. *Racial Formation in the United States*. 3rd ed. New York: Routledge, 2014.

Simmel, Georg. *On Individuality and Social Forms*. Edited by Donald N. Levine. Chicago: University of Chicago Press, (1908) 1971.

Soja, Edward. *Postmodern Geographies: The Reassertion of Space in Critical Social Theory*. London: Verso, 1989.

Trunnell, E. E., and W. E. Holt. "The Concept of Denial or Disavowal." *Journal of the American Psychoanalytic Association* 22 (1974): 769–784.

Vera, Hernan, and Andrew Gordon. "On How to Resolve Racial Taboos." *Contexts* 4, no. 4 (Fall 2005): 68–69.

Vermeulen, Timotheus. *Scenes from the Suburbs: The Suburb in Contemporary US Film and Television*. Edinburgh: Edinburgh University Press, 2014.

Wiese, Andrew. *Places of Their Own: African American Suburbanization in the Twentieth Century*. Chicago: University of Chicago Press, 2005.

6

Alienated Subjects

Suburban Failure and Aspiration in Asian American Film

HELEN HERAN JUN

ASIAN AMERICAN SUBURBANIZATION has generated a significant body of scholarship in the social sciences, providing context for the transnational forces that have transformed suburbia in the past four decades and sparking debate around questions of Asian American assimilation and racialization.[1] This chapter looks to cultural production, not as a transparent window into the "reality" of Asian American suburban experience, but rather as a complex site of mediation that enables analysis of how suburban life is being imagined and represented by Asian American filmmakers. I approach these cultural texts as an index of multiple and competing fantasies, conflicts, crises, and aspirations that are generated by and about Asian Americans in suburban space. How do these Asian American films understand what constitutes the "good life" and the American Dream and how do they animate contradictions that complicate discourses of assimilation and socioeconomic mobility that are always already implied by suburbanization?

This chapter focuses on representations of suburban life in two Asian American films, Justin Lin's *Better Luck Tomorrow* (2002) and Tze Chun's

Children of Invention (2009). I analyze how these cinematic representations of Asian American suburbanization engage with a dominant logic in which all human action and social life are reduced to an economic rationality of cost-benefit calculation, referred to as neoliberalism. These films depict vastly divergent spaces and characters, with Lin portraying the exploits of privileged Asian American teens in a gated community in suburban Orange County, while Chun's semiautobiographical screenplay captures the overwhelming economic insecurity of a Chinese immigrant mother raising two young children in a working-class industrial Boston suburb. By emphasizing the significance of neoliberalism as a political rationality that constitutes subjects as market-driven individuals of self-enterprise, I demonstrate how both films, despite their vastly different socioeconomic settings, ultimately converge in imagining Asian American suburban aspiration as dysfunction, loss, and failure.

Suburban Pathology

Justin Lin's *Better Luck Tomorrow* can be described as a comedic yet dark suburban high-school narrative that follows four high-achieving Asian American male friends during their final frenzied year of preparing for college. The hyperambitious characters are consumed by the intense process of cultivating the most competitive possible applications while they simultaneously engage in escalating criminal activity, from petty theft to burglary, commercialized cheating rings, drug sales, and finally the murder of an Asian American male rival, all of which occurs within the residential developments, schools, and commercial spaces of a wealthy suburban enclave. While the narrative can be read as a simple inversion—model minority breaking bad—I demonstrate how the characters negotiate an emasculating model minority discourse, which produces a critique that ultimately exceeds a preoccupation with suburban whiteness. In other words, their being denied membership in the high school's white masculine homosocial formation is not represented in the film as the primary obstacle for these teens; it is, rather, the neoliberal market-logic that instrumentalizes every aspect of their lives that constitutes a trajectory of profound alienation.

One of the first major studio films to feature an Asian American cast and director, *Better Luck Tomorrow* reworks the cinematic narrative of "suburban dysfunction" in which seemingly perfect neighborhoods and families are unmasked to reveal the moral deviance and inauthenticity that lie at the heart of suburbia.[2] The film opens with familiar visual signposts of the traditional iconography of the suburban cinematic landscape shot in wealthy Orange County: a slow-moving gate that invites us across the boundaries of the insulated community, neat rows of terra-cotta roofed, pastel-colored homes, young children chasing an ice cream truck, expansive athletic fields and courts, and newly paved streets are shot against the backdrop of a sunny blue sky. The opening sequence is slightly overexposed, heightening the artificial and simulacral quality of the space, while the uplifting music and fragments of young children's laughter against the refrain of the ice cream truck provide tropes of domestic security and contentment. An adjacent active oil pump, a familiar sight throughout Orange County's suburbs, cheerfully pumps for black sludge, foregrounding the dirty processes of extraction that coexist within these seemingly pristine spaces. The Filipino American protagonist and his three Asian American male friends are located within a well-established place in which a trajectory of socioeconomic mobility is an evitable part of the film's social landscape. In the film's opening line, "Are you done yet?," the absent referent (early admission Ivy League applications) punctuates the presumption underlying these characters' aspirational futures of high achievement as they lie basking in the Southern California sun, which is all jarringly interrupted by the image of a dead body under tiles of green sod.

The film's earnest main protagonist, Ben Manibag (Parry Shen), is the embodiment of a dedicated, self-driven subject with a wide range of skills and activities that he works relentlessly to cultivate. Portrayed through fast-cut editing and the frequent use of montage, Ben catalogs an endless array of college prep activities, from SAT practice, training for an academic decathlon, varsity sports, being repeatedly crowned food court "employee of the month," to more altruistic civic engagements—volunteering at the hospital, participating in canned food drives, and organizing a beach cleanup—since, as he explains, "you just can't count on good grades to get into a decent school anymore." The frenetic pace of this diversified regimen of application-building is punctuated by slow scenes that constitute Ben as a highly disciplined subject, precise and exacting with an emphasis on quantification and measurable returns—down to a hundredth of a point:

> I shoot 215 free throws a day. My goal is to beat Calvin Murphy's record of 95.85%. That's 207 baskets. Punctilious: Marked by or concerned about precise and exact accordance with the details of codes and conventions. To get a perfect score on my next SAT, I needed to improve my verbal score

by 60 points. I picked a new word every day and repeated it
over and over again. They say if you repeat something enough
times it becomes a part of you.

His disciplined formation is represented in a series of midrange shots
of Ben repetitively practicing free throws in his subdivision's immaculate
basketball court, which is set against the flat static backdrop of large
suburban homes trimmed in terra cotta. Indeed, Ben methodically records
his stats in a written chart, which is seen in close-up to underscore the
self-imposed quantification of his life (figure 6.1). Such deliberate calculation and empiricist instrumentalization of every social action (what
neoliberalism calls rational choice or alternately "freedom") is represented
not as heroic self-enterprise but as objectifying and cynical self-interest:
"As long as I could put it on my college app, it was worth it." The film's
rapid-fire fast-cuts from one scene to the next represent Ben's dizzying
range of activities as interchangeable units of instrumentalized "credit"
that can be listed on his application to Harvard, and his civic volunteerism
activities (food pantry collections, translating for Spanish speakers at the
hospital, environmentalist antilitter campaigns) are as decontextualized
as his routinized memorization of SAT vocabulary in the pursuit of a
perfect verbal score.

punc·ti'l·i·ous *adj.*
marked by or concerned about precise exact
accordance with the details of codes or conventions

Figure 6.1. Ben (Parry Shen) cataloguing his activities in *Better Luck Tomorrow*
(Justin Lin, Paramount, 2002). Digital frame enlargement.

Ben's relentless drive for self-cultivation is best understood in the context of an emergent ethos of the "entrepreneurial self" that has been dominant since the 1980s in the United States. Neoliberalism is often defined as a concrete set of "free-market" economic policies or principles (deregulation, privatization, free-trade, a "noninterventionist" state), which have generated massive concentrations of wealth for a global transnational class, while dismantling social safety nets.[3] Michel Foucault's influential theorization observes that in the United States neoliberalism is more than just technocratic economic policies, marking a radical retheorization of the human subject that replaces notions of labor and exchange with a conception of the worker "as a sort of enterprise for himself . . . being for himself his own capital, being for himself his own producer," much like Ben and his friends.[4] Foucault interprets the neoliberal mandate of the withdrawal of the state as actually a "technique for government" such that the individual subject is constituted as an economically rational actor who is "free" from so-called big government to exercise greater personal autonomy in the marketplace in exchange for being personally responsible "for social risks such as illness, unemployment, poverty, etc."[5] In this manner, the notion of citizenship as entailing entitlements to basic state provisions (e.g., education, safe drinking water, health care) has been effectively "reduced to self-care . . . divested of any orientation towards the common [good],"[6] while the "political rationality of neoliberalism is expressly about winners and losers based on entrepreneurial skill."[7] This erasure of the concept of society or common interest necessarily champions a fiercely self-enterprising individual with the initiative to cultivate the most relevant skills and forms of knowledge in a global marketplace.

Since the mid-1960s, Asian Americans such as the film's fictive characters have been increasingly constructed in dominant discourse through terms of competition, regimented discipline, and market-driven instrumentality. Model minority discourse generally posits that "Asian cultural values" (ranging from respect for authority, patriarchal family structures, and high regard for education, to forbearance and compliance, and "Confucianism") are responsible for high rates of academic and professional achievement. This discourse ignores how United States immigration law after 1965 gave selective preference to the most highly educated Asian immigrants in their nations of origin as the United States labor market suffered from a shortage of skilled workers in expanding areas of the economy, such as medicine and engineering. The ahistorical representation of Asian American "achievement" as the product of hard work and strong cultural values has been long critiqued within ethnic

studies and Asian American studies as a discourse deployed to delegiti-
matize Black and brown social justice demands while also erasing Asian
American poverty.[8] However, Victor Bascara observes that the larger context
of model minority is a neoliberal argument for the "withdrawal of the
state," which has been mounted against liberal state projects seeking to
organize or promote racial equality in the interests of a common good.[9]
While the notion of high-achieving Asian Americans is still inflected by
Yellow Peril discourse when situated in competitive relation to white
students or white workers, I contend that the characteristics that were
specifically attributed to post-1965 Asian Americans (self-enterprising,
market-driven, disciplined, competitive, and instrumentalizing) are now
constitutive of a universally idealized subject of the new global economy.[10]

Thus, the cynically market-driven and frenzied pursuit of college
admissions depicted in *Better Luck Tomorrow* is not only a representation
of a specifically Asian American model minority formation but also reflects
a dominant neoliberal epistemology of an aspirational bourgeoisie.[11] The
self-disciplined rigor to systematically constitute oneself as the ideal
candidate for the competitive market is not marked as idiosyncratic to
just Ben and his Asian American cohort, but includes a larger constituency of non-Asian students who are similarly engaged in a meaningless
frenzy of self-cultivation at this upper-income suburban high school:
"Lunchtime was club time. This was where everyone loaded up on
their extracurricular activities for their college app." Hence, white and
other non-Asian students are also present at their drug-fueled, all night
study sessions—hosted by valedictorian parachute kid, Daric Loo (Roger
Fan)—or at academic decathlon training, or are shown purchasing cheat
sheets, underscoring that the instrumentalist mandate of achievement at
any cost and the entrepreneurial ethos of college preparation adheres to
the space of the affluent suburban high school.

What distinguishes Ben and his male cohort, however, is that their
neoliberal formation is racialized as an emasculating model minority
discourse, which they subsequently negotiate through acts of criminal
transgression. The boys exploit the dominant imagining of Asian Americans as studious, compliant, rule-abiding nerds as a means to facilitate
increasingly elaborate criminal schemes. For instance, an early scene shows
the boys in the ubiquitous suburban big-box store, Best Buy, with Han
(Sung Kang) performatively approaching the customer service counter
with a sheepish apology that foregrounds a stereotypical Asian American
male interest in computers, "Hi . . . it's my little brother and he came
home with all this computer stuff he can't afford. And my mom . . . ,"

while an impatient, yet wholly unsuspicious, white worker credits back hundreds of dollars of stolen merchandise to his credit card. As the boys are egregiously filling their shopping cart, they are shot from below with the camera eye tucked safely alongside their stolen items, as opposed to an imposing, regulatory gaze of a surveillance camera from above; no one watches nor suspects these Asian Americans of criminality. As Ben tucks a bundle of cash into a box under his bed, he explains: "I guess it just felt good to do things I couldn't put on my college application. Besides it was suburbia, we had nothing better to do. Our straight As were our alibis, our passports to freedom. Going to study group would get us out of the house until 4:00 in the morning. As long as our grades were there we were trusted." While Ben references a familiar trope in which the deadening monotony of the suburbs drives teen delinquency and thrill-seeking behavior, *Better Luck Tomorrow* is distinct insofar as its high-achieving Asian American teens are wholly formed by an instrumentalist market rationality of self-improvement. Their transgressions are waged less as a rebellion against the normative mandate for high achievement, and more in defiance of the racial discourse that defines their achievement in emasculating terms of obedient compliance.

The film's representation of the boys' criminal activity expresses a sense of inviolable suburban security in which they are insulated from penal state violence, positioning school and the family ("My Dad is going to kill me") as the primary institutions of authority for these privileged teens. In contrast to the criminalization of racialized urban surplus populations, in which Black and brown male adolescents are always already dangerous threats necessitating repressive state intervention, the same illegal activities of suburban youth (e.g., drug dealing, fighting, "joy-riding") have long been narrated as benign manifestations of boredom, rather than criminal pathology. The film reifies this discourse of suburban insularity in a scene that stages a violent Asian American masculine revenge fantasy, when Ben and his friends crash a darkened backyard high school party and are met by the racial taunts of a group of white male jocks: "Hey, bible study is next door." A physical altercation culminates with Daric (Roger Fan) pulling a gun and pistol-whipping the white alpha male into fearful submission, who is now shot from the ground, lying down, as he continues to be beaten by Virgil (Jason Tobin) and Ben. The next day Ben is shown in slow motion, walking apprehensively through the high school corridors and sitting in a classroom while nervously eying the school security guard who just keeps walking: "By Monday the word had spread and pretty much everyone knew about it. I was sure the cops were gonna come and get us that morning. But it never happened." In the universe of the film, a discourse of privileged suburban protection from policing and state violence is critical to sustaining this Asian American narrative of high achievement and criminal transgression.

As their criminal activity escalates, an older discourse of Asian racial difference replaces that of model minority compliance at their high school: "We had the run of the place. Rumors came and went fast and furious. One had us linked with some Chinese mafia. It was fine with us because it just put more fear in everyone. Along with that power came greed. It just made sense to expand our business into drugs, putting the law of supply and demand into practice. I think our teacher would have been proud." While the boys enjoy the masculinist dividends of being tied to Chinese organized crime (only one character, Daric Loo, actually appears to be Chinese American), their illegal activities are explicitly not represented as a *rejection* of a normative trajectory of achievement, socioeconomic mobility, and college prep hoop jumping. Consistent with the neoliberal theorization of the "criminal" as simply another rational economic actor who weighs the possible costs and benefits of legal infraction, their profitable illegal exploits are incorporated into the boys' ever-expansive entrepreneurial capacities.[12] At one point, Ben wearily complains, "Four cheat sheets a day, the drugs, the scams—between this and all my club commitments, I couldn't even start my homework until 1:00 a.m." The film's representation of their profitable criminalized practices as a "skill set" that can be incorporated into their disciplined formations captures how the neoliberal logic of "rational choice" displaces a discourse of criminal pathology and posits its economistic episteme as both neutral and amoral.

The absence of a conventional discourse of morality in this suburban teen film is sustained throughout the narrative and remains deliberately unresolved at the film's conclusion. In the aftermath of the chaotic group murder of a wealthy Asian American male rival, Virgil's attempted suicide leaves him unconscious with a gunshot to the head, and his friends stand quietly around his bed.[13] Daric's first line when he walks into the hospital room is a market rationalist question of damage assessment, "Is he gonna be retarded or something?," before he switches into a mode of self-preservation: "Wait, Ben. Do you think Virg is going to talk? . . . Okay, let me think." Daric's shamelessly transparent self-interest, combined with an unyielding logic of cost-benefit rationality, is casually captured in peripheral dialogue all throughout the film, such as during debate practice, when he offers, "All right, the topic is population control.

Why retarded children and handicapped people should be executed in order to keep the population down. Ready?"

As Ben leaves the hospital, exasperated with Daric's self-interested preoccupation with containing the legal repercussions of the murder, the film's conclusion does not lead Ben into a police station, which would constitute a liberal resolution in which the state is reified in reestablishing moral order. Rather, the last scene shows a long shot of Ben driving down a pristine suburban street with Stephanie (Karin Anna Cheung), the murder victim's Asian American girlfriend, in her new "graduation gift" convertible as he states, "For the first time in my life, I don't know what my future will hold (figure 6.2). I don't even know what the other guys are going to do. All I know is that there's no turning back."

While *Better Luck Tomorrow* may be easy to dismiss as a masculinist teen narrative of Asian American suburban angst, the film's narration of what drives the affluent, aspirational students at an upper-income, predominantly white high school produces an unmistakable critique of the neoliberal entrepreneurial self that is constituted by market logics of rational self-interest. At earlier points in the film, characters variously

Figure 6.2. Ben (Parry Shen) driving down the road with Stephanie (Karin Anna Cheung) in *Better Luck Tomorrow* (Justin Lin, Paramount, 2002). Digital frame enlargement.

express ironic suburban teen discourses of entrapment, such as when Virgil ruminates on the possibility of Ivy League early admissions, "when all that studying pays off and you get to leave this hellhole a year early." However, the ambiguity of the film's conclusion indicates that the dehumanizing and alienated ethos of neoliberal self-enterprise cannot be so easily ascribed to the spatial confines of the suburban high school and its surrounding environs, undermining fantasies of college, the city, or the professional labor market as constituting trajectories of escape.

Agency as Failed Enterprise

In Tze Chun's critically embraced independent production, *Children of Invention* (2009), developmental discourses of Asian American immigration and assimilation are dramatically reconfigured in a working-class Boston suburb. Elaine Cheng (Cindy Cheung) is a divorced Chinese immigrant mother, raising her young US-born children, Raymond (Michael Chen) and Tina (Crystal Chiu), in Quincy, Massachusetts while their father moves to Hong Kong. Having a partial college education and working on an expired visa, Elaine survives the US gig economy by assisting Michael (Jackson Ning), a Chinese immigrant realtor, and by participating in numerous failed "network marketing" ventures. If *Better Luck Tomorrow* represents privileged Southern California suburban teens cynically engaged in seemingly infinite opportunities to cultivate the entrepreneurial self, Chun's film discloses how economic precarity is experienced as a series of humiliating displacements that discipline the Chinese immigrant mother as a "failed" enterprise who, despite her long hours, is unable to secure a home for her children.

Originally set during the 1990s in the transitioning industrial suburb of Quincy,[14] the film opens with an off-screen sales pitch that focuses on the anxiety and shame of economic uncertainty, not generally associated with suburban space: "One year ago I was just like you. Working two jobs trying to make ends meet. Worrying about money all the time. One night, my wife says to me, Rob, we can't live like this. *We can't live like this*. You know what I'm talking about. Living hand to mouth. Minute to minute, second to second." The sales narrative deploys time as both a means of underscoring the anxious temporality of scarcity and precarity while situating the failure to provide into the historical past. The camera opens onto the receptive, focused gaze of a middle-aged African American man and pans across a racially, gender, and age-diverse group of other hopeful attendees, before settling on the older white salesman in a small, generic hotel conference room. He continues, "So I went out and I looked at dozens of network marketing companies and I found the only one that could provide my family with the security it so deserves: Vitafutures vitamins." What begins as an empathetic narrative of long hours coupled with low wages and the stress of financial uncertainty cynically dissolves into a sales pitch predicated on exploiting the aspirations of those feeling trapped by economic desperation.

This opening scene powerfully captures the "depoliticization" of the capitalist economy, where the crisis of low wages, rising costs, and socioeconomic stagnation for large sectors of the US labor market, including the shrinking middle class, is somehow plausibly met with a response of "innovative products" and self-help programs promising life transformation. Political theorist Wendy Brown describes how a neoliberal political rationality reduces citizens to individual consumers "whose moral autonomy is measured by their capacity for 'self-care'—their ability to provide for their own needs and service their own ambitions."[15] Since neoliberalism defines political and social spheres through market terms, Brown observes that political and social problems are converted into "individual problems with market solutions."[16] Multilevel marketing companies are paradigmatic of such market solutions in their promotion of an array of wellness and personal improvement products tied to a sales recruitment system that promises financial freedom. As the pitch continues, Elaine, professionally dressed in a modest skirt-suit while carrying bags of unsold vitamins, forcefully argues outside the conference room with a Vitafutures representative: "Rob said that if I couldn't sell them he would give me back my two thousand dollars." In contradiction to the triumphalist narrative of family provider, Elaine's failure is compounded by her son's presence; we share his gaze as we watch her collect bottles off the lobby floor as she is forcibly removed from the midrange hotel. The film's opening pitch, which imagines that economic security and the American Dream is within reach to struggling workers, is revealed as a fraudulent promise that transforms agency into public humiliation.

The film's nuanced portrayal of the culture of multilevel marketing emphasizes how the industry relies on an entrepreneurial rhetoric of self-help and independence, "be your own boss!" combined with a "familial" discourse of community building. Elaine's persistent attraction to multilevel marketing, despite her continued losses, is a powerful expression of the distorted meaning of agency, freedom, and community under a neoliberal social formation. In response to an onslaught of economic disasters precipitated by divorce, Elaine is shown as working relentlessly, making more calls and sales pitches, reviewing more promotional materials and licensing manuals, and she is frequently shot in profile driving her late-model Altima as she shuttles back and forth across Boston and its suburbs, from sales meeting to home showing, with her children often in tow. Unlike the persistent self-cultivation of the privileged teens in *Better Luck Tomorrow*, however, whose labors generate cumulative "achievements" (higher test scores, GPAs, athletic titles) that increase their competitive advantage, Elaine's long hours in multilevel marketing and sales generate no material benefit as their economic conditions continue to deteriorate while the children increasingly resent her distracted inattention. According to neoliberal logic, the lack of "return" on her labor is not understood as labor exploitation but as entrepreneurial failure, which is also an expression of Elaine's "freedom" and "agency" since she is "free" to work as hard and for as many hours and weekends as she determines in her pursuit of the American Dream.

An upscale single family home in Lexington, a wealthy white suburb outside of Boston, is the site of Elaine's recruitment into her next multilevel marketing venture, and the house and neighborhood effectively capitalize on her aspirations as she tells the children that "maybe someday we will live here." Seen outside from a low-angle shot from Elaine's point of view, the large multistory home on an oversized lot stands in formidable contrast to the aging Quincy row house from which her family was recently evicted. Betty Cardellini, the affable white host of the large recruitment party, enthusiastically introduces Elaine to two other Chinese immigrant women: "I would like the three of you to conquer the Chinese market!" The rest of the attendees, who are mostly white women, are a combination of hopeful new recruits and well-versed veterans of the network marketing industry, and the exchanges illuminate a specialized lexicon of "break-away systems," "downstreams," "diamond levels," "front-end loading," as well as a feminist rhetoric of empowerment: "The products are amazing. But it's really more than that. It's a community, it's women helping women." Although direct sales companies like Avon and Amway have existed for nearly a century, multilevel marketing has exploded since the 1980s in a post-Fordist economy, championing an entrepreneurial discourse of "freedom" while contracting the labor of millions of unpaid "distributors" who systematically target their familial networks and social communities (whether religious, ethnic/racial, retired, and so forth) as niche markets for sales and recruitment. Research indicates that multilevel marketing companies disproportionately attract middle-class and working-class women who are seeking supplemental income and are attracted to the "flexibility" of programs offering opportunities to work from home. A paradigmatic expression of neoliberal economic instrumentality, multilevel marketing defines every person in one's community—family, friends, church, schools—as a source of revenue. After Betty temporarily "covers" her $2,500 membership fee, Elaine is shown working long days and nights, making the same pitch of entrepreneurial opportunity to a multiracial string of young, hopeful recruits and dutifully delivering their checks to Betty. But when Elaine drives back to the Cardellinis' expensive home in suburban Lexington in an attempt to collect her commission, she discovers it vacant, revealing their financial security as performative fraud. She instead encounters two imposing white male detectives who are investigating a pyramid scheme and confiscating computers, and Elaine scrambles down an elegantly paved driveway toward her car before she is taken into custody and questioned for days, leaving her children to fend for themselves in her unexplained absence.

While many viewers regard Elaine's persistent attraction to multilevel marketing as failed personal judgment (bordering on criminal behavior), network marketing is a thriving multi-billion-dollar industry that involves up to fourteen million participants in the United States alone.[17] While the Federal Trade Commission prosecuted numerous companies as illegal pyramid schemes in the 1970s, the largest multilevel marketing company in the world (Amway) defended itself as a legitimate business, and the 1980s saw a proliferation of new multilevel marketing companies.[18] The largest of these multilevel marketing companies are now publicly traded, accruing tremendous profit for "legitimate" corporate management and shareholders by directly extracting resources and labor from millions of working-class, middle-class, and retired "distributors," the vast majority of whom never receive any company compensation.[19]

The regulatory theater to prosecute a handful of businesses as "illegal pyramid schemes" positions the state as an agent of "protection" for the consumer, when in fact the state effectively constitutes relations of production that make such exploitation possible and continues to sanction it as "legal." For decades, federal regulators and academics have engaged in endless theories and proposals (e.g., algorithms and precise ratios for recruitment vs. sales) in an effort to determine the ambiguous distinction between "legitimate" multilevel marketing and illegal pyramid schemes, while corporate actors legally reap enormous profits by asserting that criminality resides in the individual "contractors" they exploit.[20] Therefore, the detectives who detain and interrogate Elaine, on the chance that she may have information about the pyramid scheme's organizers, represent themselves as protectors of the socially vulnerable while they simultaneously threaten to deport her: "Elaine, you're involved in an illegal pyramid scheme, one that targets immigrants and low-income families. . . . You're a Hong Kong national, working in the United States on an expired visa. We can hold you as long as we want." While the state hypocritically sanctions "legal" corporate actors profiting from the exploitation of the low-income immigrant families that they purport to protect, they simultaneously discipline Elaine (the low-income immigrant) as an undocumented immigrant alien whose unethical and reckless personal greed is a threat to the public good.

Working people of color were similarly figured as "irresponsible" and "reckless" when they invested in suburban home ownership, which had epitomized bourgeois fiscal responsibility until the housing market collapsed in 2008.[21] Elaine's eviction from her foreclosed suburban home immediately follows the sales pitch in the film's opening scene, as yet another instance in a series of humiliating losses, as the family's secondhand furniture and belongings are moved to the sidewalk under the awkward enforcement of a white female sheriff (figure 6.3) Raymond is seen sitting on the family's abandoned couch on the street while glumly surveying their possessions in discarded plastic bags. The camera crosscuts to the Black neighbors who peek out from adjacent row houses, underscoring the multiracial character of this older suburb defined by aging, less expensive housing stock, vinyl-siding homes without garages, uneven asphalt sidewalks, crooked driveways, and overgrown vegetation. Absent are the visual tropes of abundance and security seen in most suburb films, with their manicured lawns, protecting fences, and expensive vehicles. Instead, Quincy is represented as a suburban space produced from struggle and uncertainty, where residents precariously acquire and lose lower-market homes while mired in debt and false promise. Significantly, this foreclosed home, which the children periodically visit and longingly hope to reoccupy, is shown as being quickly resold to a Black family.[22] The film represents home ownership, therefore, not as a secure foothold into the American Dream, but rather as an index of larger exploitative market processes, in which Black and immigrant borrowers constitute profit for a mortgage industry that aggressively marketed costly subprime loans since the 1990s.[23]

These lucrative "subprime lending and securitization practices were produced and legitimated by the financial industry," generating massive profits for a wide range of financial institutions and Wall Street and global

Figure 6.3. The Cheng family's eviction in *Children of Invention* (Tze Chun, Paramount 2009). Digital frame enlargement.

investors until declining home prices led to their collapse.[24] However, after the housing bubble burst in 2008, the neoliberal mantra of personal responsibility did not apply to the most powerful corporate actors in the United States economy, as state financial architects worked with Congress to pass the most costly government bailout in history, spending over $700 billion in public funds to rescue financial institutions from the economic ruin that their unregulated business practices created. As with most working-class Americans who suffered devastating and enduring economic losses after the collapse of the housing market, Elaine receives no state assistance in recovering her foreclosed home or lost equity, nor in finding alternate housing for herself and her children, leaving her with the "entrepreneurial solutions" of the free market.

State intervention only manifests for the film's characters in the form of state repression, and after Raymond suggests to his mother that they call the police when she describes the Vitafutures representatives as "thieves," the only law enforcement in the following scene is the sheriff who is there to enforce the family's eviction from their foreclosed home. State authorities do, however, manage to detain and threaten Elaine with deportation while she is also formally reported for child negligence. After two nights, Elaine is eventually released with the assistance of a white female public attorney, who disdainfully chastises her for not telling the detectives about her children with a paternalistic tone of condescension that makes Elaine squirm uncertainly in her chair: "We have a system in this country for a reason. It's there to protect you and to protect your family. You should have told them your kids were back at the house. They would have gone and gotten them." The discourse of the detectives is repeated, in which the very state authority that detains and threatens Elaine is simultaneously constituted as an institutional agent of protection and rescue, even as she is formally disciplined for parental negligence and berated as an incompetent and failed mother. Such protectionist state concern regarding child welfare is notably absent when banks foreclose on homes and the state enforces evictions that move belongings and children out onto the street, and the very "system" that is so assuredly invoked by the attorney is precisely organized around property rights, as well as citizenship, which are the very institutional forces of Elaine's dispossession and displacement.

The family's illegitimate relation to property and suburban space is borne out in their housing in an unfinished condo development, Marina Breeze, a converted large brick factory in Quincy's industrial waterfront, which is financed by Taiwanese capital. After her eviction, Elaine's former boss, Michael, who owns a real estate company, gives Elaine unofficial access to squat in a one bedroom model unit since the Taiwanese investors have temporarily run short of capital, warning her to just keep their presence invisible since the unfinished development "isn't zoned for living yet." Quincy is represented as a suburb in transition, emerging as a so-called ethnoburb with a rapidly growing Asian immigrant population and ethnic economy since the 1990s.[25] *Children of Invention* is one of the few suburb films to take stock of the complex and changing physical character of the American suburb, showing it as a site of instability and dislocation. Sociologist Wei Li defines Asian American suburbs as "global economic outposts," emphasizing the influx of Asian capital as generating crucial economic activity and opportunity for its Asian immigrant residents; however, the small one-bedroom condo with granite countertops is clearly never intended for people like Elaine's family.[26] While she can hope to make commissions by helping Michael sell the condos to gentrifying single professionals, Elaine's location in Quincy's Chinese ethnic economy is peripheral and highly precarious. Michael is the only character who is occasionally depicted as a resource for Elaine (although this may come with unwelcome romantic interest on his part), but she otherwise seems to exist at the margins of Quincy's social networks, where she endures the humiliation of multiple displacements in relative isolation.[27] Sociological discourses of suburban Chinatowns generally narrate the force of Asian capital and the development of ethnic community in rather celebratory terms, but this formerly middle-class Chinese American family is represented as increasingly invisible and displaced from the shifting Chinese suburban landscape, with Elaine blacking out the condo windows and deflating and hiding away her air mattress every morning.

The film's most powerful negation of narratives of Chinese American progress emerges in a brief scene with the children's elderly great-grandfather, who suffers from dementia and resides in a dilapidated, cramped apartment in Boston's historic Chinatown. At the moment when detectives are threatening to report Elaine to immigration authorities, the scene cuts to the great-grandfather's tiny, battered apartment, where we learn that the family's paternal side has a long history in the United States, going back to the mid-twentieth century.[28] The great-grandfather reminisces while looking at old photographs of a Chinese laundry storefront taped to his dresser mirror—"that was when we were in Atlanta, remember?"—as he mistakes Raymond for his own son (Raymond's grandfather), who he remembers as a young child: "I washed and you stood next to me on a little stool. You said, "Papa, I can help!" And then, when you had Charles, he stood on the *same* stool. It was good when Charles went to college, so many people at the graduation . . . took their hats. Whee! whee! whee!" The moving scene is highly disorienting, as it locates three generations of their family in the United States from the 1940s onward, while the multigenerational account of sons washing laundry invokes an earlier historical formation when Chinese Americans were relegated to feminized low-wage work in a racially segregated labor market while being barred from citizenship. Charles's college education, however, does not mark a seamless narrative of assimilation or prosperity, as Raymond and Tina's father has moved to Hong Kong where he complains of "programming sixteen hour days," while sending infrequent and partial child support to their mother. The Chengs are not confined to the ghettoized urban Chinatowns and labor markets of the previous century, but the family's multiple displacements in suburban Quincy and Elaine's "freedom" to work long hours in sales, which gain her nothing but the punitive attention of the state, underscore the limits of entrepreneurial agency in the new global economy. The old man's faded photographs and fragmented historical memories of gendered racialization from the mid-twentieth century disrupt neoliberal logics that would erase how the mother's various "problems" (as Asian alien, as single mother, and as exploited immigrant worker) are, in fact, political crises that are historically produced.

The most poignant element of *Children of Invention* is the perspective of the young Chinese American children who learn that the economic and familial stability that they yearn for in the suburbs can only be secured within the individuated domain of their own entrepreneurial efforts. In the absence of alternative logics that could generate conditions for social stability and emotional connection, the children's imaginings are constrained by the anxious rubrics of cost and scarcity that have defined their lives. The children's mutual dream, that Raymond will successfully innovate his family out of homelessness and economic precarity with one of his inventions, reproduces the entrepreneurial self that is the simultaneous expression of his mother's agency and economic desperation. However, the film also beautifully fractures a privatized discourse of "personal responsibility" with a story that discloses the violence of market and state forces that relentlessly threaten displacement and dispossession. Tze Chun's film quietly counters triumphalist developmental narratives of East to West, ghetto to suburb, and immigrant to citizen, which collapse under the weight of history as the material inequalities of racialized exploitation persist under various formations of global capitalist restructuring.

Conclusion

The representations of suburban space in these two Asian American films undercut celebratory discourses of Asian American achievement and socioeconomic mobility in distinct yet related ways. For Raymond and Tina, despite their long paternal history in the United States, parents who have gone to college, and a hard-working mother who remains highly invested in the American Dream, their family emerges on the losing side of the new global economy. However, the market epistemology that constitutes these characters' economic insecurity as a private matter of personal failure also generates the dehumanized relational norms that constitute profound alienation in the divergent context of utter affluence portrayed in *Better Luck Tomorrow*. Lin's characters, who are ideally positioned to emerge as neoliberalism's "winners," nonetheless disclose that the instrumentalist logics of achievement and rational self-interest, which govern their suburban high school, produce an utterly dysfunctional and alienated formation. Even in a celebratory film such as Mira Nair's *The Namesake* (2006), which sentimentally reclaims the suburb as the "authentic" space of the Indian immigrant family (and seamlessly produces their socioeconomic mobility), the narrative still underscores how that mobility comes at the cost of an almost unbearable suburban isolation, most heavily endured by the character of the immigrant mother.[29] It is striking that Asian American film, in its depictions of a broad range of class and ethnic formations, appears to so consistently imagine suburban life through terms of dysfunction, alienation, and loss. Significantly, neither *Better Luck Tomorrow* nor *Children of Invention* figure this alienation in terms of racial isolation within the suburbs, as both films feature a critical mass of Asian Americans, whether in the form of a pan-ethnic Asian American student body or a large Chinese immigrant community in Quincy or in Boston's Chinatown. However, the presence of Asian American community in these suburban narratives cannot compensate for the profoundly individuated conditions of privatization that define the characters' relations to their social worlds, which are governed by an instrumentalist logic that would reduce communities into markets and constitute subjects as isolated individuals of self-enterprise.

Notes

1. See Becky Nicolaides, "Introduction: Asian American Suburban History," *Journal of American Ethnic History* 34, no. 2 (Winter 2015): 5–17.

2. See Douglas Muzzio and Thomas Halper, "Pleasantville? The Suburb and Its Representation in American Movies," *Urban Affairs Review* 37, no. 4 (March 2002): 543–574.

3. David Harvey, *A Brief History of Neoliberalism* (Oxford: Oxford University Press, 2005), and Lisa Duggan, *The Twilight of Equality: Neoliberalism, Cultural Politics, and the Attack on Democracy* (Boston: Beacon Press, 2008).

4. Michel Foucault, *The Birth of Biopolitics: Lectures at the Collège de France, 1978–1979* (New York: Palgrave Macmillan, 2008), 226–227. See the neoliberal classic text, Gary Becker's *Human Capital* (1964), for the concept of the individual as "entrepreneur of the self" discussed by Foucault.

5. Thomas Lemke, "The Birth of Biopolitics: Michel Foucault's Lecture at the Collège de France on Neo-liberal Governmentality," *Economy and Society* 30, no. 2 (May 2001): 201.

6. Wendy Brown, "American Nightmare: Neoliberalism, Neoconservatism, and De-Democratization," *Political Theory* 54 (December 2006): 695.

7. Brown, "American Nightmare," 701.

8. See "Success Story of One Minority Group in U.S.," *U.S. News and World Report*, December 1966, reprinted in *Asian American Studies: A Reader*, ed. Jean Yu-Wen Shen and Min Song (New Brunswick, NJ: Rutgers University Press, 2000).

9. Victor Bascara, *Model Minority Imperialism* (Minneapolis: University of Minnesota Press, 2006), 4–5.

10. Representations of Asian American productivity as "robotic" or "machine-like" (lacking American ingenuity) were Cold War articulations that would be "officially" countered by an emergent "meta-national" Pacific Rim discourse of global coprosperity.

11. The college admission fraud cases of 2019 underscore the extremes of this instrumentalist, transactional ethos with wealthy parents paying bribes, falsifying documents, and purchasing test scores to secure admission for their children. However, long before this recent scandal, an extensive public discourse has proliferated throughout popular media and (academic research) regarding the trials and tribulations of the increasingly competitive processes of college applications.

12. For Foucault's discussion of the neoliberal displacement of the psychologized, anthropological construction of criminal pathology, see *Birth of Biopolitics*, 251–260.

13. Steve is a handsome Asian American rival who they unironically call "a rich motherfucker," and whose private school, BMW motorcycle and car, house with an expansive ocean view, and multiple Ivy School acceptance letters place him in a realm of privilege that is figured as transcending their upper-income suburb and its public high school.

14. The screenplay was originally set in the 1990s, but shot in the "present" period of the 2000s to facilitate easier and less costly production. Critics note the prescient resonance of the film's narrative in the wake of the foreclosure crisis that began in 2008.

15. Brown, "American Nightmare," 694.

16. Brown, "American Nightmare," 704.

17. Michael G. Pratt and José Rosa, "Transforming Work-Family Conflict into Commitment in Network Marketing Organizations," *Academy of Management Journal* 46 (August 2003): 397.

18. William Keep and Peter Vander Nat, "Multilevel Marketing and Pyramid Schemes in the United States," *Journal of Historical Research in Marketing* 6, no. 2 (2014): 194.

19. Keep and Nat, "Multilevel Marketing," 204. The average annual gross earnings of "eligible" Herbalife distributors in 2012 was $4,358 before expenses, "though there exists no independent way to determine the percentage of the other 406,949 distributors who tried but failed to become eligible" (204).

20. Keep and Nat, "Multilevel Marketing," 205. Herbalife, for instance, defends its corporate integrity by stating that "there can be no assurance that our distributors will . . . comply with our distributor policies and procedures."

21. Discussions of the subprime mortgage industry almost always position low-income unqualified borrowers with excessive access to credit as primary agents in the crash of the US housing market. Recent research revises this dominant narrative by demonstrating how middle-class high FICO borrowers (disproportionately involved in speculation and flipping) not only had the highest increases in mortgage default delinquency but their much larger mortgages translated into the highest dollar amounts. See Antoinette Shoar,

Manuel Adelino, and Felipe Severino, "Loan Originations and Defaults in the Mortgage Crisis: The Role of the Middle Class," *Review of Financial Studies* 29, no. 7 (July 2016): 1635–1670.

22. There is no significant African American population in Quincy, which highlights the film's intervention of positioning characters from a demographic that was most significantly exploited (and endured the most significant economic losses) by the subprime mortgage and finance industry.

23. Debbie Bocian, Keith Ernst, and Wei Li, *Unfair Lending: The Effect of Race and Ethnicity on the Price of Subprime Mortgages*, Center for Responsible Lending, May 2006, 1–52. https://www.responsiblelending.org/research-publication/unfair-lending-effect-race-and-ethnicity-price-subprime-mortgages.

24. Douglas S. Massey and Jacob Rugh, "Racial Segregation and the American Foreclosure Crisis," *American Sociological Review* 75, no. 5 (October 2010): 632.

25. Marilyn Johnson, "The Metropolitan Diaspora: New Immigrants in Greater Boston," in *What's New about the "New" Immigration?*, edited by Marilyn Halter, Marilynn S. Johnson, Katheryn P. Viens, and Conrad Edick Wright (New York: Palgrave Macmillan, 2014).

26. Wei Li, *Ethnoburb: The New Ethnic Community in Urban America* (Honolulu: University of Hawai'i Press, 2009). Li's research documents high levels of class stratification within ethnoburbs, yet tends to minimize its exploitative relations and highlights the development of ethnic community identity.

27. In "The Metropolitan Diaspora," Marilyn Johnson qualifies Wei Li's general claims regarding the ethnic economic role, noting that the more working-class demographic of Quincy's Asian American community in comparison to, say, Monterey Park or Silicon Valley, means that despite the convenience and social value of an ethnic enclave economy, that "long hours and commuting left new immigrants less connected to the Quincy community" (36).

28. Owing to China's status in World War II as a US ally, the Chinese Exclusion Act of 1882 was formally repealed in 1943 by the Magnuson Act, which established a nominal annual quota of 105 Chinese immigrants and permitted some who were already in the United States to become naturalized citizens.

29. While I didn't have space to analyze Nair's *The Namesake* (2006), it serves as an interesting counterpoint due to its redemptive and sentimental imagining of the family's suburban home, which works to facilitate the film's critique of an elitist, multicultural urbanism.

References

Bascara, Victor. *Model Minority Imperialism*. Minneapolis: University of Minnesota Press, 2006.

Becker, Gary. *Human Capital: A Theoretical and Empirical Analysis with Special Emphasis on Education*. 3rd ed. Chicago: University of Chicago Press, 2002.

Block, Paula, and Ken Brusic. *The Asians: Quincy's Newest Immigrants*. Quincy, MA: Patriot Ledger, 1989.

Bocian, Debbie G., Keith Ernst, and Wei Li. *Unfair Lending: The Effect of Race and Ethnicity on the Price of Subprime Mortgages*, Center for Responsible Lending, May 2006, 1–52. https://www.responsiblelending.org/research-publication/unfair-lending-effect-race-and-ethnicity-price-subprime-mortgages.

Brown, Wendy. "American Nightmare: Neoliberalism, Neoconservatism, and De-Democratization." *Political Theory* 54 (December 2006): 690–714.

Cheng, Wendy. *The Changs Next Door to the Díazes: Remapping Race in Southern California*. Minneapolis: University of Minnesota, 2013.

Dickenson, Greg. "The Pleasantville Effect: Nostalgia and the Visual Framing of (White) Suburbia." *Western Journal of Communication* 70 (September 2006): 212–233.

Duggan, Lisa. *Twilight of Equality: Neoliberalism, Cultural Politics, and the Attack on Democracy*. Boston: Beacon Press, 2008.

Foucault, Michel. *The Birth of Biopolitics: Lectures at the Collège de France, 1978–1979*. New York: Palgrave Macmillan, 2008.

Harvey, David. *A Brief History of Neoliberalism*. Oxford: Oxford University Press, 2005.

Henwood, Doug. *After the New Economy: The Binge and the Hangover That Won't Go Away*. New York: New Press, 2003.

Iceland, John, Daniel Weinberg, and Lauren Hughes. "The Residential Segregation of Detailed Hispanic and Asian Groups in the United States: 1980–2010." *Demographic Research* 31 (September 2004): 593–624.

Jackson, Kenneth. *Crabgrass Frontier: The Suburbanization of America*. Oxford: Oxford University Press, 1987.

Johnson, Marilyn. "The Metropolitan Diaspora: New Immigrants in Greater Boston." In *What's New about the "New" Immigration?*, edited by Marilyn Halter, Marilynn S. Johnson, Katheryn P. Viens, and Conrad Edick Wright, 23–49. New York: Palgrave Macmillan, 2014.

Keep, William, and Peter Vander Nat. "Multilevel Marketing and Pyramid Schemes in the United States." *Journal of Historical Research in Marketing* 6, no. 2 (2014): 188–210.

Lai, Zenobia, and Andrew Leong. "From the Community Lawyers' Lens: The Case of the Quincy 4 and Challenges to Securing Civil Rights for Asian Americans." *Asian American Law Journal* 15 (October 1992): 73–128.

Lemke, Thomas, "The Birth of Biopolitics: Michel Foucault's Lecture at the College de France on Neoliberal Governmentality." *Economy and Society* 30, no. 2 (May 2001): 190–207.

Li, Wei. *Ethnoburb: The New Ethnic Community in Urban America*. Honolulu: University of Hawai'i Press, 2009.

Lipsitz, George. *The Possessive Investment in Whiteness: How White People Profit from Identity Politics*. Philadelphia: Temple University Press, 1998.

Lowe, Lisa. *Immigrant Acts: On Asian American Cultural Politics*. Durham, NC: Duke University Press, 1996.

Massey, Douglas S., and Jacob Rugh. "Racial Segregation and the American Foreclosure Crisis." *American Sociological Review* 75, no. 5 (October 2010): 629–651.

McGirr, Lisa. *Suburban Warriors: The Origins of the New American Right*. Princeton, NJ: Princeton University Press, 2001.

Muzzio, Douglas, and Thomas Halper. "Pleasantville? The Suburb and Its Representation in American Movies." *Urban Affairs Review* 37, no. 4 (March 2002): 543–574.

Nicolaides, Becky. "Introduction: Asian American Suburban History." *Journal of American Ethnic History* 34, no. 2 (Winter 2015): 5–17.

Ong, Aiwha. *Neoliberalism as Exception: Mutations in Citizenry and Sovereignty*. Durham, NC: Duke University Press, 2006.

Pratt, Michael G., and José Rosa. "Transforming Work-Family Conflict into Commitment in Network Marketing Organizations." *Academy of Management Journal* 46 (August 2003): 395–418.

Schloemer, Ellen, Wei Li, Keith Ernst, and Kathleen Keest. *Losing Ground: Foreclosures in the Subprime Market and Their Cost to Homeowners*. December. Durham, NC: Center for Responsible Lending, 2006.

Singer, Audrey, Susan W. Hardwick, and Caroline B. Bretell, eds. *Twentieth-First Century Gateways: Immigration Incorporation in Suburban America*. Washington, DC: Brookings Institution, 2006.

Squires, Gregory, ed. *The Fight for Fair Housing*. New York: Routledge, 2018.

Tongson, Karen. *Relocations: Queer Suburban Imaginaries*. New York: NYU Press, 2011.

Wu, Frank, "From the Perpetual Foreigner to the New Model Minority to the New Transnational Elite: The Residential Segregation of Asian Americans." In *The Fight for Fair Housing*, edited by Gregory Squires, 133–150. New York: Routledge, 2018.

7

Inhabiting the Suburban Film

Arab American Narratives of Spatial Insecurity

AMY LYNN CORBIN

CINEMATIC AND TELEVISUAL representations of the suburbs frequently reinforce a long-standing cultural ideal of suburbia: areas of single-family homes with spacious yards, where middle-class, mostly white, people live spatially separated from work or commercial districts.[1] Since the 1970s, real suburbs have become more diverse in multiple ways, including income, density of housing, family type, and mixtures of commercial and residential zones.[2] While white Americans are still the majority, the suburbs are increasingly racially diverse, with the 2010 Census showing that 30 percent of suburban residents are Hispanic, non-Hispanic Asian, or non-Hispanic Black (using the Census's categories).[3] Note, however, that because the United States government does not consider "Arab" to be a race, there is no Census information about Arab American residential patterns. This literal invisibility on the United States Census points to the complicated history of Arab immigrants assimilating into America, including the way this group has pursued the American Dream of suburban dwelling, a path of assimilation disrupted by tense United States relations with the Arab world starting in the 1970s.

Two recent films—*Towelhead* (Ball, 2007) and *Amreeka* (Dabis, 2009)—have made important contributions to the task of diversifying suburban imagery. They examine how notions of immigrant assimilation and economic prosperity play out in the specific context of the Arab American experience after the first Gulf War (1990–91) and the terrorist attacks on September 11, 2001. By tracking the way that common motifs of the suburban film are both imitated and transformed by Arab American narratives, viewers can both learn more about the particular experiences of Arab Americans and interrogate the way that the American Dream of material comfort and social integration is intertwined with suburban living, and how both of these goals are predicated on racial (in)visibility. This chapter tracks three recurrent themes in suburban film—the desire to socially conform, the isolation of the nuclear family, and teenage alienation—to demonstrate how *Towelhead* and *Amreeka* leverage these themes to offer culturally specific insights.

Towelhead is based on a novel by Alicia Erian, an American writer whose father was Egyptian, and directed by Alan Ball, who wrote the screenplay for the suburban classic *American Beauty* (Mendes, 1999) and created the HBO series *Six Feet Under* (2001–05). Ball's dark sensibility and interest in the perversity of behavior hidden behind serene suburban exteriors is evident in *Towelhead*, which follows Jasira (Summer Bishil), a thirteen-year-old girl sent to live with her strict Lebanese father, Rifat (Peter Macdissi), in the suburbs of Houston. She suffers emotional abuse by Rifat, and then sexual abuse by a white neighbor. The film's blended authorship requires us to view it as a culturally hybrid text, and one that was viewed with suspicion by some Arab American cultural groups, which critiqued its use of an ethnic slur without tackling anti-Arab sentiment in a meaningful way.[4]

Amreeka is a lower-budget film that is more easily tied to a single "author": Palestinian American writer/director Cherien Dabis. It is loosely based on her family's experience during the first Gulf War, when her physician father suffered a massive decrease in patients due to anti-Arab prejudice in a rural Ohio community that had formerly embraced him. The doctor in the film, Nabeel Halaby (Yussuf Abu-Warda), is the brother-in-law of the main character, Muna Farah (Nisreen Faour), a Palestinian mother, and her son, Fadi (Melkar Muallem), who come to Illinois to live with her sister and brother-in-law. *Amreeka* depicts the impact of anti-Arab prejudice as well as the economic struggles of immigrants in a tone both lighter and more sincere than *Towelhead*.

Amreeka's setting, a small town near Chicago, begs the question of defining the term "suburbia." While the suburbs literally refer to a residential community economically attached to a larger city, many also include aspects like neighborhood design or lifestyle patterns as part of their definition. For suburban scholars Becky M. Nicolaides and Andrew Wiese, the key principle is "decentralization," which means that some areas within municipal boundaries of a city may still feel like a suburb.[5] "Decentralization" makes sense as a defining quality for those interested in the *culture* of suburbia as depicted in fictional narratives, since having the financial resources to own a stand-alone home with a yard often enables access to high quality schools, a neighborhood that feels spacious with relatively little street activity, and family life that focuses on the private home and the yard. In one sense, it is beside the point to say that these fictional representations do not match the increasingly diverse residential patterns and economies of the suburbs. While this is an accurate critique, the traditional image of suburbia continues to dominate fictional narratives precisely because these narratives are using their settings to explicitly visualize white middle-class American ideals—not realities. A small town setting like *Amreeka*'s functions as suburban because it demonstrates the characters' desires for upscale housing, professional jobs, and the ability to be treated with respect by white residents. As David Coon puts it, the suburbs "should be analyzed less as a physical space and more as an idea, a way of life, or a state of mind," particularly one that embodies ideals about the American Dream.[6]

Similar to a genre, suburban films operate by drawing on an established set of themes and visual motifs, with newer films in dialogue with the older ones. Suburban films featuring people of color are responding to the more common white suburban films in a manner similar to Jane Gaines's theorization of the way that silent-era race films "inhabited" rather than "imitated" white Hollywood genre films. While some of these genre films, she argues, could be accused of simply substituting Black performers for white ones, this argument "misses the way in which an all-black cast performance of a white dramatic vehicle also radically alters the meaning of the original."[7] She calls this a "semiotics of substitution" in which "the result is an ensemble effect in which every character alters the meaning not only of the narrative but produces a slight shift in the system of meaning itself so that race movies are always the same but different, and different because they are white-not."[8] *Amreeka* and *Towelhead* achieve a similar effect by taking themes, imagery, and character relations that are staples of the white suburban film and adding layers of meaning specific to the cultural and political experience of Arab Americans.

Assimilation and Racialization in Post-9/11 America

The equation of the suburbs with safety is racially contingent, as revealed by scholarship on the dangers African Americans faced in so-called sundown towns or sundown suburbs.[9] Arab Americans, because of their ambiguous racial classification in the United States, have experienced both the safety of assimilating into white suburbia and the trauma of being harassed in places they felt to be safe. This precarious position requires an understanding of both racial classifications and immigration histories.

In the nineteenth century, Arab immigrants to the United States were often racially classified as "Caucasian" (i.e., white), but in the early 1900s, anti-immigrant sentiment temporarily led to reclassification as "Asian," therefore justifying limits on immigration and naturalization via the Immigration Act of 1924.[10] Arab immigrants fought to reclaim their "Caucasian" status, and between World War I and World War II most "passed" for white and their descendants assimilated into American society. Their assimilation was aided by the fact that many of these earlier immigrants were Christian, anglicized their names, and hid their ethnic origins. As subsequent generations reached middle-class status, they made the journey from city to suburbs, following the path of other white ethnic groups.[11] Significant numbers also directly settled in smaller cities or suburbs like Toledo, Ohio; Dearborn, Michigan; Cedar Rapids, Iowa; Quincy, Massachusetts; and Rochester, New York.[12]

While the United States Census still does not recognize "Arab" as a race, a complex process some scholars have compared to racialization has taken place in which many Arab and Muslim Americans are "othered" when their identities are visible due to factors including skin color, accented English, and outward signs of Muslim faith. The combined forces of the 1967 Arab-Israeli War, the United States' increasing interventions in the Middle East in support of Israel, and a growing sense of Arab nationalism as an anti-imperialist stance led many of the more recent immigrants to assert a pan-ethnic identity as Arab American.[13] The first Gulf War, the September 11 attacks, and the later wars in Iraq and Afghanistan all made the United States a more hostile climate for

Arabs, Muslims, and Middle Easterners, three distinct groups that many other Americans simply conflated with "enemy." In contemporary times, many Arab Americans do not feel "white," but are in a liminal space of "white but not quite."[14]

Research indicates that, after 9/11, a majority of Arab Americans and Muslim Americans felt "unsafe and insecure in the United States."[15] The feeling of insecurity is most extreme in places that are white-dominated; one ethnographic study of Arabs and Muslims in the metropolitan Chicago area found that suburban shopping centers and malls were frequently named as the places where people felt the most unsafe and harassed, through stares and insults. One female interviewee said, "Soccer moms scare me the most."[16] Because of the gap between the popular image of suburbia as a protected environment in which to raise a family and the reality of Arab Americans' unofficial racialization, the suburbs become a meaningful location in which to stage Arab American stories of spatial insecurity. *Towelhead* and *Amreeka* both depict families with the economic means to own houses in middle-class neighborhoods. Yet they are faced with a sense of anxiety about belonging that transcends the typical white suburban character's apprehension about being accepted by their neighbors (a proxy for belonging in the middle class).

Amreeka compares Nabeel's profession as a doctor with Muna's difficulty finding a job to illustrate economic precarity. Muna is unable to get a job in banking, her profession when she lived in Palestine, and so begins to work at a White Castle hamburger joint (figure 7.1). She

Figure 7.1. Muna (Nisreen Faour) working at White Castle in *Amreeka* (Cherien Dabis, National Geographic/Imagenation Abu Dhabi, 2009). Digital frame enlargement.

goes to great lengths to hide her place of employment from her family because she is ashamed of its low status. Instead of performing affluence to her neighbors, Muna must perform it to her family. (In contrast, consider the way that Lester [Kevin Spacey] in *American Beauty* defiantly takes a fast food job as a way to rebel against his wife's obsession with socioeconomic status.) Dabis employs the symbolism of White Castle, and its kitschy conflation of cheap food with its "castle" name, to signify the service economy that operates within the "white collar" suburbs. The White Castle restaurant is next to the bank in which Muna pretends to work, and the establishing shot of the two buildings is deliberately framed so that the gray parking lot with many empty spaces takes up the bottom two-thirds of the frame. This composition, along with the washed-out color palette of the two buildings, combines to give a sense of the generic commercial strips found throughout suburbia. Yet *Amreeka* partially "redeems" White Castle by turning it into a space of community, as Muna teaches Arabic words to a teenage fellow employee with piercings and dyed blue hair.

Muna's stress over her entry-level wages is initially contrasted with the material comfort evident in her sister and brother-in-law's home. But after Dr. Halaby loses patients due to the anti-Arab prejudice that followed the September 11, 2001 attacks, the previously well-to-do family faces financial problems as well. Financial insecurity is paired with worries about physical safety when the family gets threatening letters and phone calls that link them erroneously to Saddam Hussein. Dr. Halaby's marriage to Muna's sister, Raghda (Hiam Abbass), is tested by fights over whether to move, and he starts sleeping in the basement, spending his insomnia-fraught nights watching Arabic-language news channels, an experience likened to an "internment of the psyche."[17] The family's shock over having made a home in a community where they now feel unsafe and unwelcome illustrates the multiple types of anxiety experienced by Arab Americans, endowing the suburban trope of insecurity over belonging with an added layer of cultural politics. *Amreeka* has very few shots of the neighborhood in which the family lives and there is no sense of their immediate neighbors. The hostile racialization they face is anonymous and therefore more threatening.

Towelhead dramatizes Rifat and Jasira's racialization in a more directly confrontational manner, through their interactions with a white Army reservist and his family who live next door. The Vuoso family attempt to welcome them to the neighborhood by coming over with a pie, but their barely disguised prejudice overwhelms their attempts to be friendly.

Evelyn (Carrie Preston) speaks with a heavy Texas drawl and overper-forms politeness and Travis (Aaron Eckhart) represents the United States military, anti-Arab prejudice, and ultimately sexual predation. When Rifat serves them coffee, Evelyn awkwardly says "what tiny coffee cups . . . and no handles! How unusual!" while Travis can barely contain his hostility. Ball uses a characteristically stylized low angle at the beginning of the scene to underscore the discomfort. Following this introduction, Rifat encourages a reluctant Jasira into babysitting the Vuoso family's son, Zack (Chase Ellison), who repeatedly calls her "towelhead" and other names. The dramatic tension of the film comes from Travis's "grooming" and sexual exploitation of Jasira. In the context of the Maroun family's inse-cure place in the suburbs, however, it is notable that the threat comes from much more intimate relationships than the disembodied threats to the family in *Amreeka*.

Rifat Maroun's home in a cookie-cutter Western-style suburb signifies the middle-class lifestyle he has earned as a NASA engineer. But economic security does not bring Rifat a social or psychological sense of belonging despite his best efforts to assimilate. He reacts to the perception that his neighbors are scrutinizing him by looking down on American culture but still desperately seeks American approval. A satiric sequence shows him instructing Jasira on the need to illuminate one's American flag at night, proclaiming that he is more patriotic than their white neighbor who takes his flag down at night. The father's performance of patriotism is a riff on the familiar suburban motif of performing harmony and perfection for one's neighbors—recall Carolyn's (Annette Bening) fixation over gardening and home décor in *American Beauty*, or Beth's (Mary Tyler Moore) obses-sion with masking her family's unhappiness in *Ordinary People* (Redford, 1980). But here, the motif is used to comment on the hostile climate toward Arab Americans that compels him to perform patriotism. The scene is a microcosm of a documented response of Arab Americans to post-9/11 threats: to exaggerate their American identity through visible signs like flags that would protect them against harassment.[18] Such scenes reference the recurring suburban struggle to conform, but dramatically increase the stakes since the characters are viewed not as individuals, but as representatives of a group facing increasing hostility nationwide.

Significantly, however, the families in both films are Christian. Without head coverings, beards, or any other markers of religion, they would seem to "pass" more easily. The fact that they don't points to the American tendency to conflate "Arab" and "Muslim" identities, at the same time as the religion of Islam has become "racialized" in the United

States.[19] Both films contain scenes in which the main characters try to educate others (and by extension non-Arab American viewers) about Arab religious diversity. In *Amreeka*, the school principal, Stan (Joseph Ziegler), describes the harassment Fadi is facing at school by saying to Muna: "They hear about one Muslim extremist, and suddenly all Muslims are extremists." "We are not Muslim, even," Muna replies, and after he apologizes, she continues: "It doesn't matter, we are minority here, we are minority there." After repeatedly being called "towelhead" by young Zack Vuoso, Jasira exclaims: "Stupid! My dad doesn't wear a towel on his head. He's a Christian just like everyone else in Texas!" These scenes make visible the way that these characters get as little security from sharing the dominant religion of the United States as they do from their middle-class status.

It is striking that the two most prominent narrative films about Arab Americans in the suburbs both feature Arab Christians, when the majority of immigrants from that part of the world have been Muslim for decades. On the most literal level, this is obviously rooted in the autobiographical experiences of their creators. However, it also has to be questioned in light of the types of films that are more likely to be funded. While it might seem that the film industry would reinforce dominant tropes about Arab Americans and therefore be more inclined to fund Muslim stories, the narratives about Christian characters who are mistaken for Muslim sets up sympathy for misunderstood victims of prejudice—a common melodramatic strategy of the mainstream liberal film—and implies that they are more like "the rest of America" than they seem.

Another trope of cinematic suburbia is the depiction of individual characters who hide their psychological alienation under a veneer of success and confidence. In the Arab American context, this has important resonance with racial liminality and "passing" as middle-class Americans. Rifat exhibits an obsessive need to show his superiority over Americans he considers crude. He is polite to their faces and then insults them behind closed doors; his home décor signals elegance through marble and crystal chandeliers; and he seems primarily interested in his Greek girlfriend because she is "sophisticated . . . not a peasant like American women." Rifat performs benevolent fatherhood when he and Jasira are with other people, but privately he verbally (and sometimes physically) abuses her, as well as vents his rage at politics or discrimination. Rifat's characterization echoes a number of fictional suburban fathers who are insecure about their masculinity, but with a distinct adaptation. Instead of a white man who wants to prove he is still physically strong, to guard against stereotypes of white collar "softness" (consider the men in *The Swimmer* [Perry, 1968], *Deliverance* [John Boorman, 1972], and *American Beauty*), Rifat believes his dual experience in Middle Eastern and American cultures makes him more intelligent and cosmopolitan than his neighbors.

Suburban Isolation

In both *Towelhead* and *Amreeka*, the families appear to be the only Arab Americans in the area (figure 7.2). Additionally, the neighborhoods and schools are predominantly white, which makes their racialization all the more pointed. The situations of these two fictional families, rooted in the life stories of their creators, contrast with a more common immigrant phenomenon, which is to cluster together in specific neighborhoods or towns. While immigrant neighborhoods in major cities have long been visible in the United States, suburbs with prominent ethnic populations— what has recently been termed an "ethnoburb"[20]—have little visibility in journalism or fiction. About *Amreeka*'s setting, Dabis has explained:

> The reason for my film's setting is because I grew up in a small rural Ohio town of 10,000 people, in a family of Arab immigrants. Every time I would watch an immigrant film, I was struck that it was always immigrants in a big city. I found

Figure 7.2. Jasira (Summer Bishil) waits for the school bus in her suburban neighborhood in *Towelhead* (Alan Ball, Indian Paintbrush, 2007). Digital frame enlargement.

it really surprising that there had never been an immigrant
film set in the middle of the country. It seemed to me that if
you put immigrants in a small town their experience is that
much more dramatic, that much more heightened, because
they are really outsiders. There is no getting around the fact
that they don't belong there. So I wanted to not just reflect
my own experience, but to show a side to the immigrant story
that had never really been depicted before.[21]

Here, Dabis points to the symbolism of depicting a culturally isolated
family, instead of a family situated within an ethnoburb, which spatially
renders the psychological sense of outsider-ness felt by many immigrants
no matter where they live. The cliché of suburban anomie and isolation, represented by wide, empty streets and large lawns that separate
neighbors, can here be used to express the more profound isolation of
nationality and culture.

Towelhead leverages its setting (diegetically the Houston suburbs,
though filmed in California) to more deliberate expressionistic effect. Rifat
and Jasira's home is in a new development with single-story houses that
sprawl out horizontally and just a few young trees. Ball uses numerous
low-angle wide shots to emphasize the flatness of the landscape; the
colorlessness is literal, with white and beige stucco dominating and a
desaturated palette that drains the color out of the yards and sky. When
Rifat returns from picking up Jasira at the airport, he makes a point of
telling her that he bought this house so that she wouldn't have to go to
school in the city. When she asks why, he says "because suburban schools
are better—everyone knows that." This dialogue speaks to the way that
Rifat has internalized widely held American beliefs about the link between
place of residence and children's success. Rifat mechanistically tries to
imitate the suburban ideal, yet it is painfully clear that he doesn't provide
Jasira with the necessary tools to deal with the inevitable exclusion and
hostility she encounters in those so-called excellent schools.

Dabis's choice to set Amreeka in a small town near Chicago also
allows her to reference the sizable Palestinian community in Chicago
and its suburbs, thus providing a comparison between being isolated
in the small town with the cultural connections available in the city.
While it is difficult to get an accurate count (due to the fact that Arab
heritage is not classified as a race on the United States Census and that
people of Palestinian origin are often classified by their place of birth,
which is often another country), the metropolitan Chicago area may be

home to the largest Palestinian community in the United States.[22] One scene in *Amreeka* has Muna and Raghda quietly talking in a bedroom about being homesick, ending with a tight shot around Raghda's face and her words "You know what we should do?" The question is left open and is followed by an abrupt cut to a storefront façade, its signage a mix of Arabic and English. The soundtrack features loud instrumental Arabic music and no dialogue. There is a spatial disorientation, caused by the visual and aural contrasts between the two scenes, and a viewer unfamiliar with Arab American neighborhoods in Chicago would have no idea where the edit had moved the film. However, there is a sense of cultural *orientation*: viewers who know the neighborhood would likely recognize it as the montage of storefronts goes on (shot by a shaky, low-angle camera to simulate the sisters' view from their car window), and diegetically, Raghda has taken Muna to a place where she feels at home. The sequence ends with them walking through an Arab food store, emphasizing the importance of food to diasporic memories. However, this sequence is followed by a cut to another interior of the family's home, signaling that this brief day trip was an aberration in the family's life. The escape to the city is a fixture in several prominent white suburban films—including *Ferris Bueller's Day Off* (Hughes, 1986), *Welcome to the Dollhouse* (Solondz, 1995), and *Disturbia* (Caruso, 2007)—and there it often figures as a site of adolescent rebellion. To leave the suburbs for the city is to reject conformist values and embrace lifestyles that deviate from the moral authority of the nuclear family. The scene from *Amreeka* alters this narrative trope by instead showing the city as a potential location for cultural community, all but impossible in the suburbs.

This scene is an anomaly in *Amreeka*, and there is no parallel scene in *Towelhead*. Both films imply that their characters are anchored in suburbia, for better or for worse, and end with scenes of human connection with overtones of cultural integration. *Amreeka*'s ending is a playful, uplifting depiction of cultural hybridity. The two branches of the family, along with the school principal, Stan Novatski (Joseph Ziegler), who is of Polish Jewish origin, crowd into the Halaby's van to go to an Arabic restaurant. On the way, the kids eat cheeseburgers from White Castle and the car stereo plays Arabic music. The adults switch between English with their kids and Stan, and Arabic with each other. Raghda, the one who misses Palestine the most, tries a burger and deems it "okay," which is meant to suggest her growing acceptance of American culture through fast food. An exterior long-shot shows the van driving through an empty, flat street, characteristic of a small Midwest town, and then cuts to an interior shot of a restaurant looking out the glass door at the family's van pulling into the parking lot. The film ends with a montage of the group at dinner, sharing their cuisine, hooka pipe, and Palestinian dances with Stan. It offers a utopian, multicultural vision of the American Midwest that contrasts with the prejudice and hardship the family has undergone.

The tension is high as *Towelhead* draws to a close: Jasira has confided in a sympathetic neighboring couple, Melina (Toni Collette) and Gil Hines (Matt Letscher), about her sexual encounters with Travis, and they are helping her summon the courage to tell her father. This couple represents a version of the counterculture in the suburbs. Melina is open-minded about female sexuality and helps Jasira educate herself in a way that her conservative father never would. Gil served in the Peace Corps in Yemen and speaks Arabic, so when he stands up to Rifat, he speaks in Arabic. Melina and Gil Hines are characterized in this manner to make sure that the Vuoso family's ignorance and dysfunction does not stand for all Americans. This opens up *Towelhead* and its source novel to the critique of "self-orientalism," since Rifat, representing traditional Lebanese culture, is constructed as "an irrational and violent Arab man wielding his power over an innocent and caged virgin," who is ultimately rescued by liberal, feminist white Americans.[23] The film ends with Jasira watching Melina give birth, a redemptive moment that connects Jasira to another functional family and the idea of new life.

The choice not to set these films in Arab American communities or neighborhoods means that the characters live the experience of immigrant isolation on a very personal level, not just as citizens in a minority group of a nation. The endings further advance the idea that a solution to this isolation is to join the "melting pot" of American culture, to find connections with others across culture, ethnicity, and religion, rather than creating ethnic enclaves within the nation.

Teenage Alienation and Rebellion

A final significant way these films "inhabit" the suburban film is by endowing the recurrent suburban motif of adolescent alienation and rebellion with a specific narrative about finding a racial and political place in America. In many white suburban films, initiated by *Rebel Without a Cause* (Ray, 1956) and continuing in films like *Heathers* (Lehmann, 1988) and *Donnie Darko* (Kelly, 2001), teenagers chafe at the conformity and hypocrisy they associate with their parents' materialism, obsession with an image of perfection, and inability to act authentically.[24] *Amreeka* and *Towelhead* position their teenage characters' conflicts with their parents as a result of the older generation not understanding that their rules and values are of little use in helping the younger generation navigate the anti-Arab sentiment they face in school and in their social lives. Both Jasira and Fadi go through frequent humiliations like having their names mispronounced or being mocked for their family's origins outside the United States.

The Maroun family's cultural isolation overlaps with the distance between Jasira and her father, whose discomfort with his daughter's independence and attractiveness results in her vulnerability to sexual exploitation. Both the novel and film exhibit a complicated sense of Jasira's sexuality—on the one hand, seeming to support her right to explore her desires but on the other hand clearly depicting an abusive relationship with Travis in which the adult man takes advantage of Jasira's loneliness and sexual curiosity. To what extent is Travis's predation of her based on his sexual desire for any teenage girl versus a desire for a girl whose beauty represents an otherness that he seems to both despise and seek? And to what extent is Jasira's vulnerability similar to that of many teenage girls growing up in a culture that sexualizes their bodies, as opposed to her vulnerability being heightened because she so desperately wants to fit into American culture? Or does she seek out sexual encounters as a way to rebel against her father's culturally conservative approach toward female sexuality? The film does not provide answers to these questions, and this ambiguity means that it is not clear to what extent the story is a portrait of growing up culturally marginalized versus a sexual coming-of-age story.

While not denying these problematic elements, I would suggest another way to interpret Jasira's exploration of sexuality and resistance to her father's authority in the context of the suburban film narrative. If the second generation in immigrant families is often the site of conflicting cultural values (culture of origin versus host country), then suburban narratives about immigrant families can adapt the common suburban trope of the rebellious teenager to offer commentary not just on generational conflict but on negotiations over assimilation and cultural values. In one study of Arab Americans in Dearborn, Michigan, the teenagers generally saw gender roles and expectations as the most important division between their family's culture and the dominant culture.[25] The girls saw themselves torn between more permissive guidelines about dating and sexual activity in the wider society and their parents' very stringent rules, as well as the sense that the family's reputation depends on their choices. Thus, on the one hand Jasira's exploration of her sexuality represents a domain of her behavior she can control and can use as a weapon against her father. On the other hand, her rebellion comes in the form of making herself available to an abuser and fantasizing about herself cavorting with *Playboy* models in imaginary fashion shoots—both scenarios representing the constraining sexualization American women are subject to. When Travis flatters her by praising her beauty, she is vulnerable to his abuse because she feels rejected by both parents and stigmatized at school. Her fantasy photo shoots depict topless blonde women beckoning to her, and in one, she joins them on a golf course (these scenes reflect the addition of Ball's distinct style to Erian's narrative, as they are similar in tone to the fantasy scenes in *American Beauty* and echo that film's suggestion that "deviant" sexuality is a form of liberation from the repression and conformity of the suburbs). The mise-en-scène thus blends white-centered standards of beauty with a pastime that embodies suburban landscape and wealth. So, while the film can absolutely be critiqued for both its aestheticization of sexual abuse and its failure to interrupt Orientalist narratives, it should also be seen as an example of how formulaic suburban narratives can be appropriated to express complicated intersectional experiences. Jasira represents a young, ethnically othered girl who is not just caught between her father's strict Lebanese culture and a more permissive American culture—but her pursuit of her individuality and rebellion against her father sends her to dark places of female objectification, looking for validation as both an adolescent and an othered immigrant.

The teenagers in both films respond to the prejudice they face in school by claiming their identities as racial others and forming bonds with two African American classmates, though the friends' conversations are more overtly political in *Amreeka* than in *Towelhead*. The two African American young men express solidarity with the Arab American teenagers who are newly experiencing racism in America. In *Towelhead*, Thomas (Eugene Jones) calls Jasira a "sand n----r" after several white boys make fun of her Lebanese ancestry. Immediately afterward, however, Thomas apologizes, and it is evident he has made the connection between the racism he has experienced and what Jasira is going through. The next scene of these characters together is a family dinner in which Thomas's parents are strikingly normal in contrast to the dysfunctional adults Jasira is surrounded with. After Thomas's parents head upstairs, Thomas and Jasira have their first sexual encounter. It is in pointed contrast to Travis's predatory relationship with Jasira: Thomas touches her and brings her to orgasm without undressing her or having penetrative sex. He is depicted as gentle and loving, afterward helping her get tampons and razors from his mother because Rifat forbids Jasira to buy these items. But then Rifat comes to Thomas's house to pick her up early and when Thomas greets him politely, Rifat silently glares at him, not even deigning to get out of the car. When Jasira gets into the car, her dreamy expression falls instantly when she sees her father's anger: "You're not to see that boy again. You did not give me the full information so I could make a proper decision. Do you understand what I am referring to?" "I think so." "Good, because if you continue to visit that boy's house, no one will respect you."

This exchange makes it clear that Rifat considers African Americans off limits for his daughter. His attitude tracks with the attitudes of many earlier Arab immigrants to the United States who desired assimilation and the privileges of whiteness. In this case, assimilation means he has internalized white American racism and believes such attitudes will further his goal of belonging in American suburbia. However, Thomas's kindness and the warmth of his parents' middle-class home (emphasized by the lights of the Christmas tree and the relaxed conversation at dinner) renders the one visible African American family in the community to be the best adjusted. Most viewers will see Rifat's attempts to raise his status in American society and interpret it as exactly the opposite.

In *Amreeka*, Fadi is being harassed at school by a group of white boys and finds the misspelled phrase "Al Kada" written on his car. The scene cuts to Fadi, his cousin Salma (Alia Shawkat), and James (Andrew Sannie), her African American boyfriend, standing outside the car in an empty Midwestern field, smoking a joint and talking about how to deal with the bullying (figure 7.3). James insists that Fadi must toughen up

Figure 7.3. Fadi (Melkar Muallem), with his cousin Salma (Alia Shawkat) and classmate James (Andrew Sannie), viewing anti-Arab graffiti on his car in *Amreeka* (Cherien Dabis, National Geographic/Imagenation Abu Dhabi, 2009). Digital frame enlargement.

and proceeds to direct him to change his appearance, his walk, and his attitude to mimic African American youth culture. The implication is that James has figured out how to navigate the mostly white school and is transferring his cultural "armor" to Fadi. This impression is solidified when the trio puncture the tires of the white boys' car in the White Castle parking lot, and nondiegetic hip-hop music plays as they drive away. Fadi's defense against post- 9/11 racism is found through an alliance with African American urban youth culture.

The suggestion (implicit in *Towelhead* and explicit in *Amreeka*) that one solution to anti-Arab prejudice is to make common cause with the most visibly oppressed group in American society, African Americans, puts these teenagers at odds with their parents who aspire to "be white" or to a middle-class lifestyle that is often coded as white. Neither film is explicitly broadcasting a message that solidarity with groups classified as racial minorities in the United States is a political choice, yet this narrative similarity undoubtedly reflects the centrality of questions over racial status and "passing" in contemporary Arab American lives. The growth of anti-Arab prejudice and global senses of Arab identity has meant that growing numbers of Arab Americans are rejecting the possibility of passing, even if phenotypically possible, for the sake of political advocacy. Some activists and intellectuals have advocated that part of their movement is to advocate for official governmental classification as a racial group.[26] Among actors, it is often seen as a political choice to identify as Arab American and to accept roles that are culturally specific rather than "generic white" roles.[27] The debate over whether to pass or to join other groups that are labeled (and oppressed by their labeling) is inflected by class position, as we see with Rifat's attempts to put himself near the top of the social hierarchy and the way that Dr. Halaby achieves acceptance as an upper-middle-class professional until he is racialized post-9/11. The teenage characters are less concerned with guarding their economic and class privilege, and more with finding identities that will help them navigate the exclusion and prejudice they are experiencing. So it seems natural that the narratives use these characters as ways to explore the racialization of Arab Americans and the possible outcome of joining the pan-racial group now known as "people of color" in the United States.

Conclusion

In their differing ways, *Towelhead* and *Amreeka* redeem their suburban landscapes from hegemonic whiteness. They celebrate ethnic diversity and cultural exchange within the suburbs, rather than showing characters escaping to urban areas to find these values. The security and sense of belonging that the suburbs seem to promise only white, middle-class, American-born families are given—at least partially—to the Arab American families. But importantly, this security comes by integrating with Americans of other backgrounds, not by finding an ethnically Arab community within which to live. Thus, the films' endings are quite different than the reality of life for many recent immigrants, who live in urban neighborhoods or ethnoburbs with numerous other families from the same country or ethnic group. So for the many ways that these films add welcome diversity to images of the cinematic suburbs, they reinforce the idea that people of color are isolated in the suburbs, rather than portraying the existence of suburban immigrant communities.

Still, these films exhibit the nuanced ways that films can "inhabit" the typical suburban film, by employing much of the standard iconography, character relations, and narrative scenarios that typify the suburban film, while altering the meaning of these tropes to depict the ways in which Arab American characters experience the suburbs differently from white Americans. The pleasure of economic security and materially comfortable housing is more fraught when income is lost or verbal harassment invades the protective space of the home. Narratives of teenagers trying to find their identities, to fit in as well as be true to themselves, are suffused with the struggles of immigrant teens against racist peers. Scenarios of families trying to keep up appearances and model a perfect life are altered when it is their ethnicity or patriotism that is questioned, rather than their marriage or psychological health. And the assumed whiteness of the suburbs is destabilized by characters whose own racial classification in America has fluctuated—including characters who aspire to be white but know they are not seen that way, and characters who bond with African Americans over a shared experience of being othered.

Notes

1. Becky M. Nicolaides and Andrew Wiese, "Introduction," in *The Suburb Reader*, ed. Becky M. Nicolaides and Andrew Wiese (New York: Routledge, 2006), 7.

2. Nicolaides and Wiese, "Introduction," 5.

3. Nancy A. Denton and Joseph R. Gibbons, "Twenty-First-Century Suburban Demography: Increasing Diversity yet Lingering Exclusion," in *Social Justice in Diverse Suburbs: History, Politics, and Prospects*, ed. Christopher Niedt (Philadelphia: Temple University Press, 2013), 20.

4. Gregg Kilday, "'Towelhead' Draws Protest," *Hollywood Reporter*, August 25, 2008.

5. Nicolaides and Wiese, "Introduction," 9.

6. David R. Coon, *Look Closer: Suburban Narratives and American Values in Film and Television* (New Brunswick, NJ: Rutgers University Press, 2014), 10. Roger Silverstone agrees, writing of the "suburban imaginary": Roger Silverstone, "Introduction," in *Visions of Suburbia*, ed. Roger Silverstone (New York: Routledge, 1997), 13.

7. Jane Gaines, *Fire and Desire: Mixed Race Movies in the Silent Era* (Chicago: University of Chicago Press, 2001), 129–30.

8. Gaines, *Fire and Desire*, 131.

9. Elizabeth A. Patton, "*Get Out* and the Legacy of Sundown Suburbs in Post-Racial America," *New Review of Film and Television Studies* 17, no. 3 (2019): 349–363.

10. Nadine Naber, "Ambiguous Insiders: An Investigation of Arab American Invisibility," *Ethnic and Racial Studies* 23, no. 1 (January 2000): 37–61; Michael Suleiman, "Introduction: The Arab Immigrant Experience," in *Arabs in America: Building a New Future*, ed. Michael Suleiman (Philadelphia: Temple University Press, 1999), 6–7.

11. Naber, "Ambiguous Insiders"; Louise A. Cainkar, *Homeland Insecurity: The Arab American and Muslim American Experience after 9/11* (New York: Russell Sage Foundation, 2009); Janice J. Terry, "Community and Political Activism among Arab Americans in Detroit," in *Arabs in America: Building a New Future*, 242, 246.

12. Gaby Semaan, "Arab Americans: Stereotypes, Conflict, History, Cultural Identity and Post 9/11," *Intercultural Communication Studies* 23, no. 2 (2014): 17–32.

13. Naber, "Ambiguous Insiders," 40–41.

14. Kristine Ajrouch, "Family and Ethnic Identity in an Arab-American Community," in *Arabs in America: Building a New Future*, 15.

15. Cainkar, *Homeland Insecurity*, 1.

16. Louise A. Cainkar, "Thinking Outside the Box: Arabs and Race in the United States," in *Race and Arab Americans before and after 9/11: From Invisible Citizens to Visible Subjects*, ed. Amaney Jamal and Nadine Naber (Syracuse, NY: Syracuse University Press, 2008), 77.

17. Heike Raphael-Hernandez, "'Yes, I Will Blow Up This Place, but First I Have My Coffee'—Representations of Arab Americans in Post-9/11 Films," in *Arab American Literature and Culture*, ed. Alfred Hornung and Martina Kohl (Heidelberg: Winter GmbH, 2012), 139.

18. Semaan, "Arab Americans," 26–27.

19. Naber, "Ambiguous Insiders," 52; Sarah Gualtieri, "Strange Fruit? Syrian Immigrants, Extralegal Violence and Racial Formation in the Jim Crow South," *Arab Studies Quarterly* 26, no. 3 (Summer 2004): 64–65.

20. Wei Li, *Ethnoburb: The New Ethnic Community in Urban America* (Honolulu: University of Hawai'i Press, 2009), 1.

21. Dennis West and Joan M. West, "Coming to Amreeka: An Interview with Cherien Dabis," *Cineaste* 35 (Winter 2009): 24.

22. Cainkar, *Homeland Insecurity*, 14.

23. Laila Amine, "Alicia Erian's Towelhead: The New Face of Orientalism in the US Ethnic Bildungsroman," *College Literature* 45, no. 4 (Fall 2018): 724–746.

24. On the origin of the teenage rebellion film, see Thomas Patrick Doherty, *Teenagers and Teenpics: The Juvenilization of American Movies in the 1950s* (Philadelphia: Temple University Press, 2002); Timothy Shary, *Teen Movies: American Youth on Screen* (London: Wallflower Press, 2005).

25. Ajrouch, "Family and Ethnic Identity in an Arab-American Community."

26. Naber, "Ambiguous Insiders," 56.

27. Michael Malek Najjar, "Acting Arab/Arab Acting: Reclaiming the Arab American Identity through Aesthetic Choices," in *Arab American Aesthetics: Literature, Material Culture, Film and Theatre*, ed. Therí A. Pickens (New York: Routledge, 2018), x.

References

Ajrouch, Kristine. "Family and Ethnic Identity in an Arab-American Community." In *Arabs in America: Building a New Future*, edited by Michael Suleiman, 129–139. Philadelphia: Temple University Press, 1999.

Amine, Laila. "Alicia Erian's Towelhead: The New Face of Orientalism in the US Ethnic Bildungsroman." *College Literature* 45, no. 4 (Fall 2018): 724–746.

Cainkar, Louise A. *Homeland Insecurity: The Arab American and Muslim American Experience after 9/11*. New York: Russell Sage Foundation, 2009.

———. "Thinking Outside the Box: Arabs and Race in the United States." In *Race and Arab Americans before and after 9/11: From Invisible Citizens to Visible Subjects*, edited by Amaney Jamal and Nadine Naber, 46–80. Syracuse, NY: Syracuse University Press, 2008.

Coon, David R. *Look Closer: Suburban Narratives and American Values in Film and Television*. New Brunswick, NJ: Rutgers University Press, 2014.

Denton, Nancy A., and Joseph R. Gibbons. "Twenty-First-Century Suburban Demography: Increasing Diversity yet Lingering Exclusion." In *Social Justice in Diverse Suburbs: History, Politics, and Prospects*, edited by Christopher Niedt, 13–30. Philadelphia: Temple University Press, 2013.

Doherty, Thomas Patrick. *Teenagers and Teenpics: The Juvenilization of American Movies in the 1950s*. Philadelphia: Temple University Press, 2002.

Gaines, Jane. *Fire and Desire: Mixed Race Movies in the Silent Era*. Chicago: University of Chicago Press, 2001.

Gualtieri, Sarah. "Strange Fruit? Syrian Immigrants, Extralegal Violence and Racial Formation in the Jim Crow South." *Arab Studies Quarterly* 26, no. 3 (Summer 2004): 63–85.

Kilday, Gregg. "'Towelhead' Draws Protest." *Hollywood Reporter*, August 25, 2008.

Naber, Nadine. "Ambiguous Insiders: An Investigation of Arab American Invisibility." *Ethnic and Racial Studies* 23, no. 1 (January 2000): 37–61.

Najjar, Michael Malek. "Acting Arab/Arab Acting: Reclaiming the Arab American Identity through Aesthetic Choices." In *Arab American Aesthetics: Literature, Material Culture, Film and Theatre*, edited by Therí A. Pickens. New York: Routledge, 2018.

Nicolaides, Becky M., and Andrew Wiese, eds. *The Suburb Reader*. New York: Routledge, 2006.

Patton, Elizabeth A. "*Get Out* and the Legacy of Sundown Suburbs in Post-Racial America." *New Review of Film and Television Studies* 17, no. 3 (2019): 349–363.

Raphael-Hernandez, Heike. "'Yes, I Will Blow Up This Place, but First I Have My Coffee'—Representations of Arab Americans in Post-9/11 Films." In *Arab American Literature and Culture*, edited by Alfred Hornung and Martina Kohl, 121–149. Heidelberg: Winter GmbH, 2012.

Semaan, Gaby. "Arab Americans: Stereotypes, Conflict, History, Cultural Identity and Post 9/11." *Intercultural Communication Studies* 23, no. 2 (2014): 17–32.

Shary, Timothy. *Teen Movies: American Youth on Screen*. London: Wallflower Press, 2005.

Silverstone, Roger. "Introduction." In *Visions of Suburbia*, edited by Roger Silverstone, 1–25. New York: Routledge, 1997.

Suleiman, Michael. "Introduction: The Arab Immigrant Experience." In *Arabs in America: Building a New Future*, edited by Michael Suleiman, 1–21. Philadelphia: Temple University Press, 1999.

Terry, Janice J. "Community and Political Activism among Arab Americans in Detroit." In *Arabs in America: Building a New Future*, edited by Michael Suleiman, 241–254. Philadelphia: Temple University Press, 1999.

West, Dennis, and Joan M. West. "Coming to Amreeka: An Interview with Cherien Dabis." *Cineaste* 35 (Winter 2009): 22–26.

8

Living in Liberty City

Triangulating Space and Identity in Barry Jenkins's *Moonlight* (2016)

PAULA J. MASSOOD

> One of the most important yet least known dimensions of Black expressive culture is its consistent preoccupation with place and power. Both canonized works of art and a variety of vernacular expressive practices in Black communities speak to the spatial aspects of racial identity.[1]
>
> —George Lipsitz

≈

A CIRCULAR CAMERA MOVEMENT travels over the faces of a group of boys gathered together to play an impromptu game of soccer in a lush green field, a train passing in the distance. The camera moves with the boys as they run, kick a makeshift ball made of rags, and playfully wrestle with each other, all to the melody of Mozart's

Vesperae Solennes de Confessore in C Major on the soundtrack. Soon, one boy is singled out by the camera; apart from the rest, he wanders away from the group before being joined by another boy. The camera tracks with them, circling the pair as they walk across the playing field before wrestling with each other and falling to the ground exhausted. After they rest, the pair say goodbye and run out of the frame in a long take long shot—the camera now still—with the sounds of their laughter still audible on the soundtrack.

This scene, from early in Barry Jenkins's *Moonlight* (2016), epitomizes a conundrum of the film as a whole and of the "cruel beauty" of its suburban Miami setting.[2] The playing field, with its green grass and verdant perimeter of palm trees and other foliage, appears idyllic and safe, the perfect place for a group of boys to play without adult supervision on a summer afternoon (figure 8.1). Yet, there is an underlying menace to the scene, because Chiron (or "Little" as he's called in this first section) has left the group because they are bullying him. Thus, his exit from the game is part choice and part a necessary act of survival. Kevin, the boy who joins him, embodies this duality as well; half open and welcoming and half threat, his intentions toward Little are unclear. Meanwhile, the circling, hovering, constantly moving camera contributes to the scene's tension until it finally rests as the children leave the frame. *Moonlight's* narrative, cinematography, and soundtrack combine for an overwhelming feeling of unease in this paradise, with

Figure 8.1. Chiron/Little (Alex Hibbert) and Kevin (Jaden Piner) as children on the playing fields of Liberty City in *Moonlight* (Barry Jenkins, A24, 2016). Digital frame enlargement.

the Mozart piece acting as a punctum for the solemnity undergirding this snapshot of children at play.[3]

Moonlight is a film told in three quiet acts, with each section focusing on a different moment in Chiron's life—childhood ("Little"), adolescence ("Chiron"), and adulthood ("Black").[4] The film as a whole is marked by similar contradictions and connections as those encapsulated in the childhood soccer scene. On the one hand, such tensions communicate the beauty and danger inherent in the everyday performance of Black masculinity, particularly when it fails to meet heteronormative standards. In this case the others (including even, it is later revealed, his mother) see Little as lacking "hardness," a crucial component of being a Black male in that place, at that time. His otherness is manifold; too soft to be like the others, Little exists on the perimeters, except on the few occasions when other men in his life quietly accept his difference. But, these too, are anomalies: first is Juan, a local drug dealer who spends time with Little, teaching him to swim and to embrace his difference in the first act of the film. The other, Kevin, is a friend, foe, and love object whose presence is woven throughout the story's three acts. Like the film's Miami setting, both men are crucial figures in Little/Chiron/Black's journey of becoming. And central to this journey is the film's suburban Miami setting, which acts as a catalyst, a barrier, and an enabler of individual and community change.

Space, Race, and History

Liberty Square was planned and built in a parklike setting. The buildings were simple and inviting. The community center contained a recreation hall, a nursery, a doctor's office, a consumer cooperative store, a federal credit union, and classrooms for tenant education programs. Every family had a garden. Most grew flowers as well as vegetables.[5]

Today, Liberty Square tenants talk about rat infestations and moldy walls. Their neighborhood is known for the gangland killings that erupt along its perimeter, including a mass shooting last year [2014] across the street that wounded seven people and killed two. In the first six months of last year, 43 people were shot in and around the community. . . . It has grown from a symbol of progress for Miami's black community to a constant reminder of the city's persistent poverty and crime.[6]

Moonlight is set in Liberty City, an African American neighborhood in Miami that is home to Liberty Square (est. 1937), the oldest federally funded African American housing project in the United States. The film's location would appear to make it an outlier in a discussion of cinematic suburbia, especially since the study of American suburbanization has been based historically on the assumption that suburbs are racially and economically homogenous, with middle-class whites constituting by far the largest demographic in the heteronormative and racially uniform Levittowns of midcentury America. More recent scholarship from historians such as Becky Nicolaides and Andrew Wiese, however, has begun to address these absences.[7] According to Wiese, for example, "there are many people who assume that if visible numbers of black (or poor) people lived in a community, it was not a suburb,"[8] and yet his work reveals the rich legacy of African American and working-class suburbanization stretching from the years surrounding the Great Migration of the early 1920s and continuing into the present.

Such presumptions of white homogeneity often exist as well with American media makers, who often exclude African American suburbs from screens. Instead, Black life is most often relegated to urban, "inner city" areas defined by poverty and crime even when those areas are, in fact, suburban.[9] If not the city then African American stories are located in rural settings that connote a literal or figurative past. In what follows, however, I explore the potential of *Moonlight's* setting to help us reimagine both the definitions and the representations of suburbia, of ghettoes, and of real and imagined spaces. In the process, I also posit that Jenkins's Liberty City, like Chiron's experiences as a whole, is a web of contradictions; at one and the same time idyllic and menacing, soft and hard, and, to paraphrase Jenkins, beautiful and miserable.[10] George Lipsitz has noted that such contradictions align with African American spaces as well, arguing, "relegated to neighborhoods where zoning, policing, and investment practices make it impossible to control the exchange value of their property, ghetto residents have learned how to turn segregation into congregation."[11] Moments of congregation punctuate *Moonlight*, a text that examines the intersections of and within identity and space and place and history through understated storytelling and carefully crafted aesthetics.

At first glance, Liberty City does not appear to align neatly with normative definitions of suburban space; for example, it is in a neighborhood adjunct to Miami's central business district, not that far from the city center. Yet, as Lipsitz observes of African American suburbs more generally: "Spatial imaginaries honed in inner cities persist when Blacks move to suburbs, and for good reasons. The division between cities and suburbs does not conform exactly to the demographic concentration of whites and Blacks. Since the 1970s, Blacks have gradually started moving to suburbs. Yet Black suburbanization is largely concentrated in areas with falling rents and declining property values, most often in older inner city ring suburbs."[12] Liberty City is an anomaly of sorts. On the one hand, it aligns with Lipsitz's argument because it is located adjacent to the central city (one of the prime determinants of an inner suburb). On the other hand, it also breaks with the pattern in ways that highlight a local history "marked by Black attempts to overcome racial barriers and white attempts to sustain them."[13]

The history of Liberty City can be understood as the combined result of liberal social policies from the New Deal era and decades of real estate development focused on the growth of Miami's downtown business district and benefitting the city's white power structure. The area is defined in large part by Liberty Square, a housing project of approximately 750 units (some detached houses and some three-story apartment buildings) and over 2,000 residents. Liberty Square was intended to ease the crowding and substandard living conditions of Miami's "Colored Town"—or Overtown as it's presently known—where many people resided in shotgun shacks, lacking running water and other basic amenities. Liberty Square's construction on an empty track of land to the northwest of Overtown and the business district was also intended to help "remove the entire colored population [of Miami] to the Liberty City area," reinforcing their previous spatial segregation, while in the process opening the central city to more white businesses and residents.[14] The development, "conceived as the nucleus of a new and distant Black community outside the city limits,"[15] was lauded for its modern amenities (running water, indoor plumbing, electricity), community center, and green spaces. Soon, a "new black elite class began to develop in Liberty City as the new housing project attracted more and more middle-income blacks."[16] Despite the nefarious reasons behind its beginnings, for a few decades at least Liberty City was a thriving, though purposely contained, African American community (figure 8.2).

While Liberty Square was welcomed by an African American populace seeking to escape substandard housing, overcrowding, impoverished surroundings, and the crime and disease of Overtown, the development's creation was less a benevolent act by local officials than a longer range plan to aid in the economic expansion of Miami's white areas by moving its Black residents into areas that were already segregated and financially

Figure 8.2. Overhead shot of the Liberty Square housing development. From Roshan Nebhranjani, "A History of Liberty City," *The New Tropic*, March 13, 2017. https://thenewtropic.com/liberty-city-history-moonlight.

hobbled by redlining and other discriminatory lending practices. In his history of twentieth-century property development in Miami, historian Raymond A. Mohl identifies a number of factors related to the "whitening" of the city, much of which were rooted in New Deal policies of the 1930s. These included newly available federal funding for public housing developments and the establishment by the federal government of the Home Owner's Loan Corporation, a lending institution "designed to grant long-term, low-interest mortgages to homeowners who could not secure regular mortgages or who were in danger of losing their homes through default or foreclosure."[17] In short, federal funding was split along two axes: segregated public housing (for whites or Blacks) and home loans geared toward promoting or maintaining white neighborhoods.

According to Mohl, there were two primary ways in which federal funding—through housing construction and financing—was used by city and county leaders to limit the growth and availability of African American neighborhoods in Miami. First, city organizers had for decades imposed "'color lines' limiting black residentially to a confined section of the city." Local officials interpreted federal housing guidelines, which encouraged the "preservation rather than the disruption of community social structures which best fit the desires of the groups concerned"[18] to enforce segregation in its publicly funded housing—in effect, maintaining the Jim Crow status quo of the area. Liberty Square may have been modern in form, but it was built on decades-old anti-Black sentiment. The result was a neighborhood that embodied segregationist impulses in the composition of its residents and in a built environment that included a physical wall separating it from its white neighbors across the street.

While Liberty Square is, and remains, a physical manifestation of the municipality's discriminatory housing policies, it also bears less visible traces of boundary setting. As suggested, the 1930s was also the decade during which federally funded mortgage financing was established through the Home Owner's Loan Corporation. The immediate effects of these policies involved staff from the Home Owner's Loan Corporation and local realtors and lenders taking part in the appraisal and mapping of neighborhoods based on financial health and risk levels. The Miami area was surveyed in the late 1930s, with a number of African American neighborhoods, including the still undeveloped (but identified) location for Liberty Square, given the lowest rating of "D." To a certain extent Miami was not an anomaly: as Amy Hillier argues, in surveys of 239 cities the "areas with African Americans, as well as those with older housing and poorer households, were consistently given a fourth grade [D], or 'hazardous' rating, and colored red."[19] In Miami, possible future Black neighborhoods were also redlined, effectively premediating places like Liberty Square and its surroundings as financial risks even before they were built. "By 1938," argues Mohl, "Dade County had been redlined along racial lines by the local real estate and banking community [including] even those white neighborhoods where, over time, blacks were expected to move."[20] The effects of this racially inflected urban planning and development were manifold: the city relocated the majority of its Black residents away from the city center, maintained segregation through the construction of racially restrictive housing projects and underinvestment in Black neighborhoods, and limited actual and social African American mobility through these very same practices.

As suggested earlier, despite these policies, Liberty Square, and the surrounding Liberty City area, was a thriving Black community into the

1950s. During the latter half of the decade, however, city planners, in a continuing effort to expand downtown Miami's development, accepted federal funds to expand the construction of a massive expressway, charting a path for Interstate 95 that went directly through the Overtown area. As Mohl explains, when "the downtown leg of the expressway was completed in the mid-1960s, it ripped through the center of Overtown, wiping out black residential and business areas, the commercial and cultural heart of black Miami," and included an interchange that "took up twenty square blocks of densely settled land and destroyed the housing of about ten thousand people."[21] In all, approximately 40,000 residents were displaced from the Overtown area, with no plans for their relocation (in part because the city's continuing maintenance of racially restricted neighborhood boundaries left few options for expansion). Many of the newly homeless ended up in the Liberty City area, but with neighborhood boundaries clearly demarcated along racial lines (and limited by walls), there was little room for the increased population. The result of the drastic in-migration to the neighborhood was overcrowding and an eventual change in the demeanor of the area, one exacerbated over the following decades (like that of African American neighborhoods across the country) by an increase in poverty and crime, the appearance of drugs and gang-related violence, and a concomitant decrease in financial investment in the neighborhood, social support systems, and other services that formerly enhanced the livability of the community. By the 1990s and early 2000s, the time period in which *Moonlight* is set, Liberty City had transitioned from a functioning inner-ring suburb to a "notorious" and "crime infested" area, a scourge that the city plans on razing and, in keeping with urban planning patterns across the United States, replacing with mixed-use, mixed-income developments.[22]

Space, Race, and Identity

In *Medicine for Melancholy* the cinematic geography concerns a place impacted by redlining, urban redevelopment, gentrification, displacement, and a dwindling African American population.[23]

There's no doubt that place plays a crucial role in Jenkins's filmmaking. He chooses his locations with care, and for their "juxtapositions and ambivalences." In Jenkins's first feature film, *Medicine for Melancholy*

(2008), for example, San Francisco functions as an enabling space for its two characters, Micah and Jo, to explore their relationship to the city, to each other, and to their blackness. In the film a couple awaken following a one-night stand and spend the next twenty-four hours exploring the city. They were unacquainted prior to their night together, and the following day is spent getting to know each other while they wander the city. Micah is from San Francisco and his observations and opinions of the changing city act as both a backdrop and as a test of Jo's political affinities, along with, as Michael Boyce Gillespie suggests, acculturating and versing her "in his cultural nostalgia and lifeworld view." Jo, for her own part, is an enigmatic newcomer—an upper-middle-class artist living with her white boyfriend—who is less likely to accord with Micah's version of the city than she is a more freewheeling explorer of "urban histories and racial scripts."[24] In short, Micah and Jo experience a city that has different pasts and meanings, and the narrative tension revolves not so much around their romance as it does around the question of whether or not they will reach a cultural and political accord.

What *Medicine for Melancholy* stresses throughout its narrative are the effects of cultural geography on identity. While this spatial self-consciousness pervades the film—it is, after all, a film about urban *flânerie*—it is especially evident in a scene that occurs in Micah's apartment, where the pair, sparked by a political poster hanging on the wall, discuss San Francisco's decades-long history of development and gentrification, much of which resulted in the displacement of the working class and communities of color. The artwork includes portions of text drawn from a redevelopment survey from the early 1960s, with the word "LIES" stenciled over it. As Gillespie observes, the poster refers to the history of urban redevelopment in the city dating back to 1948 and the formation of the San Francisco Redevelopment Agency, which was created as a result of legislation providing "cities with more authority over redevelopment financing." For Gillespie, "the poster articulates San Francisco's new diaspora, those who could be or have been displaced by city initiatives that prioritize economic growth over sustaining local communities and histories."[25] For Micah, this history reflects a different San Francisco than what he experienced as a youth.

It goes without saying that San Francisco is a vastly different urban space than Miami, but both *Medicine for Melancholy* and *Moonlight* share an interest in uncovering the effects of spatial premediations, such as local and federal development initiatives, on communities of color and their impacts on the formation of individual and community identities.

The poster's explicit presence in *Medicine for Melancholy* identifies the communities in the Lower Haight and Fillmore neighborhoods as effected by the Redevelopment Agency's initiatives. In the film the changes have already occurred, and despite Micah's nostalgia for a San Francisco of the past, the narrative is located in a city of the postmillennial present, one in which African American characters, despite occupying the center of the story, are displaced from the city itself.

Moonlight's relationship to space differs in subtle yet significant ways. As suggested in my earlier discussion of Liberty City, the cultural geography of Miami, like that of San Francisco and other urban areas with significant African American populations, has changed over time, particularly following the formation of the Home Owner's Loan Corporation and federal funding of public housing in the 1930s that ensured the continuation of segregation, while enabling the growth of suburban home ownership. For Miami, and particularly for the Liberty City area, such development resulted in the construction of suburbs—not the idyllic all-white, middle class suburbs of myth, but of inner-ring African American suburban spaces that, at least for a few decades, offered better living conditions for residents moving from congested inner city areas like Overtown. The same wave of federal legislation from the 1940s and 1950s, which created the San Francisco's Redevelopment Corporation, however, also "hastened," according to Kenneth T. Jackson, "the decay of inner-city neighborhoods by stripping them of much of their middle-class constituency."[26] In short, federal protections for mortgages and residential development, combined with race-based redlining and other restrictive covenants, resulted in the further destabilization of communities like Liberty City.

While both films focus on identity and space, they differ in their approaches to narrative and aesthetics. *Medicine for Melancholy*, for example, explores the city as palimpsest, as a changing foundation upon which identities are created, shaped, changed, and questioned. Through Micah and Jo's wanderings, and in the former's constant historicizing ("mansplaining"), the film underscores "another option for cinematic place, neither strictly extradiegetic nor idle backdrop nor merely profilmic," but one rather that includes "several cartographies of urban history."[27] *Moonlight*, on the other hand, is subtler in its exploration of space. It never, for example, warns about the dangers of its drug-infested location despite the fact that it features drug dealers and addicts. Nor does it supply explicit markers of place. Instead, Liberty Square and its surroundings act as quiet, though integral, forces in Chiron's life and on his self-identity, ones that, unlike

Micah, he never articulates. In fact, it suggests that he may be wholly unaware of their lasting effects on his psyche.

Space, Race, and Aesthetics

> He's [Chiron] standing in Liberty Square, the most notorious housing project in Miami, maybe the whole southeast. . . . The paint of the buildings there was glowing and the colors were jumping off the screen. It was really lovely not to have to do the work of presenting this dark thesis about how sometimes dark childhoods can happen in beautiful places. Tarell and I are beautiful people who come from a dark circumstance and place. There is some element of this kind of imagery in pop culture and arts and letters over the past century where those things want to be in direct opposition, this sense that beauty and miserabilism can't go hand in hand.[28]

Moonlight ends on a medium shot of a young Chiron ("Little"), back to the camera, looking toward the ocean on a Miami beach. It's nighttime and his dark skin shines almost blue in the moonlight, the color palette echoing a story that Chiron was told by Juan at the beginning of the film. By this point the narrative has traveled through three acts focusing on Chiron's search for self-definition. On the face of it, *Moonlight* tells the story of Chiron's passage from "little" misfit to adult drug dealer ("Black"). But this summary is the tip of the iceberg in describing a film that quietly and beautifully explores the intersections and performance of Black masculinity and sexuality, and the impact of economics, crime, and geography on the construction of self. Near the end of the shot of Chiron on the beach he turns and looks directly at the camera. This action, combined with the film's rich color palette and layered sound design, suggests how *Moonlight's* self-conscious aesthetics are enfolded into larger meditations on the "cruel beauty" of African American life (figure 8.3).

It's become almost cliché to discuss *Moonlight's* beauty. And yet the film's aesthetics hold two keys for understanding how Liberty City functions as a chronotope of sorts: as a place that is both notoriously present in its postindustrial, neoliberal renderings as a carceral city for its Black and brown inhabitants, and enduring in its ongoing traces of community

Figure 8.3. Chiron (Ashton Sanders) on the beach at the end of *Moonlight*. (Barry Jenkins, A24, 2016). Digital frame enlargement.

building and promise from its suburban beginnings. The clue to this is in understanding Jenkins's desire to avoid the aesthetics of "miserabilism" so often attached to stories of young Black men in the hood. As he stresses, "The one thing we said on this film is that it's not neorealism. . . . It's not how I think about my childhood or the neighborhood where I grew up." Instead, Jenkins wanted to imagine Liberty City as a beautiful place that was "shiny, moist, basically revitalizing and replenishing and alive." This was accomplished through a narrative stressing, to refer to Lipsitz again, a space that allowed for a communal "congregation" of sorts, a place of hope and kindness within what Jenkins has referred to as the "darkness."[29]

The film's cinematography and sound design contribute to *Moonlight's* rendering of a space that's both sublime and threatening. The film was shot in a widescreen (2.39:1) format, which allowed Jenkins a generous canvas to "depict the expanse [of Miami], the big sky, and so much green grass."[30] Unlike earlier hood films, such as *Menace II Society* (Hughes Brothers, 1993), which stressed the lack of mobility and the boundaries that limit Black men in the city, *Moonlight* presents Miami as an open space, filled with green spaces, the expanse of the ocean, and the pastel hues of the Liberty Square houses. A fluid moving camera and careful editing adds to this expansiveness, as in, for example, the early soccer scene, which includes a montage of moving close-ups and long shots of young boys at play. The scene alternates between communal moments of joy, intimate exchanges between Chiron and Kevin, and wider shots of the verdant playing fields and a vast blue sky. Such moments illustrate what Jenkins has described as the "beautiful night-mare" of a "rough place . . . surrounded by the natural beauty of [the] environment."[31]

Another early scene perhaps more fully illustrates the film's use of cinematography and sound to create what some have called its "ecstatic aesthetic [that] opens a space for bursts of euphoric feeling in stories that are often denied them."[32] Soon after Little leaves the soccer field Juan takes him to the beach and teaches him to swim. Even before we see the water, the noise of the surf acts as a sound bridge, inviting us into the waves. As Juan and Little begin their lesson, the camera joins them, bobbing up and down with the surf, going underwater, and often framing the pair in medium close-up from water level. The cinematography picks up the green of the water, the blue of the sky, and the rich and varied browns of the characters' skin. Often considered a symbolic baptism of sorts, the scene is crucial for a number of reasons: it's the first moment when we see Little fully trust Juan; it's the first time when Little is encouraged to define himself on his own terms (as Juan says, "at some point you have to decide who you want to be"); and it's the first time we see the ocean, an ongoing aural and visual motif in *Moonlight* (the film opens with sounds of the ocean but it is not visible until seventeen minutes into the narrative).

While Liberty City is less than ten miles from the ocean, its social, economic, and cultural separation from places like Miami Beach remains vast. And yet, the ocean, and water more generally, is a crucial component to *Moonlight*. The film's sound design mixes moments of quiet (dialogue is at a minimum) with a soundtrack that features a combination of musi-cal genres (trap, gospel, classical) and the sounds of the sea. The ocean appears at three important points in the narrative, marking significant moments in Chiron's journey into becoming a Black man comfortable with himself and his sexuality. The first, his swimming session with Juan, begins his journey of self-definition as he bonds with and learns to trust his protective father figure. The scene encapsulates what Aliyyah I. Abdur-Rahman, following José Munoz, posits as the "black ecstatic," or a moment that resists "the logics of teleological progression by opening an immediate space of relational joy for black and brown people for whom the future is both yet to come and already past."[33] For Little, who later asks Juan to define the term "faggot," his path lies ahead and the swimming lesson marks the beginning of his story. And yet, it's a route that is always already determined by a cultural and geographic history that defines Black masculinity through (hetero)norms stressing hardness and emotional detachment.

The ocean returns in the second act, "Chiron," as a now-teenage Chiron goes to the beach after his crack-addicted mother, planning to score, kicks him out of their dreary apartment for the night. After an evening spent riding Miami's commuter trains, he goes to the beach. While sitting in the sand Chiron meets Kevin, who explains that he uses the spot to smoke pot. The two share a joint and talk before kissing and sharing a moment of sexual intimacy. The sexual act—Kevin masturbates Chiron—is shot from behind, in a medium close-up of the two young men sitting side by side in the sand. The soundtrack is composed of the surf and their murmurs of pleasure, and the scene ends on a shot of Chiron's blue-black hand resting on the silver sand. Not only is this Chiron's moment of sexual awakening, but it also, like the swimming lesson, takes place in a location that is both adjunct and yet metaphorically distant from Liberty City's more proscriptive personal boundaries.

The ocean returns in the third act, near the end of *Moonlight* when Chiron, now an adult answering to "Black," returns to Miami after ten years in Atlanta. The cause of the visit is an unexpected call from Kevin. Black is drawn to see Kevin again after a forced absence caused by an act of violence directed at Chiron by Kevin and then perpetrated by Chiron as an act of revenge against one of his tormentors. The majority of the third section takes place at the diner where Kevin works, but later the pair travel to Kevin's apartment, located by the very same beach from the first two acts. The men don't go onto the beach in this section, but the ocean's presence is both seen and heard; first, on the soundtrack, which layers the sounds of the surf under the action, and then in a long shot of the path leading to the beach that replicates one from the earlier scene between Chiron and Kevin.

As in the previous scenes, the ocean provides the setting for a moment of self-definition and sexual awakening for Chiron. In the past he seemed reluctant to define himself, and seemed uncertain of who he was. But, faced with Kevin's probing questions, Black articulates his identity by providing a history of his self-conscious reconstruction. While once soft and little, he "built himself hard," explains Black, acknowledging his adoption of a certain performance of (hetero)masculinity, including a buff body, gold "fronts" covering his teeth, a custom car, and a job "trapping," or selling drugs. Soon the men share an intimate, though chaste, embrace that echoes their earlier one as teens. The scene ends on a similar close-up two shot of the men's heads—Chiron's head on

Kevin's shoulder—this time shot from the front so that their faces, at peace, are visible. From this moment, *Moonlight* cuts back to the image that began the discussion at the beginning of this section, of a young Chiron in the moonlight, facing the ocean.

While the ocean scenes take up relatively little time in a film with a narrative running almost two hours, they work in conjunction with other spaces in the film to place Little/Chiron/Black in a personal as well as a communal past that helps to explain who he is in the present. Juan, for example, not only teaches Chiron to swim. The older man's mobility and welcoming house provide the young boy and teenager a respite from the cramped and ramshackle apartment shared with his increasingly drug-addled mother—and, notably, shots in the apartment are much more tightly framed. Each time Chiron visits Juan, the camera lingers on the home's lush green yard before we enter the space, which is modest, though spacious, bright, and welcoming. Likewise, the exterior shots of Liberty Square, with the buildings' pastel façades and green spaces, offer a counterpoint to more cliché images of crime-infested inner cities; by complicating the renderings of Chiron's home life, they add to the space's contradictions. To be certain, the area is marked by poverty and crime—the film opens on shots of drug dealers selling crack outside Liberty Square—but, as Jenkins reminds us, beauty and miserabilism can go hand in hand, and the contradictions and conundrums of *Moonlight* are just as much a function of the past and present of Miami's Liberty City neighborhood as they are in Chiron's search for self-definition.

So, is *Moonlight* a suburban film? If one were to define such a genre based on historical assumptions that define suburbs with clean yards, tidy houses, white picket fences, happy families, and white heteronormativity, the answer would be no. But, as this discussion of the film's setting and aesthetics underline, such clear-cut conclusions are complicated by historical and aesthetic factors that pushed many working- and middle-class families into segregated and liminal fringe areas existing next to, but not a part of, either suburban spaces or central business districts. Liberty City, with its crime, drugs, and poverty, might not present as a suburban utopia, but the area's past was built on foundations of hope and a desire for betterment that continue in *Moonlight's* soulful gestures toward community support and congregation. Chiron's story, one of becoming, is one, as well, of community acceptance of difference. *Moonlight* may not be, in the end, a suburban film, but if so, this has less to do with location and more to do with its acknowledgment of difference residing within social and cultural conformity, one that itself is much more manufactured than real.

Notes

1. George Lipsitz, *How Racism Takes Place* (Philadelphia: Temple University Press, 2011), 60.
2. Barry Jenkins, "Cruel Beauty: Filming in Miami," *Moonlight*, DVD, directed by Barry Jenkins (New York: A24, 2016).
3. Jenkins has said that his inspiration for the film's musical choices came from a number of sources, including the film's composer, Nicholas Britell, and the films of Wong Kar-Wai and Park Chul-Soo. I'd argue that this scene also bears resemblance to scenes of children's play in Charles Burnett's *Killer of Sheep* (1977), another film that explores the beauty and menace of African American life in the Los Angeles suburbs.
4. For the purposes of clarity, Chiron will be referred to by his given name when discussed generally, and by section title when specific scenes or places in the narrative are examined.
5. Marvin Dunn, *Black Miami in the Twentieth Century* (Gainesville: University Press of Florida, 1997), 165–166.
6. David Smiley and Charles Rabin, "Liberty Square Housing Project to Be Razed, Redeveloped," *Miami Herald*, January 29, 2015, https://www.miamiherald.com/news/local/community/miami-dade.
7. In her work, Becky Nicolaides focuses on the development of working-class suburbs that were built in and around Los Angeles in the early twentieth century. As she argues, such spaces "enabled families to secure the basic necessities of shelter and food cheaply and efficiently" (Becky Nicolaides and Andrew Wiese, eds., *The Suburb Reader* [New York: Routledge, 2006], 210), while also providing workers with a voice—through do it yourself home construction and landscaping—in their community. Becky Nicolaides, *My Blue Heaven: Life and Politics in the Working-Class Suburbs of Los Angeles, 1920–1965* (Chicago: University of Chicago Press, 2002). Moreover, Becky Nicolaides and Andrew Wiese's edited collection, *The Suburb Reader* (New York: Routledge, 2006), offers multiple examples of scholarship exploring the gendered, racial, ethnic, economic, and geographic diversity of suburbs.
8. Andrew Wiese, *Places of Their Own: African American Suburbanization in the Twentieth Century* (Chicago: University of Chicago Press, 2004), 5.
9. Historian Benjamin Wiggins argues that the "paratexts" surrounding films like *Boyz n the Hood* and *Menace II Society*, including marketing materials, theatrical posters, and reviews, often stressed the films' urban settings, belying their actual locations in inner-ring suburbs such as Inglewood, Compton, and Watts. As Wiggins argues, "When paratexts construct the films as 'inner-city' or 'urban,' the issues they work through become 'inner-city' and 'urban' problems . . . not issues of system[atic] racialized violence that pervade the country regardless of locale." Moreover, they work "to elide the rapid transformation and growing plight of in city-edge and inner-ring suburban areas." While Wiggins is speaking

specifically of Los Angeles, his argument pertains as well to places like Miami, whose African American suburbs have experienced similar effects of decades of deindustrialization, ebbing government support, and rising unemployment, poverty, and crime. Benjamin Wiggins, "Race and Place at the City Limits: Imaginative Geographies of South Central Los Angeles," *Ethnic and Racial Studies* 39, no. 14 (2016): 2595. It is my contention that *Moonlight's* narrative and aesthetics, as well as its paratexts, resist placing it within the urban.

10. Barry Jenkins, "One Step Ahead: A Conversation with Barry Jenkins," interview by Michael Boyce Gillespie, *Film Quarterly* 70, no. 3 (Spring 2017), https://filmquarterly.org/2017/02/28/one-step-ahead-a-conversation-with-barry-jenkins/.

11. Lipsitz, *How Racism Takes Place*, 56.

12. Lipsitz, *How Racism Takes Place*, 55–56.

13. Wiese, *Places of Their Own*, 5.

14. Raymond A. Mohl, "Whitening Miami: Race, Housing, and Government Policy in Twentieth-Century Dade County," *Florida Historical Quarterly* 79, no. 3 (Winter 2001): 321.

15. Mohl, "Whitening Miami," 322.

16. Dunn, *Black Miami in the Twentieth Century*, 168.

17. Mohl, "Whitening Miami," 325.

18. Mohl, "Whitening Miami," 320–321.

19. Amy Hillier, "Redlining and the Home Owners' Loan Corporation," *Journal of Urban History* 29, no. 4 (2003): 395.

20. Mohl, "Whitening Miami," 326.

21. Mohl, "Whitening Miami," 341–343.

22. In 1980, the Liberty City area experienced violent protests in response to the acquittal of Miami police officers accused in the beating death of an African American man named Arthur McDuffie, who had evaded arrest for a traffic violation. The violence lasted three days and resulted in three deaths, over twenty injuries, and enough damage that the federal government declared sections of the city a disaster area. In 1989 another violent protest erupted after the police killed another Black motorist. Each instance of police brutality reveals the violent strategies used by the Miami police against Miami's Black and brown residents. It is interesting that police control is almost nonexistent in the narrative of *Moonlight* (police only make one appearance in the film). Instead, the limits placed on Chiron come from other, though related, sociopolitical pressures of his surroundings, including what it means to be an African American in what can be interpreted as a life-threatening police state.

23. Michael Boyce Gillespie, *Film Blackness: American Cinema and the Idea of Black Film* (Durham, NC: Duke University Press, 2016), 122.

24. Gillespie, *Film Blackness*, 154–155.

25. Gillespie, *Film Blackness*, 136–137.

26. Kenneth T. Jackson, *Crabgrass Frontier: The Suburbanization of the United States* (New York: Oxford University Press, 1985), 206.

27. Gillespie, *Film Blackness*, 138.

28. Jenkins in Gillespie interview. Jenkins refers to Tarell Alvin McCraney, whose original play *In Moonlight Black Boys Look Blue* was adapted for the film. Both men have spoken repeatedly about the influence of their Miami upbringings on the film's narrative and visual components.

29. Jenkins in Gillespie, "*One Step Ahead.*"

30. Jenkins in Gillespie, "*One Step Ahead.*"

31. Jenkins, "Cruel Beauty."

32. Joanna DiMattia, "The Aesthetic of the Ecstatic," *Screen Education* 93 (2017): 11.

33. Aliyyah I. Abdur-Rahman, "The Black Ecstatic," *GLQ* 24, nos. 2–3 (2018): 345.

References

Abdur-Rahman, Aliyyah I. "The Black Ecstatic." *GLQ* 24, nos. 2–3 (2018): 343–365.

DiMattia, Joanna. "The Aesthetic of the Ecstatic." *Screen Education* 93 (2017): 8–15.

Dunn, Marvin. *Black Miami in the Twentieth Century*. Gainesville: University Press of Florida, 1997.

Gillespie, Michael Boyce. *Film Blackness: American Cinema and the Idea of Black Film*. Durham, NC: Duke University Press, 2016.

Hillier, Amy. "Redlining and the Home Owners' Loan Corporation." *Journal of Urban History* 29, no. 4 (2003): 394–420.

Jackson, Kenneth T. *Crabgrass Frontier: The Suburbanization of the United States.* New York: Oxford University Press, 1985.

Jenkins, Barry. "Cruel Beauty: Filming in Miami." *Moonlight*, DVD, directed by Barry Jenkins. New York: A24, 2016.

———. "One Step Ahead: A Conversation with Barry Jenkins." Interview by Michael Boyce Gillespie. *Film Quarterly* 70, no. 3 (Spring 2017). https://filmquarterly. org/2017/02/28/one-step-ahead-a-conversation-with-barry-jenkins/.

Lipsitz, George. *How Racism Takes Place*. Philadelphia: Temple University Press, 2011.

Mohl, Raymond A. "Whitening Miami: Race, Housing, and Government Policy in Twentieth-Century Dade County." *Florida Historical Quarterly* 79 (Winter 2001): 319–345.

Nicolaides, Becky. *My Blue Heaven: Life and Politics in the Working-Class Suburbs of Los Angeles, 1920–1965*. Chicago: University of Chicago Press, 2002.

———, and Andrew Wiese, eds. *The Suburb Reader.* New York: Routledge, 2006.

Smiley, David, and Charles Rabin. "Liberty Square Housing Project to Be Razed, Redeveloped." *Miami Herald*, January 29, 2015, https://www.miamiherald. com/news/local/community/miami-dade.

Wiese, Andrew. *Places of Their Own: African American Suburbanization in the Twentieth Century*. Chicago: University of Chicago Press, 2004.

Wiggins, Benjamin. "Race and Place at the City Limits: Imaginative Geographies of South Central Los Angeles." *Ethnic and Racial Studies* 39, no. 14 (2016): 2583–2600.

9

Geographies of Racism

American Suburbs as Palimpsest Spaces in *Get Out* (2017)

Elizabeth A. Patton

In America, racism exists but racists are all gone. Racists belong to the past. Racists are the thin-lipped mean white people in the movies about the civil rights era. Here's the thing: the manifestation of racism has changed but the language has not.[1]

—Chimamanda Ngozi Adichie, *Americanah*

∼

THE FILM *GET OUT* (2017) acts as a spatial palimpsest that uses collective memory to reveal the deep and masked layers of racism in places that have historically emerged from ideologies of white supremacy, especially the suburbs.[2] Writer and director Jordan Peele combines the physical violence of horror films, the emotional anguish of the psychological thriller, and the political commentary of the satire to depict the reality of people of color in white-dominated spaces in putative "postracial" America. The storyline focuses on a Black photographer named Chris Washington (Daniel Kaluuya) living in Brooklyn who agrees to meet his white girlfriend's parents for the first time at their secluded estate in an upstate suburb. Upon his arrival, he finds himself surrounded by his girlfriend's white parents, Dean and Missy Armitage, and their guests. The only Black people in the community are the family's housekeeper, live-in gardener, and a guest of the family that all appear brainwashed, evidenced by their dead stares, lack of engagement with Chris's blackness, and inability to exercise any autonomy. After an awkward visit with Rose's (Allison Williams) presumably liberal family, Chris realizes that something is terribly wrong with the Armitage household.

Geographers, urban studies, and memory studies scholars have used the metaphor of the palimpsest to describe the relationship between the physical aspects of the city and corresponding memories. Palimpsest refers to the process in which the original text of historical manuscripts has been erased and written over multiple times, but traces of the original writing remain. To recognize that "whiteness in the black imagination is often a representation of terror," bell hooks proposes "that one must face a palimpsest of written histories that erase and deny, that reinvent the past to make the present vision of racial harmony and pluralism more plausible."[3] She argues that the act of remembering the past is necessary to challenge current forms of racism that attempt to erase history. The film depicts palimpsest spaces that contain an aggregation of historical racist practices and memories of mental and physical violence experienced by people of color. I use the concept of palimpsest spaces in this chapter to describe memories and experiences of everyday life in places such as the suburbs that have been erased, while recognizing that the representations of such places also reflect "historically specific social and cultural concerns."[4] Specifically, I argue that *Get Out* challenges the construction of suburban whiteness and its spaces as seemingly natural phenomenon rather than as the result of deliberate violence and public policies since the Jim Crow era. Architectural historian Craig E. Barton claims that race "as a social construct and concept . . . has had a profound influence on the spatial development of the American landscape, creating separate, though sometimes parallel, overlapping or even superimposed cultural landscapes for black and white Americans."[5] Therefore, I draw on Barton's understanding of the role of race in spatial development, the concept of palimpsest spaces, and bell hooks's appeal to memory as a form of resistance to examine how *Get Out* recovers the historical narratives and residues of violence obscured by neoliberal forms of racism that still haunt suburban spaces. Current neoliberal forms of racism depend on a collective refusal to acknowledge the existence of race, such as colorblindness, an aspect of a "racist society that works to both reinforce the racial structure of society, while also modifying the processes of racialization."[6] Neoliberal racism bolsters the belief that racism belongs in the domain of history (the past) and therefore no longer needs to be retained in our collective memory.[7]

The Suburb's Hidden Racial Legacies of Exclusion, Violence, and Control

Peele's film counters the myth of a postracial society by revealing the racist palimpsest that bolsters suburban space, such as the hidden history of sundown practices and the public and political erasure of federal and local real estate practices that prevented the integration of most middle- and upper-middle-class suburbs. In *Get Out*, violent acts happen at night, corresponding to the temporal and spatial separation practiced by sundown towns during Jim Crow in the United States. The film opens with a scene of a Black man, who we later learn is missing Brooklyn resident Andre, walking down a suburban street at night (figure 9.1). Peele uses a horror film trope, an individual walking alone in an unfamiliar dark space, to comment on white fears and white supremacy.[8] To read this scene we must recognize that the suburbs have become a

Figure 9.1. Andre Hayworth (La Keith Stanfield) walking in a suburb at night in *Get Out* (Jordan Peele, Universal Pictures, 2017). Digital frame enlargement.

"spatial metaphor for whiteness itself."[9] Historically, television shows and films have rendered the suburbs as white middle and upper class even though the suburbs have become increasingly diverse both racially and economically since the 1970s.[10] While talking to his girlfriend on the phone, Andre expresses concern that in order to visit her, he has to travel through a "creepy confusing-ass suburb." The suburbs are synonymous with whiteness as Andre uses a comedic white-coded voice to pronounce the word "suburb." He also calls attention to his blackness by stating, "I feel like a sore thumb out here." Andre soon recognizes the danger and begins to talk to himself, voicing the inner dialogue many people of color experience in similar life-threatening situations.

As a car follows him, we hear Andre say aloud: "Okay, I just keep on walking and don't do anything stupid. Fuck this, I'm going the other way. Not today, not me! You know how they like to do motherfuckers out here. I'm gone." Andre's suspicion is confirmed. A white vintage sports car comes into view and passes by, but shortly turns around and starts to follow Andre. The audience hears the car stereo playing "Run Rabbit Run" (1939), a World War II song that eerily transports us to the Jim Crow era and foreshadows the necessity for Andre to run and try to escape. A white man chokes him until he passes out and places him in the trunk of the white car. This scene references the practice of controlling the movement of Black men in public spaces. It also points to the colonial roots of this brutal racial practice in sundown towns and the common violence acted on African Americans during Jim Crow while equating "whiteness with the bringing of death" to people of color.[11] Andre's words reflect the experiences of people of color who traversed spaces designated as "whites only." African Americans were not only terrorized by residents and police, their experiences were omitted in public and popular discourses regarding life in the suburbs.

To make this system of racial violence and discrimination work, racism was organized as a social-spatial system primarily through practices of exclusion (e.g., redlining), temporal separation (e.g., sundown towns), or duplication (e.g., separate bathrooms for white and Black people).[12] Sundown towns and suburbs across the country represented one of many strategies to spatially segregate minorities from white populations. Peele acknowledges that the suburbs are represented as "rigidly controlled place[s], protected by modes of surveillance and discipline."[13] The scene renders the suburbs as a de facto sundown town, which historically operated as spaces of surveillance and exclusion throughout the United

States. This relationship continues because de facto segregation has given "whites privileged access to opportunities for social inclusion and upward mobility" and simultaneously excluded communities of color.[14] Preventing minorities from spending the night in towns and suburbs through intimidation, violence, and discriminatory laws meant that physically and symbolically such spaces remained white and predominantly Christian, cementing the association of the suburbs as spaces of whiteness.

Sundown towns, which also included newly incorporated suburbs, appeared between 1890 and 1940 during the Jim Crow era in the United States.[15] These places obtained their name because of the signs that were posted on the main roadways at the town boundaries with statements such as "Nigger, Don't Let the Sun Go Down on You in ___," which were displayed by officials and by residents who were enabled by town or county ordinances.[16] In these racially segregated places, people of color, especially African Americans, Hispanics, and Asian Americans, and sometimes Jews were not allowed within the town limits after sunset even though they often worked or shopped there during the day. Middle-class and upper-middle-class white residents depended on African Americans and other minorities to tend their gardens and take care of other domestic tasks, such as cooking and cleaning; however, most domestic servants did not reside in the same town or suburb. Instead, they lived in communities adjacent to the white suburbs and towns of their employers.[17] Therefore, if African Americans lived in whites-only places they were servants that did not reside on their own, avoiding the violation of sundown town rules.[18]

The Armitages live with two Black servants in a large, lakeside upper-middle-class home in the exurbs that is architecturally reminiscent of an antebellum plantation. When Rose and Chris arrive at her parents' house, they encounter Walter, a Black man in his thirties, slowly raking the front yard. Rose waves and tells Chris that Walter is her parents' groundskeeper. Later, as Chris tours the house he meets the other servant, Georgina—also in her thirties—cleaning the kitchen with a pleasant smile on her face. The image of the exterior of the home as well as the depiction of imprisoned Black servants is associated both with the use of slaves to perform domestic labor and the practice of having live-in Black servants through the postwar period.

Upon his arrival at the house, Chris appears uncomfortable and tries to engage Georgina, who he perceives as a potential Black ally, in conversation. This interaction seems to be an attempt to make sense of his position as both a Black man and guest in a white household that employs Black domestic workers. However, Georgina never responds as Dean (Bradley Whitford), Rose's father, speaks on her behalf by telling Chris who she is and stating that "my mother loved her kitchen, so we kept a piece of her in here." At the time this seems like an extemporaneous remark, but the audience later learns its insidious meaning. Dean recognizes that, as a purported liberal family, employing Black live-in servants may seem problematic to Chris. Dean denies his racism while upholding racist practices, which represents a common neoliberal racist tactic to silence antiracist voices. He tells Chris, "I know what you're thinking. . . . Come on, I get it. White family, Black servants. It's a total cliché." Chris responds that he "wasn't going to take it there." Dean replies, "Well, you didn't have to, believe me. Now, we hired Georgina and Walter to help care for my parents. When they died, I just couldn't bear to let them go. But, boy, I hate how it looks." Dean's family has managed to find a way keep a piece of both of his dead white parents. The audience later learns that Dean's mother and father are actually alive, and their conscious minds control Georgina's and Walter's bodies, respectively.

From the onset, Peele connects the colonial roots of what Richard Dyer describes as "whiteness as death" with racist practices of spatial violence and exclusion.[19] The servants represent the period of human chattel enslavement in the United States when Blacks were forced to live and labor on plantations—a space of white supremacy. Almost one hundred years after the abolition of slavery, African Americans that attempted to move into suburban white neighborhoods during the postwar period often faced "a guerrilla war of death threats, property destruction, and physical violence."[20] Initially, racial violence is concealed in *Get Out*, much like the "hidden violence" of post–World War II racism described by Arnold R. Hirsch.[21] For example, Dean, Rose's father, secretly auctions Chris to party guests while Chris discusses his unease with Rose by the lake. Initially, the spectator's view is limited to a close-up of Dean standing silently outside with his hand raised. The camera turns and we see the party guests sitting on lawn chairs with raised bingo cards that are already stamped. Dean continues to raise his hand with one, then two, then three fingers extended as he uses his other hand to point to the crowd. As viewers, we begin to realize that Dean is holding an auction and his guests are bidding on something, using their bingo cards. The camera pulls back and we see that Dean is standing under a gazebo painted black next to a framed picture of Chris with his camera (figure

9.2). The silent auction represents overt violence during the period of slavery and also the hidden violence that emerged during the postwar period. The film portrays racial palimpsests that contain an accumulation of historical accounts of physical and mental violence experienced by people of color that are obscured under the layers of our contemporary moment of postracial ideology, which claims that all people are treated equally in the United States because structural forms of racial violence supposedly no longer exist.

Peele's decision to depict imprisoned Black bodies also alludes to the history of Black Codes in controlling the movement of African Americans and the issue of mass incarceration in the United States. Before the Civil War, some northern states such as Ohio, which abolished slavery in 1802, enacted Black Laws prohibiting free Blacks from living in the state.[22] In 1865 and 1866, after the Civil War, southern states adopted Black Codes, which replaced slave codes, and vagrancy laws "to establish another system of forced labor."[23] According to legal scholar Michelle Alexander, African Americans were convicted as vagrants if they were found to be unemployed. These laws constricted the freedom of African American by forcing them to work for low wages or no pay if convicted.[24] Likewise, the imprisoned Black servants at the Dean family home are forced to work for the Armitage family. Alexander also connects Jim Crow practices

Figure 9.2. Screenshot of Dean Armitage (Bradley Whitford) auctioning off Chris Washington (Daniel Kaluuya) to guests in *Get Out* (Jordan Peele, Universal Pictures, 2017). Digital Frame Enlargement.

to the current practice of mass incarceration in the United States. She argues that mass incarceration is a form of neoliberal "racialized social control . . . that functions in a manner strikingly similar to Jim Crow."[25] Although less visible in a postracial society, mass incarceration marginalizes large numbers of African Americans similar to the earlier system of Jim Crow. Upon release from prison, people are denied the right to vote and often racially segregated as they are often unable to participate in the economy, in housing, and in other public benefits, similar to the system of exclusion under Jim Crow.[26] If he remains in the Armitage household, Chris will be enslaved just like Georgina and Walter who have lost their autonomy as their minds are imprisoned and their bodies controlled by their white masters.

Racial Geographies of Institutional Segregation

Although filmed in Alabama, *Get Out* is set in an upper-middle-class white suburb in the North to show the continuity of old forms of racism, such as spatial exclusion and racial terror that have supposedly ceased in the era of postracism. Peele's decision to locate the story in a northeastern suburb is significant as he deploys a racial palimpsest traditionally associated with the South in many Hollywood films.[27] For example, the recent film *Green Book* (Farrelly, 2018) firmly situates the geography of racism in the South despite well-documented instances of racism in the North and entries in *The Negro Motorist Green Book*, an annual guidebook, that helped Black travelers navigate segregation while traveling throughout the United States during the Jim Crow era.[28] Set in the early 1960s, the film tells the story of Italian American Frank "Tony Lip" Vallelonga (Viggo Mortensen), who drives Dr. Don Shirley (Mahershala Ali), an accomplished African American musician, on an eight-week concert tour in the Midwest and South. In order to safely navigate the trip, Shirley hires Tony to act as a driver and bodyguard. His record label representatives give Tony a copy of *The Green Book*. Tony and Dr. Shirley's encounters with overt racism intensify as they travel deeper into the South. During a pivotal scene in the film, they are pulled over by a police officer for being within the town limits after dark. The landscape signals to the audience that they are in a sundown town by briefly showing a sign that permits "whites only" within the town after dark. To reinforce the point, a racist police officer mocks Dr. Shirley in jail, telling him "you let the sun set on your black ass," evoking the reality of sundown towns throughout the country during Jim Crow.

In contrast to films such as the *Green Book*, Peele highlights geographies of racism in the North, which is often associated as a space inhabited by liberals and progressives in films depicting racial relations in the United States. Peele confirms this interpretation in an interview, stating that "it was really important for me to not have the villains in this film reflect the typical red state type who is usually categorized as being racist. It felt like that was too easy," he said. "I wanted this film to explore the false sense of security one can have with the, sort of, New York liberal type."[29] Although there were no official Jim Crow laws in the North, people of color that lived and traveled in the suburban and rural spaces north of the Mason-Dixon Line also had to navigate the socio-spatial practices of racism. According to historian Thomas Sugrue, negotiating "northern Jim Crow was exhausting, demoralizing, and dangerous" for Black people.[30] Peele seems to be arguing that racial injustice still exists in so-called liberal places of the country, "sutured to geographies of race and racism in ways that reproduce inequality."[31] The continued act of associating racism with the South and Jim Crow and consequently the past allows the neoliberal myth to persist—that the rest of the United States has moved past racial injustice and violence.

Peele's *Get Out* challenges the myth of the postracial Northern suburb, which obscures the lingering impact of the institutional racism that prevented people of color from living in the suburbs during the postwar boom. According to sociologist James Loewen, "all-white suburbs were *achieved*" through exclusionary real estate practices.[32] Although hidden under the racist palimpsest of the suburbs, spatial exclusion extended beyond the early period of Jim Crow. African Americans were unable to participate in the postwar suburban boom because of widespread racist lending practices, such as redlining, discriminatory real estate strategies of steering Black home buyers away from white neighborhoods, and community covenants that prevented white owners from selling houses to Black homebuyers. Between 1950 and 1960, homeownership rates in the United States increased from 55 to 62 percent compared to the 1940s. Population growth in the suburbs was the main cause as the suburbs saw a 35 percent increase in the 1950s and 1960s compared to a 5 percent increase in population in major cities.[33]

During this period, 85 percent of homes built were located in the suburbs. This was primarily due to government measures such as the

Federal Housing Administration (FHA) and Veterans Administration (VA)-backed mortgages that financed the construction and purchase of ten million homes between 1946 and 1953.[34] The GI Bill ensured that college-educated, white veterans like Rose's grandfather Roman Armitage "were best prepared to undertake the high-earning, white-collar work of the new postwar economy."[35] African Americans were technically entitled to the mortgage benefits of the GI Bill and also sought the American Dream of purchasing a home in the suburbs. However, most African American veterans did not apply for an FHA mortgage to purchase suburban homes because the VA routinely rejected applications based on race to uphold FHA housing appraisal standards, which required most of the new suburban neighborhoods to remain white in order to ensure government-backed funding.[36]

Consequently, the enforcement of suburban segregation through racist real estate practices mirrored the sundown policies of exclusion during the Jim Crow era. Thus, the suburbs by their very nature are sundown towns. Sundown towns throughout the United States have virtually been erased from the historical record. But according to James Loewen, these places existed and were an open secret among residents, which is analogous to the present refusal to dismantle through public policy the legacy of redlining and other racist housing practices that continue to influence de facto housing segregation in the present. Consequently, many African Americans remained in the city or created suburban communities of their own in places such as the metropolitan areas of Atlanta, New Orleans, and Washington, DC to avoid the racial violence of sundown suburbs experienced by Andre in the opening scene of *Get Out*.[37]

The Sunken Place, Racial Amnesia, and the Importance of Collective Memory

Get Out is an example of the "expressive artifacts" that African Americans have created to chronicle "history with memories" that supplement the erasure of Black culture and the suppression of racist practices in official historical narratives that homogenize "the diverse cultural forces resident in the landscape, thus reinforcing a peculiar sense of collective amnesia."[38] In this case, the whiteness of American suburbs and the continued threat to Black bodies did not happen by accident in such spaces. For example, in *Get Out's* title sequence, Peele addresses the Black audience by asking them to remember the past. Peele hails spectators through music—within the intermediate space of the woods—to transport the audience from the threatening space of the suburbs to Chris's familiar and protective apartment in the city. As we move along with the camera, we hear the song "Sikiliza kwa wahenga" (2017) by Michael Abels, which is Swahili for "listen to your ancestors."

The African song of remembrance is significantly followed by "Redbone" (2016) by Donald Glover (also known as the Childish Gambino) asking spectators to "stay woke!" because "They gon' find you, Gon' catch you sleepin', put your hands up baby . . . Now, don't you close your eyes." Peele confirms his intent in an interview, stating: "Well, first of all, I love the 'Stay Woke' [lyric]—that's what this movie is about."[39] To stay woke is to be aware, to vigilantly look past the given narrative, to question the apparatuses of white supremacy. Peele prompts us to remember the history of African Americans traveling through or attempting to reside in such racially charged spaces, required to be ever vigilant to possible threats, which rendered and still render such spaces potentially horrifying. Chris expresses such alarm when he realizes that his girlfriend Rose did not disclose to her parents that he is Black, reminding the audience of the history of racism toward African Americans and other people of color if they turned up in spaces of whiteness unannounced.

Rod (Lil Rel Howery), Chris's best friend, expresses the need to stay woke. He is suspicious of Rose and her white family and raises the alarm bell by attempting to use deductive reasoning and common sense to convince Chris that he is in danger. Significantly, in the final scene, the audience expects the worst for Chris because he has killed the Armitage family in self-defense. However, Peele counters this expectation by making Rod the hero, who arrives in his police car and saves Chris from incarceration and potential death. Chris tells Rod over his cellphone that he was hypnotized by Rose's mother (Catherine Keener), a psychiatrist, the night before to help him quit smoking. Rod responds by asking him, "Bruh, how you not scared of this, man? Look they could have made you do all types of stupid shit. They have you fuckin' barking like a dog. Flyin' around like you a fuckin' pigeon, lookin' ridiculous. Okay? Or, I don't know if you know this, white people love making people sex slaves and shit." In this exchange, Rod is appealing to their shared identity as Black men to help Chris remember and acknowledge the racial violence that Black people have experienced in the past in majority-white spaces. Chris argues that the Armitages are not a kinky family but shares his strange interactions with other Black people at the party. Earlier in the day, Chris encounters Andre, the missing Black man from Brooklyn, who now goes by the name Logan and appears to be romantically involved with an older white woman. Chris sends a picture to Rod to confirm that this is in fact Andre, Rod's missing friend. He calls Rod again, explaining that Andre is acting strangely along with Georgina and Walter, stating that "it's like all of them missed the movement." Rod responds, saying, "Oh, shit! Chris, you gotta get the fuck up outta there, man! You in some 'Eyes Wide Shut' situation. Leave, motherfuck . . ." but does not get a response from Chris because the cellphone battery goes dead.

In the film, Rod represents the collective wisdom and memories of African Americans, as he is the only person who recognizes the threat to people of color in spaces of white supremacy, but to no avail. Rod goes to the police station to report Chris as missing as he is unable to reach him by phone for two days. He tells Detective Latoya the following regarding the Armitages: "They're probably abducting Black people, brainwashing them and making them slaves . . . or sex slaves. Not just regular slaves, but sex slaves and shit. See? I don't know if it's the hypnosis that's making 'em slaves or what not, but all I know is they already got two brothers we know and there could be a whole bunch of brothers they got already." The detective and her colleagues, as well as Chris, believe that Rod's theory is absurd and could not possibly happen in an affluent suburb populated by liberal, upper-middle-class white families. Although this exchange is used for comic effect, the audience realizes that Rod's concern is justifiable because Chris's life is in jeopardy. Actually, Rod's anxieties are not that far-fetched considering the long history of violence to Black bodies in the United States. Enslaved Black women and men were subjected to sexual violation, which included "outright physical penetrative assault, forced reproduction, sexual coercion and manipulation, and psychic abuse."[40] Rod's assertions represent a collective legacy of distrust that African Americans have inherited from the shared remembrance of white "fascination with black sexuality as exotic."[41] The stereotypical belief in Black masculinity as hypersexualized led to horrible acts against Black bodies such as the Tuskegee Syphilis Study, which was conducted on Black men without their knowledge and consent between 1932 and 1972.[42]

Notably, Rose's mother is a psychiatrist, and her father is a doctor, professionals who symbolize the psychological and physical violence historically committed against African American bodies in domestic spaces. Rose's brother, Jeremy (Caleb Landry Jones), who openly discusses stereotypes about Black bodies at the dinner table, using terms such as "genetic makeup" to argue that Chris "would be a fucking beast" if he trained his body. Jeremy embodies racist attitudes of racial essentialism and violence—in other words, older forms of racism rooted in colonialism and slavery. Chris is unable to escape the Armitage home because he was hypnotized by Rose's mother the night before as part of a ruse to help him stop smoking. He finds himself mentally trapped in the sunken place—a dark void—and physically tied to an armchair and forced to watch a short video on an old television console in the basement by Rose's grandfather, Roman Armitage (Richard Herd). In the video, titled "Behold the Coagula," Roman explains that Chris was chosen for his "natural gifts," another reference to racial essentialism. Arguably, Rose's grandfather represents the generational bridge between Jim Crow forms of racism and colorblind ideology. In these collective scenes, Peele pushes back at neoliberal racism, which supposedly embraces African Americans by disseminating postracial narratives that assert that racism is a thing of the past—a period in United States history to be forgotten—despite evidence to the contrary.

The collective wisdom and memories of African Americans are further suppressed in the sunken place, which Peele conceptualizes as a space of marginalization where people of color are silenced no matter how much they scream.[43] In its lowly environs, Chris is forced to view his life on a screen as his body is trapped in a void. Jim Hudson, the gallery owner who is designated to occupy his body, describes Chris's limited existence in the sunken place as the following: "A sliver of you will still be in there somewhere; limited consciousness; you'll be able to see and hear what your body is doing, but your existence will be as a passenger . . . an audience." Peele's description of the sunken place is similar to Sigmund Freud's use of the palimpsest to describe the function of the unconscious. Freud employed the metaphor of Rome as palimpsest to describe the function of memory as it relates to his topographical model of the mind: the conscious, preconscious, and unconscious levels.[44] He theorized that the mind accumulates memories in the unconscious by likening it to the layers of the built environment: "Let us make the fantastic supposition that Rome were not a human dwelling-place, but a mental entity with just as long and varied a past history: that is, *in which nothing once constructed had perished*, and all the earlier stages of development had survived alongside the latest" (emphasis added).[45] Most of the feelings, beliefs, and memories that drive human behavior are buried in the unconscious, mostly inaccessible to our conscious minds but at times they surface like older writing on a palimpsest.[46] Like the historical remnants of the built environment, Chris's conscious mind will not perish; that is, his memories, beliefs, and thoughts will continue to exist but in limited form as his consciousness will be buried, presumably in Jim's unconscious mind.

This conceptualization of the mind is helpful in understanding the servant Georgina, who exists in the sunken place, and explains her reaction when Chris confronts her about his dead cellphone. Georgina apologies to Chris, claiming that she must have accidently unplugged it when cleaning the desk in the bedroom. Chris again attempts to connect with Georgina as a Black person in a white space by stating, "All I know is sometimes if there's too many white people, I get nervous, you know." Georgina responds with prolonged silence, then a strange smile, laughter, and tears, followed by "No, no, no, no, no, no. That is not my experience, not at all. The Armitages are good to us—they treat us like family." In this scene, Georgina appears to be experiencing internal conflict as her unconscious mind seems to break through the surface, but only for a moment before Rose's transplanted grandmother regains control and presents as a conforming Black woman. In the sunken place, Chris and Georgina will be silenced through total assimilation, trapped under the layers of consciousness (Freud's level of awareness). Their experiences reference those Black families who purchased homes in majority white spaces and were expected to deny their cultural identities through assimilation and neutralization—to embrace whiteness and to be subservient.[47]

In our current era of neoliberal racism, people of color are often expected to accept colorblind ideology, which argues that all people have equal opportunity regardless of their race or ethnic origins. The sunken place acts as a metaphor to understand how neoliberal racism in the form of colorblindness attempts to negate and ultimately to forget the legacy of structural racism. For example, individual failings and prejudice are offered as the reason why people of color do not achieve the American Dream instead of institutional racism, which prevented African Americans from buying homes in the suburbs and continues to construct and support racial inequality. The following exchange between Chris and the gallery owner uncovers the racism that undergirds colorblind ideology:

CHRIS: Why Black people . . . ?

JIM: Who knows? Some people want to change. Some people wanna be stronger, faster, cooler. Blah blah blah, but don't lump me in with that ignorant shit. *I couldn't give two shits about race. I don't care if you are black, brown, green, purple . . . whatever* [emphasis added]. People are people. What I want is deeper: Your eye, man. I want those things you see through.

CHRIS: That's crazy.

JIM: Is there a greater compliment?[48]

Jim articulates the colorblind credo, claiming that race does not matter, but he ultimately embraces the violence of racism by the silencing of Black voices. Ultimately, Chris is expected to willingly accept his fate and not question white supremacy. In *Get Out*, Black people are terrorized and silenced in predominantly white spaces, analogous to historical experiences of people of color in suburban spaces of whiteness.

Conclusion

Get Out depicts the reality of people of color in wealthy, white-dominated suburbs in "postracial" America after the election of Barack Obama. It can be read as a representation of a palimpsest space, signifying the temporal and spatial layers of violence and psychic trauma experienced by African Americans in white spaces in the United States both past and present. The film reveals neoliberal racist tactics that deprive people of color of their voices and tries to erase them. These strategies echo the racist practices of the postwar period that excluded African Americans from the suburbs and sundown towns and through official histories that failed to acknowledge their memories and historical experiences during Jim Crow. Neoliberal colorblind ideology maintains existing power structures by downplaying and ultimately negating the lived experience of violence and discrimination of people of color, a repression that Peele seeks to make manifest. The film represents the social-spatial practice of racism in the United States and challenges neoliberal racism by mobilizing collective memory and history to confront the horrors of historical forms of racism. It also engages the audience through fear, allowing spectators to recognize contemporary forms of racism that comprise the real terror that people of color continue to face in predominantly white spaces such as the suburbs.

Notes

1. Chimamanda Ngozi Adichie, *Americanah* (New York: Alfred A. Knopf, 2013), 390.

2. This chapter represents an expansion and reframing of arguments in a previously published article: Elizabeth A. Patton, "*Get Out* and the Legacy of Sundown Suburbs in Post-racial America," *New Review of Film and Television Studies* 17, no. 3 (2019): 349–363.

3. bell hooks, "Representing Whiteness in the Black Imagination," in *Cultural Studies*, edited by Lawrence Grossberg, Cary Nelson, and Paula Treichler, 338–346 (London: Routledge, 1992).

4. Robert A. Beuka, *SuburbiaNation: Reading Suburban Landscape in Twentieth-Century American Fiction and Film* (New York: Palgrave Macmillan, 2004), 19.

5. Craig E. Barton, *Sites of Memory: Perspectives on Architecture and Race* (New York: Princeton Architectural Press, 2001), xv.

6. David Roberts and Minelle Mahtani, "Neoliberalizing Race, Racing Neoliberalism: Placing 'Race' in Neoliberal Discourses," *Antipode* 42, no. 2 (March 2010): 250.

7. See Michael Omi and Howard Winant, *Racial Formation in the United States*, 3rd ed. (New York: Routledge, 2014), 55, 152.

8. For a detailed discussion of the role of race in the history of Black horror films, see Robin R. Means Coleman, *Horror Noire: Blacks in American Horror Films from the 1890s to Present* (New York: Routledge, 2011).

9. Andrew Wiese, *Places of Their Own: African American Suburbanization in the Twentieth Century* (Chicago: University of Chicago Press, 2009), 109.

10. Amy Lynn Corbin, *Cinematic Geographies and Multicultural Spectatorship in America* (New York: Palgrave Macmillan, 2015), 170.

11. Richard Dyer, *White: Essays on Race and Culture* (London: Routledge, 1997), 209.

12. Robert R. Weyeneth, "The Architecture of Racial Segregation: The Challenges of Preserving the Problematical Past," *Public Historian* 27, no. 4 (2015): 11–44.

13. Beuka, *SuburbiaNation*, 220–221.

14. George Lipsitz, *How Racism Takes Place* (Philadelphia: Temple University Press, 2011), 6.

15. Sometimes they are referred to as sunset towns; James W. Loewen, *Sundown Towns* (New York: New Press, 2005), 6.

16. Loewen, *Sundown Towns*, 3.

17. Thomas J. Sugrue, *Sweet Land of Liberty: The Forgotten Struggle for Civil Rights in the North* (New York: Random House, 2009), 208.

18. Loewen, *Sundown Towns*, 281.

19. Dyer, *White*, 209.

20. Wiese, *Places of Their Own*, 100.

21. Arnold R. Hirsch, *Making the Second Ghetto: Race and Housing in Chicago, 1940–1960* (Chicago: University of Chicago Press, 1998), 40.

22. Stephen Middleton, *The Black Laws: Race and the Legal Process in Early Ohio* (Athens: Ohio University Press, 2005), 74–75.

23. For an in-depth discussion of the relationship between the history of slavery in the United States and the adoption of Black Codes in southern states, see Douglas A. Blackmon, *Slavery by Another Name: The Re-enslavement of Black Americans from the Civil War to World War II* (London: Icon Books, 2012); Michelle Alexander, *The New Jim Crow: Mass Incarceration in the Age of Colorblindness* (New York: New Press, 2012), 28.

24. Alexander, *The New Jim Crow*, 28.

25. Alexander, *The New Jim Crow*, 4.

26. Alexander, *The New Jim* Crow.

27. Hollywood has historically depicted sundown towns in the southern region of the United States. For example, in *The Fugitive Kind* (1960), the sheriff evokes the image of a sundown to threaten a white drifter, Valentine Xavier (Marlon Brando), if he does not immediately leave town. *Sudie and Simpson* (Tewksbury, 1990) is set in a fictional Georgia town with a sign that says "Nigger!! Don't let the sun set on you in Linlow," and *Freedom Song* (Robinson, 2000) is set in a Mississippi town with a large billboard that says "Nigger, Read and Run / If you can't read, run anyway."

28. The guidebook was published by Victor Hugo Green, a New York City mailman, from 1936 to 1966.

29. Bethonie Butler, "Jordan Peele Made a Woke Horror Film," *Washington Post*, February 23, 2017. https://www.washingtonpost.com/lifestyle/style/jordan-peele-made-a-woke-horror-film/2017/02/22/5162f21e-f549-11e6-a9b0-ecee7ce475fc_story.html?utm_term=.235135dddbc8.

30. Sugrue, *Sweet Land of Liberty*, 132.

31. Joshua F. J. Inwood, "Neoliberal Racism: The 'Southern Strategy' and the Expanding Geographies of White Supremacy," *Social & Cultural Geography* 16, no. 4 (January 1015), http://doi.org/10.1080/14649365.2014.994670.

32. Loewen, *Sundown Towns*, 109.

33. Frank Hobbs and Nicole Stoops, U.S. Census Bureau, *Census 2000 Special Reports, Series CENSR-4, Demographic Trends in the 20th Century* (Washington, DC: U.S. Government Printing Office, 2002), 31.

34. Dolores Hayden. *Building Suburbia: Green Fields and Urban Growth, 1820–2000* (New York: Vintage, 2004), 132; Barbara M. Kelly, *Expanding the American Dream: Building and Rebuilding Levittown* (Albany: State University of New York Press, 1993), 17–18.

35. Lizabeth Cohen, *Consumers' Republic: The Politics of Mass Consumption in Postwar America* (New York: Vintage, 2008), 141.

36. Richard Rothstein, *The Color of Law: A Forgotten History of How Our Government Segregated America* (New York: Liveright Publishing, 2017), xi.

37. Jonathan Fricker and Donna Fricker, "Louisiana Architecture: 1945–1965 Post-War Subdivisions and the Ranch House" (Baton Rouge: Louisiana Division of Historic Preservation, 2010), 7–8, http://www.crt.state.la.us/hp/nationalregister/historic_contexts/ranchhousefinalrevised.pdf.

38. Barton, *Sites of Memory*, xv–xvi.

39. Trent Clark, "Jordan Peele Explains Why Childish Gambino's 'Redbone' Was Perfect for 'Get Out'," *HipHopDX*, February 23, 2017, https://hiphopdx.com/news/id.42476/title.jordan-peele-explains-why-childish-gambinos-redbone-was-perfect-for-get-out.

40. Thomas A. Foster, "The Sexual Abuse of Black Men under American Slavery," *Journal of the History of Sexuality* 20, no. 3 (September 2011): 445–464.

41. Alankaar Sharma, "Diseased Race, Racialized Disease: The Story of the Negro Project of American Social Hygiene Association against the Backdrop of the Tuskegee Syphilis Experiment," *Journal of African American Studies* 14, no. 2 (2010): 259.

42. Sharma, "Diseased Race, Racialized Disease."

43. Jordan Peele, Twitter Post. March 16, 2017, 9:12 PM. https://twitter.com/jordanpeele/status/842589407521595393?lang=en.

44. See also Freud's description of a child's writing toy, the "Mystic Writing-pad," to describe the function of memory. Sigmund Freud, "A Note upon the 'Mystic Writing-Pad,' " in *Organization and Pathology of Thought: Selected Sources*, ed. D. Rapaport (New York: Columbia University Press, 1951), 329–337.

45. Sigmund Freud, *Civilization and Its Discontents* (New York: Dover Publications, [1929] 2016), 6.

46. For a detailed discussion, see Thomas Parisi, "The Unconscious: Dynamic, Conflictual, Transformative," in *Civilization and Its Discontents: An Anthropology for the Future?* Twayne's Masterwork Studies 171 (New York: Twayne Publishers, 1988), 44–57.

47. For an in-depth discussion of the experience of Black families moving to and living in white suburbs during the postwar era, see also Daisy D. Myers, *Sticks 'n Stones: The Myers Family in Levittown* (York, PA: York County Heritage Trust, 2005), and Sugrue, *Sweet Land of Liberty*.

48. Jordan Peele and Tananarive Due, *Get Out* (Los Angeles: Inventory Press, 2019), 128.

References

Adichie, Chimamanda Ngozi. *Americanah*. New York: Alfred A. Knopf, 2013.

Barton, Craig E. *Sites of Memory: Perspectives on Architecture and Race*. New York: Princeton Architectural Press, 2001.

Beuka, Robert A. *SuburbiaNation: Reading Suburban Landscape in Twentieth-Century American Fiction and Film*. New York: Palgrave Macmillan, 2004.

Butler, Bethonie. "Jordan Peele Made a Woke Horror Film." *Washington Post*, February 23, 2017. https://www.washingtonpost.com/lifestyle/style/jordan-peele-made-a-woke-horror-film/2017/02/22/5162f21e-f549-11e6-a9b0-ecee7ce475fc_story.html?utm_term=.235135dddbc8.

Clark, Trent. "Jordan Peele Explains Why Childish Gambino's 'Redbone' Was Perfect for 'Get Out'." *HipHopDX*, February 23, 2017. https://hiphopdx.

com/news/id.42476/title.jordan-peele-explains-why-childish-gambinos-red-bone-was-perfect-for-get-out.

Cohen, Lizabeth. *Consumers' Republic: The Politics of Mass Consumption in Postwar America*. New York: Vintage, 2008.

Corbin, Amy Lynn. *Cinematic Geographies and Multicultural Spectatorship in America*. New York: Palgrave Macmillan, 2015.

Dyer, Richard. *White: Essays on Race and Culture*. London: Routledge, 1997.

Feldman, Keith P. "The Globality of Whiteness in Post-Racial Visual Culture." *Cultural Studies* 30 (2016): 289–311.

Foster, Thomas A. "The Sexual Abuse of Black Men under American Slavery." *Journal of the History of Sexuality* 20, no. 3 (September 2011): 445–464.

Frankowski, Alfred. "The Violence of Post-Racial Memory and the Political Sense of Mourning." *Contemporary Aesthetics*, October 7, 2013, https://contempaesthetics.org/newvolume/pages/article.php?articleID=676.

Freud, Sigmund. *Civilization and Its Discontents*. New York: Dover Publications, (1929) 2016.

Fricker, Jonathan, and Donna Fricker. "Louisiana Architecture: 1945–1965 Post-War Subdivisions and the Ranch House." Louisiana Division of Historic Preservation, 2010, http://www.crt.state.la.us/hp/nationalregister/historic_contexts/ranchhousefinalrevised.pdf.

Hayden, Dolores. *Building Suburbia: Green Fields and Urban Growth, 1820–2000*. New York: Vintage, 2004.

Hirsch, Arnold R. *Making the Second Ghetto: Race and Housing in Chicago, 1940–1960*. Chicago: University of Chicago Press, 1998.

Hobbs, Frank, and Nicole Stoops, U.S. Census Bureau. *Census 2000 Special Reports, Series CENSR-4, Demographic Trends in the 20th Century*. Washington, DC: U.S. Government Printing Office, 2002.

hooks, bell. "Representing Whiteness in the Black Imagination." In *Cultural Studies*, edited by Lawrence Grossberg, Cary Nelson, and Paula Treichler, 338–346. London: Routledge, 1992.

Inwood, Joshua F. J. "Neoliberal Racism: The 'Southern Strategy' and the Expanding Geographies of White Supremacy." *Social & Cultural Geography* 16, no. 4 (January 2015): 407–423, doi:10.1080/14649365.2014.994670.

Kelly, Barbara M. *Expanding the American Dream: Building and Rebuilding Levittown*. Albany: State University of New York Press, 1993.

Loewen, James W. *Sundown Towns*. New York: New Press, 2005.

Mele, Christopher. "Neoliberalism, Race and the Redefining of Urban Redevelopment." *International Journal of Urban & Regional Research* 37 (2013): 598–617.

Myers, Daisy. *Sticks 'n Stones: The Myers Family in Levittown*. York, PA: York County Heritage Trust, 2005.

Omi, Michael, and Howard Winant. *Racial Formation in the United States*. 3rd ed. New York: Routledge, 2014.

Ono, Kent A. "Postracism: A Theory of the 'Post'—as Political Strategy." *Journal of Communication Inquiry* 34 (2010): 227–33.

Roberts, David, and Minelle Mahtani. "Neoliberalizing Race, Racing Neoliberalism: Placing 'Race' in Neoliberal Discourses." *Antipode* 42, no. 2 (March 2010): 248–257.

Sugrue, Thomas J. *Sweet Land of Liberty: The Forgotten Struggle for Civil Rights in the North*. New York: Random House, 2009.

Weyeneth, Robert R. "The Architecture of Racial Segregation: The Challenges of Preserving the Problematical Past." *Public Historian* 27, no. 4 (2015): 11–44.

Wiese, Andrew. *Places of Their Own: African American Suburbanization in the Twentieth Century*. Chicago: University of Chicago Press, 2009.

10

The Limits and Possibilities of Suburban Iconoclasm

Suburbicon and 99 Homes

NATHAN HOLMES

ERIAL VIEWS OF ITERATIVE landscapes, slow-motion tracking shots of men waving from behind garden hoses, impossibly coiffed and crinolined housewives laboring effortlessly in kitchens, buzz-cut white children gathered around television sets. These images are the familiar preludes to iconoclastic narratives in which the charming façades of white middle-class life—often the literal front lawns and exterior walls of suburban homes—conceal dark, psychically corrupt, and oppressive interiors. The familiar gesture of suburban iconoclasm is performed within a range of late twentieth and early twenty-first century popular films. In various ways, these films sustain what has become a common sense idea, that the suburbs are a zone of artifice and inauthenticity, a false appearance containing a secret history. This common sense is the effect of an endlessly repeated technique of defamiliarization in which, as Timotheus Vermeulen puts it, "the pretty white fence secretes a grave-yard, or the spectacular picture window hides abuse in plain sight."[1] Such representations are typically expressionistic or surreal and set *outside* any historical reality directly related to social geography or the built environment. The sense of isolation or nowhere-ness in *The 'Burbs* (Dante, 1989), *Edward Scissorhands* (Burton, 1990), *The Virgin Suicides* (Coppola, 1999), and *It Follows* (Mitchell, 2014), the artificially televisual settings of *Pleasantville* (Ross 1998) and *The Truman Show* (Weir, 1998), and the constant return to "the 1950s" as either a setting or an aesthetic sensibility connoting middle-class whiteness make sense within the terms of suburban iconoclasm, which has typically sought a controlled, agreeably kitschy, false appearance on which to stage its revelatory gesture.

While the racial geography and class structure of the suburbs has changed dramatically, on-screen and in the popular imagination the suburbs remain blindingly white and middle class. In part, this has had to do with the whiteness of Hollywood itself and its economic calculation that Black casts do not attract mass audiences. But one danger in understanding the suburbs as synonymous with whiteness is the ease with which racial ontology—whiteness as a transhistorical essence—becomes substituted for the historically dynamic assemblage of the political, economic, and social forces that constitute it.[2] This "racecraft," Barbara and Karen Fields argue, "transforms racism into race, disguising collective social practice as inborn individual traits."[3] For Barbara and Karen Fields and other historical materialist scholars of American racism, whiteness is less an explanation for racism—including the exclusionary and predatory practices of American housing—than its result. The diverse groups of Americans who moved to the suburbs in the postwar era, many of whom were recent immigrants, didn't necessarily think of themselves as white until they were interpellated as such by federal policies and real estate practices.[4] Claims of racial ontology are also susceptible of seeing race to the exclusion of class structures, with "whiteness" frequently functioning as a metaphor for class power.[5] *Get Out*, for example, was primarily seen by critics (if not by Jordan Peele himself) as an iconoclastic indictment of the emboldened racism of white liberals in the putatively "postracial" era of the Obama presidency. Yet, as Touré F. Reed notes, hardly any mention was made of the obvious affluence of the household in which Chris (Daniel Kaluuya) becomes trapped, or the ways that upper-class suburban insularity, entitlement, and acquisitiveness could be seen as an animating factor in their monstrous racial essentialism.[6] The use of the suburbs to conjoin white and middle-class categories persists in cultural and political discourse (consider, for example, what the oft-invoked "suburban voter" is meant to connote) despite the fact that the majority of metropolitan Black Americans now live in the suburbs and despite the fact that in the contemporary economy "the middle class" is an increasingly meaningless term.[7]

The degree to which suburban iconoclasm has helped to either mystify or describe the historical processes and effects of racial inequality is ambiguous. Films such as *The Virgin Suicides* and *Revolutionary Road* portray idyllic white enclaves marred by profound but nebulous internal disturbances that seem immanent to racial homogeneity or ideologies of exclusion, a return of the repressed that rhymes with suburban horror formulas. In these instances, suburban iconoclasm aims not so much at the suburban dream but at the essence of suburbia itself as a historical, geographic, and, in the terms of Omi and Winant, "racial formation" (following the Fields's critique of the ways race is substituted for racism, we might correct this to "racist formation") predicated on segregation. But suburban iconoclasm is less trenchant when its critique centers the suburbs as a solely *cultural* formation, one which imagines those who live there as naively identifying with the suburban dream. *Revolutionary Road* and *American Beauty* (both directed by Sam Mendes) snidely regard the suburbs as an individual lifestyle choice, one that is available to critique primarily on the grounds of inauthenticity. In racial terms, the perniciousness of such representations is in the way they give ground to the idea that the suburbs are an *effect* of whiteness or white identity rather than spaces that, inasmuch as they are white enclaves, *produce* or help to constitute the mistaken assumption that whiteness is an inborn trait.[8] Jettisoning racial ontology not only brings the socioeconomic dynamics of the suburbs into focus, it also makes them available to be seen not simply as a social space to be cast off, but to be built upon.

In what follows I examine two recent films that attempt to make sense of the suburbs as a social space. The first, *Suburbicon*, is set within the Levittown, Pennsylvania race riots of 1957 but mystifies the suburban history it attempts to represent by psychologizing whiteness. The second, *99 Homes*, adopts a melodramatic-realist mode that engages the psychic and economic dynamics of the 2008 housing crisis. While there is no question that suburban iconoclasm has become a banal repudiation of white suburbia, this chapter argues that its essential impetus holds the potential to interpret suburban life and expand our understanding of the dynamics that shape it. The stakes of recognizing this impetus lie in the necessity of recognizing that the suburbs are not an elective culture but a social reality. This makes the suburbs crucial to any mass social transformation oriented around questions of racial inequality and class politics, not to mention climate change or the politics of gender. In order to explore the possibilities and limitations of suburban iconoclasm as the site of such transformation, I propose that we see it as an aesthetic expression of what Marshall Berman identified as the "avidity" characterizing suburban life.[9] Countering the political activists of his generation who had written off the suburbs, Berman argued for seeing avidity—a combination of restless energy and ardent fervor—rather than apathy as a defining quality of suburban life. In Berman's view avidity helps to clarify the suburbs as a dynamically contradictory social space whose history generates forms of collectivism and class solidarity alongside racism, conservative reaction, and nugatory consumerism.

Suburbicon opens on the Mayers, a Black family moving into the all-white community of Suburbicon (a fictionalized version of Levittown, Pennsylvania), an event that shows their new white neighbors to be visibly stunned (figure 10.1). Although the film does not explicitly acknowledge the true events on which it is based (this was only done in publicity discourse for the film), the Mayers are based on the real-life Myers family, who moved to Levittown in August 1957 as part of a civil rights campaign to integrate the suburbs and then faced virulent opposition to their presence by local residents, culminating in violent protests. *Suburbicon*'s version of the Myerses' story is told in brief episodes between the film's

Figure 10.1. Mrs. Mayers (Karimah Westbrook) in front of her new home in *Suburbicon* (George Clooney, Black Bear Pictures, Dark Castle Entertainment, Huahua Media, Silver Pictures, Smokehouse Pictures, 2017). Digital frame enlargement.

more dominant plotline focusing on their neighbors, the white Lodge family. This storyline unfolds a noir-ish plotline in which Gardner Lodge (Matt Damon) engineers the kidnapping and murder of his wife by a pair of cartoonish hoodlums, Rose (Julianne Moore) and her sister (also played, for uncanny effect, by Moore) as part of an insurance scheme. This narrative focalization effectively sidelines the Mayerses' story and the bigotry they face becomes overshadowed by a darkly comic tale involving the Lodges. The Lodge story is primarily told from the point of view of young Nicky Lodge (Noah Jupe), who slowly discovers his father's designs. As Nicky pieces together the plot and begins to fear for his own safety, next door Mrs. and Mr. Mayers (Karimah Westbrook and Leith M. Burke) and their son, Andy (Tony Espinosa), face growing hostility from their white neighbors, who build fences and gather outside their house in increasing numbers to loudly jeer at them, pound on musical instruments, and sing "Dixie." While the Lodge family plot unravels, the film crosscuts to bigoted protestors who begin to riot. As the police fruitlessly attempt to restrain them, they jump on the Mayerses' car, throw rocks through windows, and, finally, place a Confederate flag on the front of their house. When the sun rises the next morning Nicky's scheming father and aunt, his heroic uncle Mitch (Gary Basaraba), an insurance investigator (Oscar Isaac), and the two hoodlums hired for the home invasion (Glenn Feshler and Alex Hassell) have been, respectively, poisoned, strangled, stabbed, bludgeoned by a fire poker, shot, and run over by a fire engine. As the Mayers silently pick up the detritus of the previous night's riots, Nicky heads outside with his baseball glove to play with young Andy Mayer.

Suburbicon's dualized storyline was designed to form a meaningful counterpoint between private and public sagas. The message of the film, as Ann Hornaday summarized it in her review for the *Washington Post*, is that "the performative wholesomeness of the Lodge household is just as bogus as the self-proclaimed virtue of the racists terrorizing the black family next door."[10] Yet for many critics this construction was received as imbalanced or even tone deaf for the way its centering of white characters in a historical representation reproduced the Hollywood tendency to whitewash history. In the *New York Times*, Wesley Morris echoed the feelings of many critics by saying that *Suburbicon* amounted to a misguided attempt to express America's racist past that was apparently driven more by Clooney's white guilt than the need to tell the Mayerses' side of the story. *Suburbicon*, that is, smacked of a

Hollywood liberalism "where showing a problem tends to be confused with addressing it." Clooney, Morris bluntly states, is "not humanizing the Mayers . . . he is using them."[11]

It's also possible to see *Suburbicon*'s failure in more formal or generic terms. *Suburbicon* is the result of a combination of two scripts, George Clooney and Grant Heslov's on the Levittown riots and an unused script written by Joel and Ethan Coen from 1986 that had been languishing in a Warner Brothers vault. Clooney and Heslov's work arguably contributed to the film's sober historicist style, while the Coens, from the distance of a few decades, supplied their recognizable combination of noir and screwball. Along with John Waters and Tim Burton, the Coens' visual aesthetic, as much as their writing, has contributed to the retro, midcentury iconography of suburban iconoclasm, and in films such as *Fargo* (1996) and *A Serious Man* (2009) they rely on suburban settings to suggest the banality of American desperation, a theme more directly tackled in the visually Coen-esque *Suburbicon*.

Yet the inadequacy of *Suburbicon* goes even further than issues of formal proportion or normative ideas regarding the "humanization" of characters. It has also to do with the film's approach to historical representation, which simplistically flattens the events surrounding the Levittown riots into a presentist vision of instinctive racism. In the film, the Mayers family appear in town ex nihilo to face unremitting white prejudice. The events to which *Suburbicon* refers, in fact, have been amply documented, and would not have been difficult to locate or dramatize.[12] In fact, the film reproduces a number of scenes from *Crisis in Levittown* (1957), an NAACP-produced documentary that sought to demonstrate a plurality of opinion—from opposition to support—among the white residents of the suburb to the Myerses' presence. The Myerses' decision to move to Levittown was not a private one, and the vocal, violent reaction of a group of white homeowners was not a kind of primal bigotry; it was mediated by the anxious precarity (rather than solidity) that attached to property ownership. As Thomas Sugrue has shown, the Myerses' residency in Levittown was part of a larger civil-rights campaign to integrate the suburbs spearheaded by the American Friends Service Committee, a Quaker group committed to civil rights and racial freedom with deep roots in southeastern Pennsylvania.[13] In *Suburbicon*, there is no mention of the planning of the project to integrate Levittown, the interracial coalition of activists that spurred the Myerses' move, the numerous Levittown supporters of the Myers (some of whom are interviewed in *Crisis in Levittown*), the neighbors who agreed to stay with them and to watch

their house so that the Myerses could sleep soundly, or, finally, the fact
that the news media were present in the suburb from the very beginning
of the Myerses' move (not arriving, as the film implies, in response to
the riot). Instead, the collective politics of civil rights are transmuted
into private feeling, such as when Nicky talks with Andy about how
his parents are dealing with the protests. "My dad says you don't show
'em nothing . . . and you don't show 'em you're scared." In *Suburbicon*'s
representation, the Mayerses quietly embody the ethos and resolve of
the civil rights movement, but only in a highly individualized and almost
prosaic (one might say *suburban*) way. Consonant with the liberal view
of racism, their attachment to civil rights is a matter of personal choice
rather than part of a larger struggle.

It's perhaps the case that historical representation and suburban
iconoclasm are narrative discourses simply too disparate to be paired.
In contrast to the diffuse solemnity marking the Mayerses' storyline,
the story that unfolds within the walls of the Lodge household adopts
the sharp angles and high-contrast lighting redolent of noir—more
specifically, the cartoonishly menacing color interiors of Nicholas Ray's
Bigger Than Life (1956)—to lend a gleeful wackiness to Gardner Lodge's
avarice. In one scene, Nicky—a variation on Christopher Olsen's Richie
in *Bigger Than Life*—returns home from a Little League game to discover
pamphlets for military school. After hearing a muffled scream Nicky
grabs a steak knife and walks bravely down the basement stairs, pulling
on a light to reveal his aunt Emily bent over the pool table, his father,
pants around his ankles, spanking her with a table tennis paddle. After
Nicky quickly shuts off the lights in shock, the scene pointedly cuts to
the ongoing construction of fences by the Mayerses' neighbors. In this
(primal) scene and others, everyday consumer objects are rendered darkly
absurd, just as public prejudice indexes private sexual deviance. Later,
Gardner delivers a stern lecture to Nicky in his den about "discipline,"
a gurgling aquarium featuring an underwater treasure scene behind him
mocking his seriousness. After his murder plot unravels, Gardner kills
an insurance investigator with a fire poker in the middle of a nighttime
street, then, after disposing his body at a construction site, flees the scene
on a comically tiny children's bicycle. He dies, finally, after eating a
poisoned peanut butter sandwich. In short, the entire suburban lifeworld,
all of the mass-produced kitsch that fills and surrounds middle-class
existence—from Ping-Pong paddles and fire pokers to peanut butter
sandwiches—is shown as easily converted into nightmarish instruments
of malevolence, perversion, and death.

The incommensurability of the film's storylines has to do with the divergence of the lifeworlds each implies. The Lodge storyline describes an uncanny, psychologically distorted, and fundamentally surreal environment that seems drawn from a vigorous Oedipal imagination (Julianne Moore plays both Nicky's mother and aunt and is thus figured as both his mom and his not-mom replacement mom). This plasticity of mise-en-scène, however, is at odds with Hollywood's conventional mode of historical representation, particularly in recent films, that depicts the histories of American racism. Flamboyant stylization would be at odds with the aims of films like *42* (Helgeland, 2013), *Selma* (DuVernay, 2014), or *Hidden Figures* (Melfi, 2016), which employ psychological realism as a way to restore dignity to historical figures entangled in the irrationalities of racism.[14] In this register, racism is typically embodied in baleful individuals, even if they are representatives of larger structures of power, and it is never imbued in the physical world itself. The represented historical world in these films cannot be plastic because its goal is to convince us of its unmediated transparency to history's actuality. *Suburbicon*'s gamble is that it can make these ends meet. The saga of the Lodge family is not just meant to ironically undermine the rumors that a Black family will bring the problems of the inner city to peaceful Levittown, but also to help psychologize the irrational prejudice of the white protestors. Racism, in this view, is fundamentally displacement—behind every angry white bigot is a tawdry tale of perversion and avarice. The protests are merely the epiphenomenal surface; probe deeper, go inside the home, and you will find the truth.

Such a structure aligns with a fundamentally narrow, but long-standing liberal view of racist animus that *Suburbicon* unwittingly reproduces. As historian Lily Geismer writes: "The increasing popularity of psychology in the 1940s and 1950s accentuated [a] focus on individualism. . . . Psychoanalytic theories became especially important to liberal ideas about race and racism during the postwar period, and reinforced the idea that racism was the product of personal prejudice and moral deficiencies, rather than public policy or the directives of the market."[15] The movement between the outside of violent protest and the life of the Mayerses (who are never pictured inside their house) to the inside/interior story of the Lodges mirrors the surface to depth movements of psychoanalysis. Without reference to the federal policies or real estate markets shaping suburban life, the viewer of *Suburbicon* can trace racism back only to the congenital immorality of the family or a craven patriarch like Gardner Lodge.

Is it possible to disavow the false promises made for the suburbs and the perils of property relations with their connections to racist violence, and yet also acknowledge and sustain a relationship to "home," however we may define it? If the only legitimate way to cinematically interpret suburban experience is to couch it within frames of individual shame, irony, or contempt (a position clearly implying a distanced, undoubtedly urbane, even white, authenticity) then on what grounds can we imagine a better world that takes into account the existence of the suburbs?

Some such questions underpin Marshall Berman's "Notes toward a New Society," a ranging account of the pitfalls of the New Left's understanding of American society and its possibilities for transformation published in the early 1970s. For Berman, this era was marked by radical activism, partially derived from Marcuse's *One-Dimensional Man*, in which "a people that is internally monolithic is opposed by radical forces from the 'outside.' "[16] Vanguardist revolutionary groups such as the Weathermen adopted a condemnatory stance toward America as a whole, including, Berman notes, quoting from their first manifesto, "not only the rich, the owners of wealth and property, the bourgeoisie, but 'virtually all of the white working class,' blue- and white collar alike, who enjoy 'privileges, but very real ones, which give them an edge of vested interests and tie them to the imperialists.' "[17] Such radical groups, composed of members that were highly educated, middle class, and mostly suburban, identified themselves with the oppressed peoples of colonized Third World countries, whom they understood to be in the best position to overthrow not just American imperialism, but the American people themselves. In the words of the late Weatherman Ted Gold, "If it will take fascism, we'll have to have fascism"[18] For Berman, the Weatherpeople's extremism was simply the logical extension of "[the] idea of the American people as 'one-dimensional' which most American radicals had accepted uncritically for years," and that "by taking it seriously—dead seriously—the Weatherpeople made it plain to all of us how cruel, how antihuman an idea it was."[19] The problem, as Berman saw it, was the lack of political alternatives that do not take up a simplistic inside-outside dynamic, and which sought out "a theory of 'modern' people, of the men and women who highly developed societies create; a theory of the tensions and contradictions in the life we live, of our strengths and limitations, of our hidden capacities and potentialities."[20]

To develop such a theory would mean not looking to faraway places and peoples in order to "get outside ourselves," but rather, starting, as it were, at home. To answer these questions, Berman looks to the writings of Jean-Jacques Rousseau, which interpreted the turmoil of the modern urban age as animating a "free-floating avidity" among individuals, an ambiguous mix of creative and destructive impulses, a pursuit of sex or profit that made them "noisy, brilliant, and fearsome." Although Rousseau saw avidity as a signature obstacle to democracy or even happiness, he understood that there was no going back, no return to more innocent modes of traditional rural life. As Berman explains, "*avidity* is at the heart of Rousseau's dialectic": "On the one hand, avidity compels man to pursue profit and power, to compete against and exploit one another. On the other, avidity alone can infuse men with the daring to get through the masks, to feel and know themselves and each other, and to fight to fulfill their real potentialities. . . . it will take avidity to liberate human energy *from* bourgeois society—so that people working together, in a more genuine community, can develop themselves and each other more fully than possible."[21] Essentially, Berman's reading of Rousseau encourages us to look at the spaces of American middle-class life cast as least revolutionary—namely, the suburbs—to find evidence of a motive force for experimenting with new social formations.

The American suburbs *have* been such an experiment, although this has not been the dominant representation. As Herbert Gans's famous study of Long Island's Levittown illustrated, the suburbs fomented both an avid consumer culture and new forms of communitarianism and political resistance.[22] These were built on the basis of midcentury comforts, much of the security of which was forged in the class struggles of previous decades and, in turn, into the New Deal programs that underwrote the suburban hegira. Although these programs also codified segregation, the conviction of the interracial coalition of Quakers, Communists, writers, and artists who fought to integrate Levittown was that the suburbs were simply a new site of ongoing struggle. So, too, the impulse to undermine the commodified image of the suburbs and the will to traverse suburban boundaries were born out of an avidity stimulated by media and mass culture. In short, the one-dimensionality so often ascribed to the suburbs, as well as the sense that their putative whiteness makes them terminal spaces of alienation, is, itself, another suburban projection.

Avid energy is apparent across a range of suburban representation, even that which reproduces the familiar gesture of the fully enclosed, ahistorical suburban world. We see it in the fervor of Jim Carrey as Truman Burbank in *The Truman Show* (Weir, 1998) just as much as in Richard Pryor's nervy Arlo Pear in *Moving* (Mettner, 1988) and in the giddiness of *Pleasantville's* teens who will colorize and add jazz and new realms of sexual feeling into their world. Even in *Suburbicon*, Gardner Lodge's murderous plot is born of restless dissatisfaction with what is, as is the violent energy of those opposing the Mayerses' presence. Avidity isn't tied to virtue, but is, according to Berman, a "frighteningly ambiguous" impulse born of the contradictions of capitalist culture. In practice, it is joined with another Rousseauean concept, *perfectibility*—"the unwillingness to settle back and rest content, the need to change constantly one's life for the better."[23] Berman shares an anecdote about a meeting of Students for a Democratic Society (SDS) in 1966 in which a white radical disavowed his suburban origins by citing a litany of preferable affiliations: "I have more in common with oppressed blacks in the ghetto . . . sharecroppers in Georgia, Indians on the reservation, Bolivian tin miners, Vietnamese—for Christ's sake I have more in common with *anybody* than with my parents!"[24] His protest was in response to a Black attendee from the Student Nonviolent Coordinating Committee (SNCC) who advised that it would be more politically efficacious for him go back and "work with our own kind." The lesson for Berman here resonates with Rousseau's view that social transformation cannot be driven by a disavowal, which seeks only to distance oneself from one's origins. This means not simply physically relocating to the suburbs, but acknowledging how the impulses to perfectibility are shaped within it:

> It is perfectibility and avidity that lead our parents, in Scarsdale or wherever they are stuck, to trade in their car for a new one every year. How to judge them? Is it absurd to think that a new car will make them happy? Of course, this is precisely the sort of absurdity that makes the American economy and our middle-class life run. But it is not at all absurd for our parents to feel that their old car and all the other things they have now do not make them happy. Indeed, it is the beginning of wisdom. . . . What *we* have to make clear to them is that it's not so much the car as the system that built it, that needs changing—and that we can't trade a social system in, we must build a new one.[25]

The rhetorical "we" here has particular generational overtones; it is the voice of the 1960s left and the baby boom—the same generation as Nicky and Andy in *Suburbicon*, George Clooney, and the Coen Brothers. It is arguably, too, this generation that experiences suburban alienation most intensely, develops a fascination with Cold War culture, and, in turn, formulates the gesture of suburban iconoclasm.

Suburban iconoclasm, although it partakes of the depthless aesthetic Fredric Jameson attributed to postmodernism, is in fact rooted in the avidity of the site it represents. One can see this, for example, in the expressionistic middle-class interiors of Douglas Sirk and Nicholas Ray, which are adapted into the visual vocabulary of Tim Burton (particularly the world of Pee-Wee Herman [Paul Reubens]), the grotesquerie of John Waters, the Coens, even the acid-tinged animation of Jon Kricfa-lusi's *Ren & Stimpy* (1991–96). The sensuous designs of décor and the plastic physiognomy of performers (think of William H. Macy's rictus of desperation in *Fargo*) in the works of these filmmakers convey not just the lie or secret of suburbia but the ways that the sustaining of the lie produces an animating avidity. Following Barbara Ehrenreich, the roots of this avidity may lie in the industrious anxieties of the middle class, a "fear of falling" either back into poverty or upward into the "numbing haze" of material affluence.[26] As the events in Levittown in 1957 and Charlottesville in 2017 show (and what could be more suburban or more Coen-esque than white men in khakis carrying tiki torches from Home Depot?), avidity can manifest in terrifying ways, particularly when gathered into the projective fantasies of white supremacy and right-wing ideology.

In the last years of the twentieth century and into the twenty-first housing prices continued to rise while income levels have remained relatively flat.[27] Meanwhile the centrality of real estate and the housing industry to nonproductive forms of finance capitalism culminated in the 2008 housing crisis. As is well known, this crisis resulted in millions of home foreclosures. Black homeowners, who were 50 percent more likely than whites to receive one of the subprime loans that led to the crisis, felt the brunt of the crisis. Whereas the midcentury housing boom was marked by racial exclusion, since the 1970s American housing has been marked by what Keeanga-Yamahtta Taylor has termed a "predatory inclusion," wherein previously excluded minority groups are targeted by the banks and the real estate industry as candidates for expensive, high-interest rate loans. The ease with which these loans could be defaulted only served to confirm racist myths about Black people and money. As Taylor puts it, "The real estate industry created the idea that Black homeowners posed a risk to the housing market and then profited from financial tools pro-moted as mitigating that risk."[28] The horizon of Black homeownership and the widespread experience of dispossession and disillusionment (particularly after President Barack Obama's decision to bail out banks but not homeowners) presents a historical intrusion on suburban iconoclasm as a form of cultural representation. Simply put, what does a satire of the psychic pitfalls of homeownership and the suburban dream provide in the context of widespread dispossession? The end of *Suburbicon*-style suburban iconoclasm might be seen as part of a larger reawakening to history (which also includes an acknowledgment of our ongoing entanglements with the environment) in which the myth of "end-of-history" neoliberalism lies in ruin. Such a context, however, produces new forms of avidity and requires new modes of representation.

One of the only films to confront the aftermath of the 2008 housing crisis, Ramin Bahrani's *99 Homes* (2014), depicts a demographically diverse suburban milieu riven by economic precariousness.[29] The film bracingly portrays the effects of home foreclosure on Nash (Andrew Garfield), a single father and out-of-work construction worker in Orlando, an area at the epicenter of the crisis. After being forcibly removed from his house, Nash brings his son (Noah Lomax) and mother (Laura Dern) to a hotel occupied by other recent casualties of foreclosure. In an ironic twist Nash begins to work for the realtor who evicted him, Rick Carver (Michael Shannon). Under Carver, Nash steals air conditioning units and pool pumps from foreclosed homes and moves kitchen cabinetry from houses of the recently evicted to houses Carver has sold. Eventually Nash is given the job of offering "cash for keys" (a quick payment of $3,500 from the bank to foreclosed residents for their keys) and soon of conducting the evictions himself with local police in tow. As Nash follows Carver's beacon of upward mobility, his new roles distance him from both his class and his family, a divide that is arrestingly depicted when Nash is accosted in the parking lot of the hotel in front of his son, mother, and other tenants by a recently arrived evictee who shouts "I know you, RICK CARVER REALTY!" *99 Homes* thus becomes a Faustian tale of the forms of avidity generated within neoliberal precarity, specifically its demand that each of us become an atomized entrepreneur and coldly calculating *homo economicus*. In doing so, it shows how home ownership entangles affective attachments to property relations. And while this story is not told through the lens of Black homeowners in particular, the film is careful to detail the suburbs as a racially and ethnically diverse landscape, revealing the colorblind dissolution of housing foreclosure within particular class strata.

Shannon's e-cigarette-smoking Carver is an indefatigable wraith who evicts people and then strips their homes for parts (invoicing them to

Fannie Mae to double his profits). His business is the perfect emblem of the inversions of financialization: where once he worked to put people in houses, now he removes them; where we once built houses, now Carver disassembles them. A municipal Gordon Gekko (Michael Douglas in Oliver Stone's *Wall Street* of 1987), he sneers at Nash's desire to buy back his family home, advising him not to get emotional about real estate. Houses to Carver are "big boxes and small boxes. What matters is how many you've got." He spends his life in two gaudy McMansions, one with his family and another, steps across the golf course that his property backs into, with a college-age mistress. Taking Carver's advice, Nash purchases a new, bigger house with a pool. But when he shows it to his family they're appalled. It's not *their* home and it has been purchased on the backs of the evictions of others. The new home's generic surfaces mark it as a product, one that is fundamentally undomesticated and unpossessable.

99 Homes is a departure from the conventional mode of suburban iconoclasm and its predilection for zany 1950s kitsch even as it employs a range of expressive techniques to expose how property relations undo the sanctity and solidity typically ascribed to "home." John David Rhodes theorizes that much of cinema involves a complex spectatorial relationship to property, one in which we often find ourselves paying a ticket price to look at places that we do not, and cannot, occupy or possess. Rhodes argues that when cinema and property communicate with each other—as when, for example, a film devotedly attends to the furnishings of a penthouse apartment, the landscaped lawns of a country manor, or even the rustic beams of a farmhouse—the film image becomes endowed with property's origins in alienated labor. "The cinematic image's sensuous evidence of private property compels us—to look! to enjoy!," writes Rhodes, "but also condemns this image of property" through its ephemerality.[30] In the cinematic image of property the evanescence of moving images doubles our sense of an inability to truly possess property—both in the sense that we likely cannot afford the property on display and in the sense that the product of another's alienated labor is never truly ours to possess—creating a spectacle of property that divulges property's function in a capitalist system.

The materialist-realist aesthetic of *99 Homes* foregrounds the house as a site of labor and property as an ongoing transaction within a fluid marketplace. Nash is introduced working in the open trestles of a partially built home—a quick signification of the labor embedded in dwelling places. But a foreman, announcing the bankruptcy of the builder, stops work at the site, sending Nash home without pay. The home that Nash will soon be evicted from doubles as a salon, where his mother Lynn conducts hair appointments. The atypical family structure draws attention to the multiple variations of social reproduction and gendered labor that have become sited in what was once a straightforwardly heteropatriarchal space. So, too, property and labor become inextricably entwined. In showing us front lawns piled with furnishings, belongings strapped to the tops of cars, and interiors outfitted with interchangeable fixtures (from cabinetry to pools), *99 Homes* evinces how the capricious nature of property undoes the integrity we attribute to home. Thus, when Nash introduces his family to the house with a pool that he's bought for them we share their appalled distrust of the surroundings, which become for all their opulence de-sensualized real estate.

Although everyday settings, a mixture of professional and non-professional actors, and handheld camera work mark it as an inheritor of neorealism, *99 Homes* reserves space for melodramatic expressivity in the form of Carver (figure 10.2). Where suburban iconoclasm relies on expressionistic techniques to cartoonishly distort the suburban diegesis, here visual exuberance is condensed into Carver's colorful suits and campy brashness. His sartorial presence and brusque style outline him against the kitchen sink naturalism of the film's setting and other characters, but unlike in *Suburbicon* this counterpoint helps to both cohere the film's world and interpret its underlying structure. For Carver comes to embody the piratic rapacity of capital itself, particularly its ability to

Figure 10.2. Rick Carver (Michael Shannon) taking a drag from his e-cigarette in *99 Homes* (Ramin Bahrani, Broad Green Pictures, Hyde Park Entertainment, Imagenation Abu Dhabi FZ, Noruz Films, 2014). Digital frame enlargement.

dissolve the bonds formed through work (often here across racial difference), friendship, and family.

Carver's villainy, however over-the-top, is itself generated within
the tragic ferment of American capitalism. As he explains to Nash in a
monologue, he's not an aristocrat, his father was a roofer who fell off
a townhouse, "a lifetime of insurance payments and they dropped him
before he could buy a wheelchair, but only after they got him hooked on
painkillers." Carver is therefore an avatar of avidity for the Trump era: a
restless, cynical, petty bourgeois entrepreneur. Such avidity is transferred
to Nash unevenly throughout the film, and, at the film's climax, ultimately
rejected as Nash reveals Carver's conspiracy with the banks to the FBI.
In a departure from both classical Hollywood melodramatic style and
the meritocratic myths of contemporary neoliberalism, however, Nash's
moral virtue offers him no material advantage; the film ends with his
own future uncertain.

99 Homes does not lay the problems of suburbia at the door of
what George Lipsitz has called a "possessive investment in whiteness."
The film does show the ways that race limns class stratification via the
Hispanic day laborers that Nash works with and subsequently hires.
Nash's promotion would likely be unavailable to these characters and it
seems clear that Carver's developing paternal interest in Nash is based
in their shared whiteness. The film also delineates the fundamentally
multiracial character of the victims of the housing crisis, both at the hotel
where Nash's family lives with other dispossessed former homeowners
and through a montage that shows Nash delivering eviction notices
to a series of residents. As Nash evicts people of all colors, ages, and
backgrounds from their homes (always with the help of local police), as
the contents of their interiors are unceremoniously dumped onto front
lawns, the duality of property, its status as both a domestic space and, as
Rhodes puts it, "a little bit of capital" is revealed.[31] In a bitter reversal,
the exclusionary housing practices of the postwar era are replaced by
the indiscrimination of financialized real estate (one which, it should be
noted, adversely affected the low-income Black home buyers who saw
subprime mortgages as an opportunity to enter the housing market).
Highlighting the connections between Carver and Trump, particularly
the casually racist commentary that both employ toward "immigrants,"
director Ramin Bahrani says in an interview that he sees contemporary
forms of racism (now increasingly articulated in the language of white
supremacy) as connected to economic uncertainty: "People are still strug-

gling economically, and that will only continue to get worse. And when that happens, people want someone to blame. There are other reasons, of course. There's racism, and that's increasingly coming to light thanks to the Black Lives Matter movement. But I think a lot of that comes down to economics. They're looking for someone to blame."[32] Bahrani's film makes clear where this blame properly lies as it traces how money is made through foreclosures back through investment groups acting as "bulk buyers" in a depressed housing market.

Although it attempts to represent historical racism, *Suburbicon* jumbles production detail, visual technique, and parochial liberalism, depicting suburban avidity as the product of something as vague as the white suburban soul. *99 Homes*, however, renews the possibility of suburban iconoclasm by attuning itself to the lies of property and its capacity to dissolve social bonds. A ravaged housing market, soaring health care costs, and new modes of labor exploitation produce forms of populist avidity, evidenced in phenomena as politically contradictory as teachers' strikes, support for border walls and violence against immigrants, enthusiasm for white supremacy, and support for politicians espousing previously taboo socialist orientations. Within this emergent political landscape it has become fashionable for liberals to repudiate the center of America as the locus of support for Trump, just as in Berman's day it was popular to repudiate the suburbs as site of conformist inauthenticity. In the wake of Trump's election, *Saturday Night Live* even aired a mock commercial that promoted the idea of the East and West Coasts, putative liberal domains, seceding from the rest of the country. Such a position is both inaccurate (wherever the middle of the country is said to be, it is incredibly diverse, never mind that support for Trump was particularly strong in places like Long Island) and casually immoral, but notable for the way it repeats the political perspectives Berman described. As in *99 Homes* the task should be to face the suburbs, developing expressive modes that create a space for seeing the claims that property makes on us.

Notes

1. Timotheus Vermeulen, *Scenes from the Suburbs: The Suburb in Contemporary US Film and Television* (Edinburgh: Edinburgh University Press, 2014), 2.

2. The claim for transhistorical whiteness has been popularized by the work of Ta-Nehisi Coates, particularly in "The Case for Reparations." For a

response to Coates that advances a historically situated critique of Coates's racial ontology in relation to housing inequality, see Touré F. Reed, "Between Obama and Coates," *Catalyst* 1, no. 4 (Winter 2018), https://catalyst-journal.com/vol1/no4/between-obama-and-coates.

3. Barbara J. Fields and Karen E. Fields, *Racecraft: The Soul of Inequality in American Life* (London: Verso, 2014), 261.

4. See Dianne Harris, *Little White Houses: How the Postwar Home Constructed Race in America* (Minneapolis: University of Minnesota Press, 2013); David Roediger, *Working toward Whiteness: How America's Immigrants Became White* (New York: Basic Books, 2005).

5. The race vs. class debate is ongoing, and by no means settled among scholars on the left. For a recent and clarifying view, see Asad Haider, *Mistaken Identity: Race and Class in Trump's America* (London: Verso, 2018).

6. Touré F. Reed, "Dr. Touré Reed, Illinois State University, on the 'Black Experience,' as seen in *Get Out* and *Atlanta*," February 21, 2018, podcast audio, *WJBC Interviews*. https://player.fm/series/wjbc-interviews/dr-toure-reed-illinois-state-university-on-the-black-experience-as-seen-in-get-out-and-atlanta.

7. Caitlin Zaloom, "Does the U.S. Still Have a 'Middle Class'?," *Atlantic*, November 4, 2018, https://www.theatlantic.com/ideas/archive/2018/11/what-does-middle-class-really-mean/574534/.

8. Such an assumption, of course, reproduces the spurious claims of nineteenth and early twentieth-century race science.

9. Marshall Berman, "Notes toward a New Society," *Partisan Review* 30, no. 4 (1971): 404–422.

10. "George Clooney's *Suburbicon* Bristles with Rage and Bitter Humor," *Washington Post*, October 24, 2017, https://www.washingtonpost.com/goingoutguide/movies/george-clooneys-suburbicon-bristles-with-rage-and-bitter-humor/2017/10/24/04be771c-b43e-.

11. Wesley Morris, "George Clooney's Awkward White Guilt in 'Suburbicon,'" *New York Times*, November 3, 2017, https://www.nytimes.com/2017/11/03/movies/george-clooney-suburbicon-racism.html.

12. See Dianne Harris, ed., *Second Suburb: Levittown, Pennsylvania* (Pittsburgh: University of Pittsburgh Press, 2010), in particular Thomas Sugrue's chapter "Jim Crow's Last Stand: The Struggle to Integrate Levittown," 175–199, and Daisy Myers's own firsthand account.

13. Thomas Sugrue, "Jim Crow's Last Stand," 180–182.

14. In contrast to the formal and stylistic inventiveness seen in work by filmmakers such as Spike Lee, Steve McQueen, Dee Rees, Barry Jenkins, or Boots Riley.

15. Lily Geismer, *Don't Blame Us: Suburban Liberalism and the Transformation of the Democratic Party* (Princeton: Princeton University Press, 2015), 9.

16. Berman, "Notes toward a New Society," 406.

17. Berman, "Notes toward a New Society," 406.

18. Qtd. in Berman, "Notes toward a New Society," 408.

19. Berman, "Notes toward a New Society," 108.

20. Berman, "Notes toward a New Society," 408.

21. Berman, "Notes toward a New Society," 418.

22. Herbert Gans, *The Levittowners: Ways of Life and Politics in a New Suburban Community* (New York: Columbia University Press, 1967). See also Amanda Kolson Hurely's *Radical Suburbs: Experimental Living on the Fringes of the American City* (Cleveland, OH: Belt Publishing, 2019).

23. Berman, "Notes toward a New Society," 420.

24. Berman, "Notes toward a New Society," 420.

25. Berman, "Notes toward a New Society," 420.

26. Barbara Ehrenreich, *Fear of Falling: The Inner Life of the Middle Class* (New York: Pantheon, 1989), 29–30.

27. Organization for Economic Co-operation (OECD), "Under Pressure: The Squeezed Middle Class," May 1, 2019, http://www.oecd.org/social/under-pressure-the-squeezed-middle-class-689afed1-en.htm, accessed June 1, 2019.

28. Keeanga-Yamahtta Taylor, "How Real Estate Segregated America," *Dissent*, Fall 2018, https://www.dissentmagazine.org/article/how-real-estate-segregated-america-fair-housing-act-race.

29. *The Big Short* (McKay, 2015) also explores the crisis, particularly its origins in the world of finance capital, and in a few key scenes illustrates how real estate markets subsist on subprime mortgage lending.

30. John David Rhodes, *The Spectacle of Property: The House in American Film* (Minneapolis: University of Minnesota Press, 2017), 20.

31. Rhodes, *The Spectacle of Property*, 19.

32. Ramin Bahrani, in Elise Nakhnikian, "Interview: Ramin Bahrani Talks *99 Homes*," *Slant*, September 24, 2015, https://www.slantmagazine.com/film/interview-ramin-bahrani/.

References

Berman, Marshall. "Notes toward a New Society." *Partisan Review* 30, no. 4 (1971): 404–422.

Ehrenreich, Barbara. *Fear of Falling: The Inner Life of the Middle Class*. New York: Pantheon, 1989.

Geismer, Lily. *Don't Blame Us: Suburban Liberalism and the Transformation of the Democratic Party*. Princeton: Princeton University Press, 2015.

Hornaday, Ann. "George Clooney's *Suburbicon* Bristles with Rage and Bitter Humor." *Washington Post*, October 24, 2017, https://www.washingtonpost.com/goingoutguide/movies/george-clooneys-suburbicon-bristles-with-rage-and-bitter-humor/2017/10/24/04be771c-b43e-11e7-a908-a3470754bbb9_story.html?utm_term=.fe4fa97ec34a.

Morris, Wesley. "George Clooney's Awkward White Guilt in 'Suburbicon.'" *New York Times*, November 3, 2017. https://www.nytimes.com/2017/11/03/movies/george-clooney-suburbicon-racism.html.

Nicolaides, Becky. "How Hell Moved from the City to the Suburbs: Urban Scholars and Changing Perceptions of Authentic Community." In *The New Suburban History*, edited by Kevin Kruse and Thomas J. Sugrue, 80–98. Chicago: University of Chicago Press, 2006.

Organization for Economic Co-operation (OECD). "Under Pressure: The Squeezed Middle Class." May 1, 2019. http://www.oecd.org/social/under-pressure-the-squeezed-middle-class-689afed1-en.htm.

Rhodes, John David. *The Spectacle of Property: The House in American Film*. Minneapolis: University of Minnesota Press, 2017.

Sims, David. "George Clooney Explains How *Suburbicon* Happened." *Atlantic*, October 31, 2017. https://www.theatlantic.com/entertainment/archive/2017/10/george-clooney-explains-how-suburbicon-happened/544397/.

Sugrue, Thomas. "Jim Crow's Last Stand: The Struggle to Integrate Levittown." In *Second Suburb: Levittown, Pennsylvania*, edited by Dianne Harris, 175–199. Pittsburgh: University of Pittsburgh Press, 2010.

Vermeulen, Timotheus. *Scenes from the Suburbs: The Suburb in Contemporary US Film and Television*. Edinburgh: Edinburgh University Press, 2014.

11

"A Perfectly Normal Life"?

Suburban Space, Automobility, and Ideological Whiteness in *Love, Simon*

ANGEL DANIEL MATOS

O<small>N THE SURFACE,</small> *LOVE, SIMON* (Berlanti, 2018) is a formulaic teen romance centered on the coming out process of a white, middle-class gay teenager who embodies potentially conservative and regressive attitudes toward queerness and gender variation.[1] The normative frameworks embedded in this film become even more tangible, and unsurprising, when we consider its spatial dimensions, in that most of its events are set in suburban spaces—which historically, imaginatively, and ideologically have been associated with notions of white supremacy, homogenization, and heteronormativity. For instance, George Lipsitz highlights how a post–World War II United States was characterized by urban revitalizations that "helped construct a new 'white' identity in the suburbs by helping to destroy ethnically specific European American urban inner-city neighborhoods," leading to a rising number of minority communities in cities and a noticeable increase in dynamics of residential segregation.[2] Given the historical and ideological ties between whiteness and suburban spaces, and considering how these spaces were often developed with the purpose of further marginalizing minority communities, this chapter will examine how this spatiality, its metonymic extensions, and its enabling mechanisms affect the representation of queer whiteness in the film.

Queer and media critics have suggested that racial discourse has been fundamental in shaping both queer identities and their representations, even though foundational studies in the field have excluded race from their analyses. Siobhan B. Somerville, for instance, has argued that "the structures and methodologies that drove dominant ideologies of race also fueled the pursuit of knowledge about the homosexual body," and that both sympathetic and oppressive discourses on queerness were "steeped in assumptions that had driven previous scientific studies of race."[3] Melanie Kohnen echoes these sentiments by highlighting how the emergence of the homo/heterosexual binary can be traced to "previous and concurrent discourses that defined 'white' against 'Black' racial identities," and how whiteness is central to historical accounts of queer identities and their increasing visibility in past centuries.[4] Historical resonances of these dynamics of exclusion and invisibility are absolutely present in contemporary cinematic representations of queer thought and experience. Oftentimes, both films and scholarship disregard the fact that queerness is intricately linked to racial and sexual discourse, thus leading to "a screening of race" that sidelines "the importance of race and racialization in the construction of queer visibility" and that elevates discourses of whiteness that perpetuate "a history of willful forgetfulness."[5] The stakes of these claims gain even more prominence in analysis of teen cinema, which frequently centers the experiences of mostly straight and white teens, further fueling these enterprises of normativity and forgetfulness. As such, this discussion will be mindful of the ways that whiteness and race inform the representation of queer teen experience in *Love, Simon*, especially given the fact that this film is staged within the context of a suburb located in Atlanta, Georgia.

Keeping in mind the historical and cultural ties between queer and racial discourse, I want to make the case for the film being more nuanced in its treatment of race, sexuality, and identity than a surface viewing might suggest. I demonstrate how *Love, Simon's* implementations of space and mobility highlight ways of approaching the film that can potentially pressure values such as homogenization and normativity. More specifically, I argue that *Love, Simon* uses suburban space and automobility to self-reflexively highlight and negotiate the unsustainability of normative thinking and the difficulties (and consequent impossibilities) of maintaining a semblance of homogeny in a culture with rapidly evolving sociocultural circumstances.[6] Through a close examination of the film's representations of automobility and suburban space, it becomes apparent that *Love, Simon* is a film in crisis: its attempts to foster a normative, "universal" appeal are ultimately pressured by the very presence of suburban spaces and automobility. The elements used to stage the film's plot thus become the very components that partially undermine the white and normative frameworks that haunt the entire film.

Love, Simon is notable for being the first major studio film focused on the social and romantic life of a gay teen, created mostly for a teen and young adult audience. The film focuses on a closeted Simon Spier (Nick Robinson), who falls in love with an anonymous student that he regularly corresponds with via email. Simon's attempts to negotiate the boundaries of the closet, his relationships, and his budding romantic feelings become increasingly difficult when Simon is blackmailed by his classmate Martin (Logan Miller). Simon is thus coerced to help Martin win over the affections of their friend, Abby (Alexandra Shipp), or risk having his secret exposed to the entire school via social media. While celebrated for circulating gay teen romance to a widespread, mainstream audience, the film was also the object of countless critiques, especially in terms of how it elevates models of queerness that are contingent on white, masculinist, and middle-to-upper-class ideologies. In his widely circulated review of the film, Daniel D'Addario points out that while some viewers might find affirmation in watching the film, others might "find its stabs at relatability fairly ludicrous." D'Addario further questions the film's potential to "appeal to a generation that's boldly reinventing gender and sexuality on its own terms" and states that *Love, Simon* is ultimately a belated film, one that "simply feels like looking back in time."[7] I cannot help but see how the critiques raised by D'Addario mesh with the ideological issues that frequently surface in cinematic representations and critiques of suburban spaces. By focusing on the notion of "looking back" raised in this review in conjunction with matters of spatiality, we can develop a more holistic understanding of the film's self-reflexive use of space, temporality, race, and sexuality.

Unpacking Suburban Spatiality and Whiteness in *Love, Simon*

In her phenomenological examination of whiteness, Sara Ahmed discusses how spaces shape, accommodate, and extend the reach of certain people while simultaneously excluding others: "Spaces acquire the 'skin' of the bodies that inhabit them. What is important to note here is that it is not just bodies that are orientated. Spaces also take shape by being oriented around some bodies more than others."[8] Here, Ahmed's phenomenological approach to spatiality echoes Henri Lefebvre's views on the production of social space: "any space implies, contains and dissimulates social relationships—and this despite the fact that a space is not a thing but rather a set of relations between things (objects and products)."[9] *Love, Simon*'s introductory scene exemplifies such processes of spatial orientation and production, in that it uses the suburban home to not only imbue the film with a sense of normality and homogenization but to also demonstrate how these spaces are shaped by the social relationships and interactions staged within them. In the introduction of the film, for instance, Simon speaks to the audience in a voice-over and claims: "I'm just like you. For the most part my life is totally normal."[10] But it doesn't take long for the audience to grow uneasy with Simon's assertion, especially when considering that his perspectives on what is considered "normal" differ immensely from the realities of many queer teenagers, and many minority communities for that matter. Simon lives in a large, middle-class suburban home and seems to be part of a normative, nuclear family. He has access to material and emotional comforts that distance him from the difficulties faced by many of today's youths, who are, as Alexander J. Means puts it, "a generation of young people struggling to secure livelihoods in the most dismal labor market since the Great Depression."[11] The film's introductory scenes give us little, if no sense, that Simon is dealing with the repercussions of said struggles.

Contextual clues offered by the film indicate that it is mostly set in a mixed-race suburb in Atlanta, Georgia, one that is heavily marked by class due to the presence of both apartment complexes and detached private homes. This suburb is also surrounded by comforts and amenities that also signal a spectrum of middle- and upper-class residents present in this context, including an independently owned coffee bar with a drive-through service and a Waffle House (an affordable breakfast chain that originated in an Atlanta suburb). These first scenes show Simon walking out of his suburban home with his eyes covered by his mother's hands. As they step outside of their large, detached, and private house, adorned with large white columns and a perfectly landscaped front yard, his eyes are uncovered as his father tosses him a set of car keys, and Simon stands in awe in front of a burgundy station wagon topped with a giant red bow. These characters and the suburban home work in tandem to convey a sense of stability and normality, especially since the large house in the background and the white family standing gleefully in front of Simon's car inflect our perception of the film's events. The imagery invoked in these first scenes spotlights a close-knit family that benefits significantly from the perks and affordances granted by their middle-class suburban life. This introduction painstakingly attempts to convey a sense of family and nostalgia that is both wholesome and aspirational. Various moments in this scene are presented as video footage that Simon and his family record through their phones. Through the use of muted and blurry colors and a shaky cam, these clips are presented as amateurish, unedited footage that invokes associations with home videos recorded by a handheld video cassette camera (figure 11.1). This presentation style therefore emphasizes the backwardness and antiquation that D'Addario's brings up in his review of the film—a nostalgic sense of "pastness" further compounded through the implementation of Brenton Wood's 1967 hit single "The Oogum Boogum Song" nondiegetically playing in the background.[12] The use of shots reminiscent of home video footage and a song from the 1960s indicate that these introductory shots are very much a product of the past: a time different and distinct from our contemporary moment.

This introductory scene uses the backdrop of a suburban home to frame images of a white, seemingly normative, nuclear suburban family that are filtered through the temporal and affective trappings of nostalgia. The film is set during our contemporary moment, yet the consistent dragging of the past into the present induces a sense of timelessness,

Figure 11.1. Simon (Nick Robinson) and his family in front of their suburban home in *Love, Simon* (Greg Berlanti, Twentieth Century Fox, 2018). Digital frame enlargement.

placelessness, and tradition that critics such as Greg Dickinson and Robert Beuka approach as quintessential components of American films set in suburban spaces. Dickinson has pointed out how suburban films appeal to, and at times reject, nostalgic memories in order to convey a sense of well-being and belonging: "the films choose safety and security, offering images of white heterosexuality leavened with just a bit of danger and risk offered by 'aberrant' sexuality and the authenticity of 'other' racial and ethnic identities."[13] This introduction meticulously mobilizes and reifies material and visual elements that are common in suburban films created since the postwar years, elements that elevate middle-class white values, "a heightened valorization of the nuclear family," the reification of gender norms, and "a collapsing distinction between public and private spaces."[14] Along these lines, the suburbs—and as will be discussed later, its mobile extensions such as the station wagon and the minivan—generate tensions and blur the boundaries between public and private space, especially since "residents establish their place in the public sphere by owning private property."[15] The material, normative, and spatial effects that these suburban spaces produce are further bolstered through the montage of clips presented in *Love, Simon*'s introduction, which include shots of Simon's family happily gathered around in the kitchen as his sister attempts to prepare a meal, and Simon and his friends playfully tossing food at each other in the high school cafeteria. This montage is crowned by Simon's (perhaps ironic) proclamation that he has "a perfectly normal life."[16]

In his examination of *New Queer Cinema*, José Esteban Muñoz approaches the presentation of whiteness in these films as slippery, in that it cannot be reduced to "to a single set of mechanisms" and it often calls "attention to its universalizing and camouflaging properties."[17] Regardless of whether or not *Love, Simon* can also be situated within this tradition of New Queer Cinema, there are two important notions to keep in mind. First, *Love, Simon* is similar to a strand of New Queer Cinema films that emerged during the 1990s in that it also contributes "to the continual reproduction of the normative imprint—the idealized white prototype that forms not only gay male desire but, beyond that, gay male sociality."[18] Second, *Love, Simon* seems to be self-conscious of this notion, especially when considering how it actively calls attention to universalizing claims through its ironic representation of a white teen who simultaneously has a perfectly normal life but is nonetheless "just like [us]." We are presented with a fictional life that is not only perfectly normal, but perhaps *too* picture-perfect in its construction—imbued with a nostalgic sense of wholesomeness that is overwhelming, potentially parodic, and at times downright unbelievable.

David R. Coon argues that nostalgic suburban films often invoke reflective versions of the past that are initially presented as desirable and appealing, but that are ultimately shown to be unsustainable precisely because they exude values that "clash with human desires for freedom, knowledge, and growth."[19] Coon further points out that contemporary suburban films, similar to the self-reflexive nature of whiteness in New Queer Cinema posited by Muñoz, are self-aware of their implementation of nostalgia and are often straightforward about the ways in which the past is manipulated in order to "reveal the dangers and complications of turning a nostalgic view of the past into a seemingly utopian version of the present."[20] *Love, Simon* partakes in this tradition because its nostalgia is framed as a deliberate and palpable construction as seen through the implementation of the home video "filter" and the choice of background music. We are showered with a series of arguably normative shots, images, and messages, but the nostalgic tinge of these elements suggests that the moment we are witnessing is a product of the past that might not have much clout or currency in our contemporary moment. These moments of nostalgia are framed as deliberately and consciously fictional. They are presented to us as snapshots of a story that has a dwindling influence in a society that has diverging and evolving understandings of identity and being.

The clash between traditional values, nostalgia, and the desire for freedom and growth is further mobilized in this introductory scene through the spatiality and mobility granted by automobiles—more specifically through the contrast and parallels established through the space of the suburban home and Simon's station wagon. Whereas suburban spaces commonly reify the values of homogenization, stagnancy, normativity, and the nuclear family, cars evoke connotations of freedom, privacy, and mobility. This clash is best exemplified not only through Simon's placement between the space of the suburban home and his vehicle but also through the shot of Simon's family spectating his departure in his station wagon—with their suburban home looming in the background. Peter Merriman approaches cars as mobile, personal, enclosed, and private spaces present amid "the public spaces of the street and the road," and he points out how these associations led driving and car ownership to be viewed as rites of passage for young people, which partially explains why cars "emerged as spaces of sexual encounter" and freedom for youth cultures in the twentieth century.[21] The ideological dyad between the space of the suburbs and the space of the car has frequently been represented in teen cinema, most notably in *Rebel Without a Cause* (Ray, 1955). Susan White suggests that the suburban home in *Rebel* represents the "utopian family and the stability sought by Ray's characters" while also serving as "a symbol of failure for men who have succumbed to society's demand for stasis and predictability."[22] White further suggests that cars in this film often convey ideas that combat those of the suburban home, especially since Nicholas Ray's use of vehicles "becomes a kind of shorthand image for the rootlessness and potential violence of men."[23]

The representation of automobiles and automobility in *Love, Simon* is more complex than a surface interpretation would suggest and departs from the ways in which cars have traditionally been represented in teen cinema. I want to avoid falling into the trap of implementing and reinforcing a divide between the film's seemingly conservative depiction of the suburban home and the freedoms and affordances granted by the mobile space of the car. As scholars such as Dickinson have noted, "The automobile seems nearly as important as the houses in defining suburban space in general and particular characters' place within the space."[24] Thus, it is important for us to know how and why Simon's car serves as both an extension and reification of a suburban ethos. Simon is gifted a first-generation Subaru Outback, a station wagon that not only conveys the family-oriented values of suburban spaces through its traditional use and even the name of its make, but that also invokes a sense of nostalgia through the very fact that the vehicle is a used first-generation model and not a newer vehicle.

As discussed by Cindy Donatelli, "Station wagons were models that set out many of the goals that were later taken up in the minivan: they offered extended space to accommodate family members rather than goods or passengers being delivered."[25] Donatelli goes as far as to approach station wagons as objects that embodied "an idealized suburban domesticity," especially during the peak popularity of these vehicles in the 1950s.[26] We can also consider historical events such as the 1956 Federal-Aid Highway Act , which further exemplifies the inextricable link between suburban space, automobility, and matters of race. LaGarrett J. King and Shakealia Y. Finley have pointed out that while the Federal-Aid Highway Act connected the United States through interstate highway systems, facilitated suburban expansion, and led to the expansion of several industries, it did so by expediting "the deterioration of inner cities with large African American populations" and ultimately serves as an instance of "racist policy enacted through fiscal policy."[27] Simon's vehicle therefore serves as a mobile space that carries the symbolic and historical weight of normative suburban ideologies, further bolstering the film's nostalgic presentation of a past that is losing its grip over the present by using a vehicle that predates the family-oriented minivan.

In accordance with Ahmed's assertion regarding the synergetic relationship between spaces and bodies, it is impossible to view Simon's vehicle as immune from the influences of suburban space. Symbolically layered, Simon's Subaru station wagon represents ideals that pressure the conservative connotations of suburban space while also functioning as a metonymic extension of the suburban home. This ideological duality is not limited to suburban influence, especially since it can be traced to the very connotations of automobility, which frame vehicles as both a source of freedom and limitation: "Automobility is a Frankenstein-created monster, extending the individual into realms of freedom and flexibility whereby one's time in the car can be positively viewed, but also structuring and constraining the 'users' of cars to live their lives in particular spatially stretched and time-compressed ways. . . . [It coerces drivers] to juggle tiny fragments of time in order to put together complex, fragile and contingent patterns of social life, which constitute self-created narratives of the reflective self."[28] Since the vehicle in *Love, Simon* is symbolically imbued with a suburban ethos, it is worth exploring how it marshals these aforementioned tensions, thus revealing the crises and anxieties that characterize the film's stance on matters of identity. We must further bear in mind that automobility presents particular affordances and privileges that are frequently celebrated in teen cinema—but let us not forget that these privileges are partially granted to Simon due to his white, middle-class background. Simon's station wagon thus grants him a sense of privacy and mobility that teenagers from different backgrounds and upbringings might not have access to. For instance, consider Dee Rees's film *Pariah* (2011), which focuses on the experiences of Alike, a black butch lesbian teen who uses forms of public transportation such as buses, rather than a private vehicle, to travel around the city—and who is not granted the privacy and freedom of mobility that a car can potentially bestow to teens.[29]

The Critical Limits and Potentialities of Automobility in *Love, Simon*

Simon's Subaru station wagon is a looming presence in various scenes in the film. The car, as mentioned previously, is a symbolic marker of suburban space that reifies the affordances and normative ideologies

that are often attached to these spaces. Through his vehicle, Simon is
provided with opportunities to bond with his friends, offer them rides
to school, and drive them to their local coffee bar to pick up beverages
before heading to class. The car's early associations with the ideals of
suburbia heavily inflect our understanding of the film's major tensions,
and *Love, Simon* uses this inflection to mobilize avenues of critique that
interrogate the ideals of homogeneity and normativity associated with
the suburbs. The potentialities of these critiques become palpable when
the station wagon is juxtaposed with people who pressure the suburban
ideals that Simon embodies through their filmic presence.

Early in the film's narrative, we are introduced to the character
of Ethan (Clark Moore), the only openly queer student at Simon's high
school and someone who is very much Simon's foil. Ethan is a queer
person of color who shuns the traditional and hegemonic masculinist
models of identity that Simon appears to perform and embody. Simon,
broadly speaking, is a character who is reserved, nonconfrontational,
obsessed with normality, and aspires to assimilate. All of these traits can
be observed from the way he acts, his way of speaking, and even his
attire, which mostly consists of jeans, hoodies, and limited color options
such as dark and gray hues. Simon's constant rejection of flamboyance, as
pointed out by Mason P. Sands, can be approached as "a reflection of a
greater internal desire to embrace his all-hoodie wardrobe and be more
straight-acting," a desire that is not overtly contested in the film.[30] This
wardrobe also highlights Simon's whiteness because, to draw from the
language of Kohnen, it ultimately "signifies his body as unmarked and
unremarkable."[31] Ethan, conversely, speaks openly about his queerness,
shows no desire to fit in, and directly confronts bullies who threaten him.
These notions are especially salient when someone tries to undermine
Ethan's fashion accessories through the use of antiqueer and transphobic
remarks. Ethan retorts by questioning the bully's taste in clothing:

> BULLY: Cool scarf, Ethan. Hope it doesn't get caught in your
> vagina.
>
> ETHAN: Great choice on the cargo pants, by the way. It looks
> like you got gangbanged by a T.J. Maxx.
>
> BULLY: Whatever, fag.
>
> ETHAN: Honestly, it's just not even a challenge anymore.

Ethan's presence is very much evocative of an intersectional model of queer youth that actively rejects norms of gender and sexuality. Ethan is also an embodiment of multiple forms of oppression that Simon does not have to deal with on an everyday basis, based not only on his public queerness and nonnormative gender expression, but also his race. Later in the film, Ethan discloses that he also has to deal with issues that Simon does not have to deal with as a white, middle-class, nonreligious teen-ager—especially when Ethan's conflicts with his family come to light: "My mom still tells my grandparents about all the girls I'm dating when we go over their house for dinner, every Sunday. She says it's 'cause they're old and religious, and it's easier that way. I don't know, maybe that's true. But you should hear her voice when she talks about the girls."[32] In a film that is so fixated on notions of normalcy and belonging, Ethan is quite a refreshing character.

When Ethan is introduced in the film, we are shown a close-up shot of him as he talks about potential Halloween costumes with his friends. He brings up the idea of dressing up as "sexy Pokémon" for Halloween, and as he utters this statement, Simon's station wagon appears unfocused in the background—a ghostly presence of the nor-mative and homogenizing values of suburbia. This shot can be read as an argument about Ethan's character: he is the focal point of this shot and he represents an intersectional and antioppressive model of queer being, whereas the station wagon, which carries the weight of tradition, homogenization, and privilege, remains blurred in the background (fig-ure 11.2). As Ethan confronts the aforementioned bully, we are shown

Figure 11.2. Ethan (Clark Moore) in front of Simon's station wagon in *Love, Simon* (Greg Berlanti, Twentieth Century Fox, 2018). Digital frame enlargement.

a shot of Simon getting out of his car, expressing how he wishes that "Ethan wouldn't make it so easy for" people to bully and target him.[33] This scene operates in a twofold fashion. It highlights Simon's privilege and demonstrates how his purview of the world is very much informed by conservative and homonormative frameworks—the implication being that Ethan should do his best to conceal his queerness, blend in, and not stand out. Additionally, this scene creates a contrast between Simon and Ethan: whereas the former embodies a suburban ethos and tries his best to, as Coon would put it, preserve "the illusion of homogeneity,"[34] the latter feels free to express queer desires and attack various forms of oppression. In this scene, Simon is framed as a person who is privileged due to his race, his class, and his ability to pass as straight and "normal," a presentation augmented by the haunting presence of the Subaru station wagon in the background and challenged by Ethan's placement in front of it.

The spatial and ideological significance of the station wagon accommodates Simon, yet these ideological attachments do not extend to Ethan. Ahmed's perspectives toward the experiences of people of color and comfort are particularly illuminating in this instance: "To be not white is to be not extended by the spaces you inhabit. This is an uncomfortable feeling. Comfort is a feeling that tends not to be consciously felt, as I have suggested. You sink. When you don't sink, when you fidget and move around, then what is in the background becomes in front of you, as a world that is gathered in a specific way."[35] In the aforementioned scene, it is not Ethan who is uncomfortable, but rather it is Simon who avidly expresses distress when confronting Ethan's unabashed desire to resist and openly exist. This shot focuses on Ethan whereas Simon and his station wagon remain blurred in the background. These normative elements remain in the background and do not interfere with Ethan's being. The spatiality that Ethan embodies does not extend itself to Simon, thus putting into question whose attitudes, identities, and purview are ultimately out of focus in this scene.

In addition to the ghostly presence of the station wagon, the film also stages various moments inside of Simon's vehicle. These scenes further complicate this station wagon as both a metonymic extension of normative suburban ideologies and a means for escaping the homogenizing pressures of suburban space. Simon's car is a mobile space, one that initially grants him access to moments of privacy, secrecy, and intimacy that allow him to conceal and preserve the illusion of normalcy and homogeneity fostered in many suburban spaces. For instance, when Simon first receives an email from Blue, the anonymous teen that he becomes romantically interested in, he escapes his school and rushes to his car, eager to read the email. Simon's car functions as a mobile safe space of sorts: a self-contained semisecluded area that allows him to privately engage with his queer yearnings without having to experience the public judgment or scorn that Ethan experiences in an earlier scene. The car, however, is a space that is similar to suburban locations in that it disrupts the distinction between public and private space—for although Simon feels enclosed and safe in his station wagon, this moment of privacy is disrupted as another driver shows up behind Simon's car and starts blaring its horn—thus unsettling the false sense of privacy granted through this ephemeral safe space. Simon's car is a marker of privilege that is initially emblematic of the ideals and affordances commonly associated with white, suburban spaces. As the film develops, however, so do the symbolic applications of this vehicle. The station wagon eventually oscillates from being a mobile space that carries the ideological baggage of the suburbs into a space of freedom and mobility, one that enables Simon's queerness to transition from a being a source of foreclosure to one of connectivity.

Scholars have pointed out that bodies "do not move through a neutral space in neutral cars, but instead bodies, spaces and cars are embedded within power geometries along the lines of gender as well as how they intersect with age, ethnicity and class, that configure and reconfigure the driving subject."[36] These power geometries are not only established between drivers and the spaces they travel through but also between the people dwelling inside of these vehicles at a given moment. Along these lines, Eric Laurier, Barry Brown, Hayden Lorimer, et al. have suggested that cars often serve as sites where important conversations take place because of their spatiality, the sense of privacy that they enable, and the way they position people side by side. The physical confines of the car "are a useful place to raise difficult issues. Individuals cannot walk away from the conversation, and the stretched out silence that the car enables allows for slow and considered responses to complex or difficult issues."[37] In a pivotal scene in *Love, Simon*, the car exemplifies this notion, in that it enables Simon to prompt a difficult conversation and helps him to move beyond his desire to "fit in" and pass as straight. In this scene, Simon comes out to one of his friends for the first time. Abby and Simon begin discussing their family life and their relationships as Simon is driving his station wagon through the suburbs at night. Abby asks Simon, "Have you ever been in love?," and this question causes him to stall his vehicle near a grassy patch of the suburban neighborhood he is driving through. The two teens sit in awkward silence. After a moment of hesitation, Simon utters the words "I'm gay" for the first time to another person. Abby is very accepting, claiming that she is not surprised and that she loves Simon (figure 11.3).

After hearing Abby's words of affection and acceptance, Simon lets out a sigh of relief, turns on the blinkers of his car and proceeds to move forward. Although connotations of privacy and secrecy are still in place, the car nonetheless provides Simon with the means to disclose his queerness to another person within the space of the suburbs and provides him with the means to negotiate, "assess and contest the forms of interaction between" himself and his "own subcultures and mainstream society," a characteristic trope found in gay suburban narratives.[38] The car serves as a site of negotiation, one that carries the ideological baggage of the suburban home while nonetheless granting him the ability to escape the pressures of secrecy and homogenization, which is notable since Simon's station wagon is still located in the suburbs—a nonneutral space—as this coming out scene unfolds. The spatiality of the car's interior during this scene is also not neutral, especially when one considers that Abby is a person of color, she recently moved to Simon's town, and is the only one of Simon's friends who lives in an apartment complex rather than a detached suburban home. Furthermore, the film stresses that Abby does not live with a normative nuclear family, since she moved away from Washington, DC into her current residence after her parents' divorce. In many ways, Abby mobilizes visual and ideological elements

Figure 11.3. Simon (Nick Robinson) comes out to Abby in *Love, Simon* (Alexandra Shipp) (Greg Berlanti, Twentieth Century Fox, 2018). Digital frame enlargement.

that contest fundamental components of suburban films. Most notably, she does not dwell in the quintessential "single-family detached house"[39] nor is she part of a normative white family. Taking into consideration that people both shape and are shaped by the spaces they dwell in and given the tendency of apartment living to counter the ideals of suburban life, it comes as no surprise that her presence in the car pressures and challenges the suburban values of assimilation exalted by Simon and his Subaru station wagon.

An Unsustainable Fantasy

An important scene that is staged in Simon's station wagon is the film's conclusion, for it presents viewers with another instance that illustrates the extent to which the homogenizing grasp of the suburbs further dwindles. Harkening back to scenes present in the beginning of the film, Simon ventures from suburban home to suburban home and to Abby's apartment on the way to school, picking up his friends and his new boyfriend, Bram, a queer teen of color who is also the anonymous teen that he was corresponding with throughout most of the narrative. But rather than heading out to school, Simon decides to play hooky and drive out for an "adventure." His friends cheer and hoot at the act of rebellion and we are presented with a shot of Simon's car driving out of the suburbs. The shot transitions to a bird's-eye perspective, and the camera continues to shift upward until we get a view of skyscrapers in the background. The camera then focuses on the city lurking in the distance and freezes as this image is painted over in a red hue, implying that the adventure that they are seeking awaits somewhere beyond the influence of suburban space.

Dickinson has suggested that white suburban films commonly represent the suburban home as a place of safety, acceptance, and belonging—and even though characters may depart from these spaces, they almost always return to the safety and the normality promised by the suburban home: "the films offer audiences escapes from the boredom of suburban life but return the audience to that very same suburb, the same relationships."[40] However, I argue that we see something different occur in the ending to *Love, Simon*, and that we can approach this scene as another attempt to self-reflexively pressure the ideals of homogenization and normativity associated with the suburbs. We observe a departure from a space of illusion and conformity into a space of flux and adventure. The city becomes a site on the horizon full of promise and joy while the suburbs become a space that is left behind and relegated to nondiegetic space. And while all of the teens in Simon's car will eventually return to the safety of suburban space after their adventure in the city, the film's conclusion does not show this moment of return to audiences, thus foreclosing a visual representation of the characters' return to safety and normality. Of course, this "escape" raises metronormative concerns and perpetuates a troubling dichotomy between the suburbs as a space of oppression and the city as a space of freedom. Although a discussion of these concerns is beyond the scope of this chapter, the film's conclusion ultimately rejects an exaltation of suburban space in favor of a location that is stereotypically more open and accommodating toward queer and people of color.

To return to D'Addario's claim, *Love, Simon* is indeed a film that looks back in time, a film that in many regards may seem "belated." However, it is too simplistic to claim that the film simply glorifies the past and offers us a completely uncritical, nostalgic view that venerates normative ideals, aspirations, and the conservative trappings of suburban space. The film's spatiality can be interpreted as reflexive and self-conscious, enabling critiques of nostalgic views of the past while opening different possibilities for futurity. At the end of the day, *Love, Simon* is, to some extent, a formulaic teen film that elevates normativity and the ideological whiteness present in suburban spaces. However, a closer examination of this space in conjunction with notions of automobility suggests that *Love, Simon* toys around with these elements to challenge the fragility and failures of homogenization and normative thinking. *Love, Simon* suggests that the ideals of suburbia are not only unsustainable for queer being but are also very much in tension with evolving and nuanced understandings of identity, race, and sexuality. In due course, many of the film's spectators are still *not* like Simon. But toward the film's conclusion, we just might realize that the person who claimed to have a perfectly normal life, the person who claimed that Ethan should assimilate, the person who claimed to be "just like us" is not the same one who is driving away from the suburbs.

Love, Simon's status as a major studio film undoubtedly gave rise to various compromises, especially when it came to the presentation of queer content to mainstream audiences in a "palatable" and "accessible" fashion. Therefore, it is perfectly understandable why and how the film generated substantial tensions between audiences who crave more mainstream queer representations and people who desire queer (teen) cinema with a political, countercultural bite. But as Richard T. Rodríguez has suggested, queer cinema that is frequently dismissed as mainstream, "multiplex trash," and lacking in political viability can help us to better ascertain "the politics of fantasy mirrored from everyday life practices and the ideologies of whiteness that interminably circumscribe them."[41] On various levels, *Love, Simon* perpetuates a fantasy of normality imbued with ideologies of whiteness—a depiction of a queer teen who fits in, who is loved by his family and peers, who wins over the object of his affection, who succeeds in almost every facet of his life, who owns a private vehicle, and who is part of a nuclear family that accepts him. But a close examination of the film's reflexive implementation of suburban spatiality and automobility demonstrates the fragility of this fantasy.

When this fiction is juxtaposed with the realities of teens who cannot and will not fit in, it becomes nothing short of a blur in the background. When this fantasy tries to uphold a universalizing narrative of normalcy through the manipulative frameworks of nostalgia, it ultimately becomes as muted, shaky, and dated as home video footage—a desperate attempt at a normative past to cling to in the present. But as Andrew Baldwin reminds us, although the past is an important temporal construct that must be taken into consideration when critically examining whiteness, we must not disregard the conceptual mobility that is inherently part of ideological whiteness: "whiteness moves. It *disaffiliates* from 'old' racisms."[42] *Love, Simon* was groundbreaking. It circulated a queer teen narrative to audiences that might not have encountered queer representation in a mainstream film, or in *any* film for that matter. But now that we are living a moment where queer teen representations are receiving increased exposure and recognition, we could only imagine how ideological whiteness will continue to circulate in queer teen cinema and how these films could potentially pressure, if not dismantle, these ideologies through reflexive uses of spatiality.

Notes

1. *Love, Simon*, Blu-ray, directed by Greg Berlanti (Los Angeles: Twentieth Century Fox, 2018).

2. George Lipsitz, *The Possessive Investment in Whiteness* (Philadelphia: Temple University Press, 1998), 7.

3. Siobhan B. Somerville, *Queering the Color Line: Race and the Invention of Homosexuality in American Culture* (Durham, NC: Duke University Press, 2000), 17.

4. Melanie Kohnen, *Queer Representation, Visibility, and Race in American Film and Television* (New York: Routledge, 2015), 17–18.

5. Kohnen, *Queer Representation*, 20.

6. Mimi Sheller and John Urry, "The City and the Car," *International Journal of Urban and Regional Research* 24, no. 4 (2000): 739. According to Sheller and Urry, automobility refers to "a complex amalgam of interlocking machines, social practices and ways of dwelling, not in a stationary home, but in a mobile, semi-privatized and hugely dangerous capsule."

7. Daniel D'Addario, "*Love, Simon* Is a Groundbreaking Gay Movie: But Do Today's Teens Actually Need It?," *Time*, March 8, 2018, http://time.com/5190982/love-simon-groundbreaking-gay-movie/.

8. Sara Ahmed, "A Phenomenology of Whiteness," *Feminist Theory* 8, no. 2 (2007): 157.

9. Henri Lefebvre, *The Production of Space*, trans. Donald Nicholson-Smith (Oxford: Blackwell, 1991), 82–83.

10. *Love, Simon*.

11. Alexander J. Means, "Generational Precarity, Education, and the Crisis of Capitalism: Conventional, Neo-Keynesian, and Marxian Perspectives," *Critical Sociology* 43, no. 3 (2017): 341.

12. Brenton Wood, "The Oogum Boogum Song," *Oogum Boogum*, Double Shot Records, 1967.

13. Greg Dickinson, "The *Pleasantville* Effect: Nostalgia and the Visual Framing of (White) Suburbia," *Western Journal of Communication* 70, no. 3 (2006): 217.

14. Robert Beuka, *SuburbiaNation: Reading Suburban Landscape in Twentieth-Century American Fiction and Film* (New York: Palgrave Macmillan, 2004), 2.

15. David R. Coon, *Look Closer: Suburban Narratives and American Values in Film and Television* (New Brunswick, NJ: Rutgers University Press, 2013), 10.

16. *Love, Simon*.

17. José Esteban Muñoz, "Dead White: Notes on the Whiteness of New Queer Cinema," *GLQ* 4, no. 1 (1998): 137.

18. Muñoz, "Dead White," 137.

19. Coon, *Look Closer*, 32.

20. Coon, *Look Closer*, 34–35.

21. Peter Merriman, *Mobility, Space and Culture* (London: Routledge, 2012), 65.

22. Susan White, " 'You Want a Good Crack in the Mouth?' *Rebel Without a Cause*, Violence, and the Cinema of Nicholas Ray," in *Rebel Without a Cause: Approaches to a Maverick Masterwork*, ed. J. David Slocum (New York: State University of New York Press, 2005), 54.

23. White, " 'You Want a Good Crack in the Mouth,' " 59.

24. Dickinson, "The *Pleasantville* Effect," 219.

25. Cindy Donatelli, "Driving the Suburbs: Minivans, Gender, and Family Values," *Material History Review* 54 (Fall 2001): 85.

26. Donatelli, "Driving the Suburbs," 88.

27. LaGarrett J. King and Shakealia Y. Finley, "Race Is a Highway: Towards a Critical Race Approach in Economics Classrooms," in *Doing Race in Social Studies: Critical Perspectives*, ed. Prentice T. Chandler (Charlotte, NC: Information Age Publishing, 2015), 197.

28. Sheller and Urry, "The City and the Car," 744.

29. *Pariah*, DVD, directed by Dee Rees (Universal City, CA: Universal Pictures, 2012).

30. Mason P. Sands, "From Page to Screen 'Love, Simon' Forgets It's a Coming Out Story," *Harvard Crimson* (March 27, 2018), https://www.thecrimson.com/article/2018/3/27/love-simon-page-screen/.

31. Kohnen, *Queer Representation*, 177.

32. *Love, Simon*.

33. *Love, Simon*.

34. Coon, *Look Closer*, 105.

35. Ahmed, "A Phenomenology," 163.

36. Gordon Waitt, Theresa Harada, and Michelle Duffy, "'Let's Have Some Music': Sound, Gender, and Car Mobility," *Mobilities* 12, no. 3 (2015): 4.

37. Eric Laurier, Barry Brown, and Hayden Lorimer, et al., "Driving and 'Passengering': Notes on the Ordinary Organization of Car Travel," *Mobilities* 3, no. 1 (2008): 12.

38. Martin Dines, "Sacrilege in the Sitting Room: Contesting Suburban Domesticity in Contemporary Gay Literature," *Home Cultures* 2, no. 2 (2005): 179.

39. Dickinson, "The *Pleasantville* Effect," 219.

40. Dickinson, "The *Pleasantville* Effect," 228.

41. Richard T. Rodríguez, "Undead White," *GLQ* 25, no. 1 (2019): 65.

42. Andrew Baldwin, "Whiteness and Futurity: Towards a Research Agenda," *Progress in Human Geography* 36, no. 2 (2012): 183.

References

Ahmed, Sara. "A Phenomenology of Whiteness." *Feminist Theory* 8, no. 2 (2007): 149–168.

Baldwin, Andrew. "Whiteness and Futurity: Towards a Research Agenda." *Progress in Human Geography* 36, no. 2 (2012): 172–187.

Beuka, Robert. *SuburbiaNation: Reading Suburban Landscape in Twentieth-Century American Fiction and Film*. New York: Palgrave Macmillan, 2004.

Coon, David R. *Look Closer: Suburban Narratives and American Values in Film and Television*. New Brunswick, NJ: Rutgers University Press, 2013.

D'Addario, Daniel. "*Love, Simon* Is a Groundbreaking Gay Movie: But Do Today's Teens Actually Need It?" *Time*, March 8, 2018. http://time.com/5190982/love-simon-groundbreaking-gay-movie/.

Dickinson, Greg. "The *Pleasantville* Effect: Nostalgia and the Visual Framing of (White) Suburbia." *Western Journal of Communication* 70, no. 3 (2006): 212–233.

Dines, Martin. "Sacrilege in the Sitting Room: Contesting Suburban Domesticity in Contemporary Gay Literature." *Home Cultures* 2, no. 2 (2005): 175–194.

Donatelli, Cindy. "Driving the Suburbs: Minivans, Gender, and Family Values." *Material History Review* 54 (Fall 2001): 84–95.

King, LaGarrett J., and Shakealia Y. Finley. "Race Is a Highway: Towards a Critical Race Approach in Economics Classrooms." In *Doing Race in Social Studies: Critical Perspectives*, edited by Prentice T. Chandler, 195–228. Charlotte, NC: Information Age Publishing, 2015.

Kohnen, Melanie. *Queer Representation, Visibility, and Race in American Film and Television: Screening the Closet.* New York: Routledge, 2015.

Laurier, Eric, Barry Brown, and Hayden Lorimer, et al. "Driving and 'Passengering': Notes on the Ordinary Organization of Car Travel." *Mobilities* 3, no. 1 (2008): 1–23.

Lefebvre, Henri. *The Production of Space.* Translated by Donald Nicholson-Smith. Oxford: Blackwell, 1991.

Lipsitz, George. *The Possessive Investment in Whiteness.* Philadelphia: Temple University Press, 1998.

Love, Simon. Directed by Greg Berlanti. 2018. Los Angeles: Twentieth Century Fox. Blu-ray.

Means, Alexander J. "Generational Precarity, Education, and the Crisis of Capitalism: Conventional, Neo-Keynesian, and Marxian Perspectives." *Critical Sociology* 43, no. 3 (2017): 339–354.

Merriman, Peter. *Mobility, Space and Culture.* London: Routledge, 2012.

Muñoz, José Esteban. "Dead White: Notes on the Whiteness of New Queer Cinema." *GLQ* 4, no. 1 (1998): 127–138.

Pariah. Directed by Dee Rees. 2012. Universal City, CA: Universal Pictures. DVD.

Rodríguez, Richard T. "Undead White." *GLQ* 25, no. 1 (2019): 63–66.

Sands, Mason P. "From Page to Screen 'Love, Simon' Forgets It's a Coming Out Story." *Harvard Crimson*, March 27, 2018. https://www.thecrimson.com/article/2018/3/27/love-simon-page-screen/.

Sheller, Mimi, and John Urry. "The City and the Car." *International Journal of Urban and Regional Research* 24, no. 4 (2000): 737–757.

Somerville, Siobhan B. *Queering the Color Line: Race and the Invention of Homosexuality in American Culture.* Durham, NC: Duke University Press, 2000.

Waitt, Gordon, Theresa Harada, and Michelle Duffy, " 'Let's Have Some Music': Sound, Gender, and Car Mobility." *Mobilities* 12, no. 3 (2017): 324–342.

White, Susan. " 'You Want a Good Crack in the Mouth?' *Rebel Without a Cause*, Violence, and the Cinema of Nicholas Ray." In *Rebel Without a Cause: Approaches to a Maverick Masterwork*, edited by J. David Slocum, 53–88. New York: State University of New York Press, 2005.

Wood, Brenton. "The Oogum Boogum Song." *Oogum Boogum*. Double Shot Records, 1967, vinyl record.

Contributors

Amy Lynn Corbin is Associate Professor of Film Studies and Media & Communication at Muhlenberg College. Her book, *Cinematic Geographies and Multicultural Spectatorship in America* (2016), explores the intersection of spectatorship and place in the post–civil rights era.

Joshua Glick is Assistant Professor of Film & Media Studies and English at Hendrix College and a member of Columbia University's summer faculty. He is the author of *Los Angeles Documentary and the Production of Public History, 1958–1977* (2018). He is working on a book on current documentary and social movements.

Nathan Holmes is an Assistant Professor of Cinema Studies at SUNY Purchase College. He is the author of *Welcome to Fear City: Crime Film, Crisis, and the Urban Imagination* (2018) and several chapters and articles exploring cinema's relationship to the built and natural environment.

Helen Heran Jun is Associate Professor of English and African American Studies at the University of Illinois, Chicago. She is the author of *Race for Citizenship: Black Orientalism and Asian Uplift from Post-Reconstruction to Neoliberal America* (2011). Her current research examines discourses of slavery and human trafficking in relation to the prison industrial complex.

Paula J. Massood is Professor of Film Studies at Brooklyn College, CUNY, and the Graduate Center, CUNY. She is the author of *Black City Cinema: African American Urban Experiences in Film* (2003), *Making a Promised Land: Harlem in 20th-Century Photography and Film* (2013), and coeditor of *The Spike Lee Reader* (2007). She is a coeditor with Angel

Daniel Matos and Pamela Robertson Wojcik of *Crossroads: Intersections of Space and Identity in Screen Cultures* (2021).

Angel Daniel Matos is an Assistant Professor of Gender, Sexuality, and Women's Studies at Bowdoin College who specializes in youth literatures, queer studies, and screen cultures. He is a coeditor with Paula Massood and Pamela Robertson Wojcik of *Crossroads: Intersections of Space and Identity in Screen Cultures* (2021).

Elizabeth A. Patton is an Assistant Professor of Media and Communication Studies at the University of Maryland, Baltimore County. She is coeditor of *Home Sweat Home: Perspectives on Housework and Modern Domestic Relationships* (2014). She is the author of *Easy Living: The Rise of the Home Office* (2020).

John David Rhodes is a founding editor of the journal *World Picture* and is Reader in Film Studies and Visual Culture at the University of Cambridge, where he is also the Director of the Center for Film and Screen. His most recent book is *The Spectacle of Property: The House in American Film* (2017).

Merrill Schleier is Professor Emeritus of Art and Architectural History and Cinema Studies at the University of the Pacific. She is the author of *The Skyscraper in American Art* (1990) and *Skyscraper Cinema: Architecture and Gender in American Film* (2009). She has published numerous articles and chapters on cinema and the built environment.

Ellen C. Scott is Vice Chair of Cinema and Media Studies at UCLA. She is the author of *Cinema Civil Rights* (2015) and is working on two book projects: a history of slavery on the American screen and the Black women film critics of the Classical Hollywood era.

Timotheus Vermeulen is an Associate Professor in Media, Culture, and Society at the University of Oslo, Norway. He is the author of *Scenes from the Suburbs* (2014), and is editor with Martin Dines of *New Suburban Stories* (2013).

Index